Reminiscences

of

Admiral John J. Hyland, Jr.

U.S. Navy (Retired)

Volume I

Copyright © 1989
U.S. Naval Institute
Annapolis, Maryland

Preface

One will not read far into the oral history of Admiral John Hyland before being struck by his considerable enthusiasm for naval aviation. He got into pilot training as a result of his experience as an ensign on board the aircraft carrier Lexington in the mid-1930s. Because of that enthusiasm--and his talent--he continued his flying longer than most of his contemporaries. Included, along with squadron duty in fighters and patrol planes, were service as Admiral Ernest J. King's personal pilot; command of the air group of the carrier Intrepid in the closing stages of the Pacific war; and several tours as a test pilot. He was involved in active combat service at both the beginning and end of the war; the contrast between the two periods was dramatic as U.S. naval capability advanced markedly.

In addition to the flying billets, several of Admiral Hyland's other tours of duty involved aviation. He was air officer of the carrier Lake Champlain, operations officer of the carrier Kearsarge, air officer for the Operational Development Force, air operations officer on the staff of Commander in Chief Pacific Fleet, commanding officer of the seaplane tender Onslow and the carrier Saratoga, and Commander Atlantic Barrier Wing. He was also involved as a nuclear weapons planner when the Navy was getting more and more involved in that discipline in the late 1950s and early 1960s. His comments on duty with the Joint Strategic Target Planning Staff are revealing concerning the often adversarial relationship with the Air Force.

This first volume covers Admiral Hyland's career up through his years as a junior flag officer. The upcoming second volume will deal with his concluding service as Commander Seventh Fleet and Commander in Chief Pacific Fleet during the Vietnam War. At the same time Admiral Hyland tells his story with considerable enthusiasm, he also displays a becoming sense of modesty, which is refreshing for so senior an officer. His memoir is interesting throughout and adds valuable information for the benefit of historians and other readers.

The initial interviews were done by Dr. John T. Mason, Jr., former director of the Naval Institute's oral history program. He performed a valuable service by getting the series started. Admiral Hyland completed the interviews while in Annapolis for the 50th anniversary reunion of his Naval Academy graduating class. Admiral Hyland has done some slight editing to the transcript, and he has provided some followup information. Other than those changes, the transcript is largely a record of the way he originally spoke during the interviews. John Hoshko provided some inputs on the annotating footnotes, and Susan Sweeney compiled the detailed index.

Paul Stillwell
Director of Oral History
U.S. Naval Institute
August 1989

Admiral John J. Hyland, United States Navy (Retired)

John Joseph Hyland was born in Philadelphia, Pennsylvania, on 1 September 1912, son of Captain John Hyland, USN, now deceased, and Mrs. Josephine (Walker) Hyland. He attended Brookline (Massachusetts) High School, prior to entering the U. S. Naval Academy, Annapolis, Maryland, on appointment from the Thirteenth District of Massachusetts in 1930. Graduated and commissioned ensign on 31 May 1934, he subsequently advanced in rank attaining that of vice admiral, to date from 1 December 1965 and admiral, to date from 1 December 1967.

Following graduation from the Naval Academy in 1934, he joined the USS Lexington (CV-2) and a year later transferred to the USS Elliot (DD-146). Detached from that destroyer in June 1936, he was ordered to the Naval Air Station, Pensacola, Florida, for flight training and on 12 May 1937 was designated naval aviator. After service with Fighting Squadron Six, operating off the USS Enterprise (CV-6), he had duty from July to September 1940 with Patrol Squadron 26. Transferred to Patrol Squadron 102, he was stationed at Olongapo, Philippine Islands, at the outbreak of World War II, and subsequently participated in the defense of the Philippines, engagements in the Netherlands East Indies, and in the final retreat to Australia.

"For extraordinary flying achievement in command of a PBY type airplane, December 20, 1941 to March 3, 1942 . . ." he was awarded the Distinguished Flying Cross. The citation further states in part:

"During that time, Lieutenant Hyland participated in the bombing attack on enemy Japanese Naval forces at Jolo Harbor, Philippine Islands; he also successfully landed his PBY airplane in rough seas to effect the rescue of the one surviving member of an R.A.A.F. Hudson airplane which had crashed in the Malucca Sea on January 1, 1942 . . ."

He is also entitled to the Ribbon for, and a facsimile of, the Presidential Unit Citation awarded Patrol Squadron 102 for outstanding service in the Netherlands East Indies and Philippine areas from 8 December 1941 to 3 March 1942.

Between March and June 1942 he was attached to Patrol Squadron 101 and in August reported as Assistant Operations Officer at the Naval Air Station, Anacostia, D.C., where he remained until September 1944. There he also served for 16 months as private pilot for Admiral Ernest J. King, USN, the Chief of Naval Operations and Commander in Chief U.S.

Fleet. He then became Commander Air Group Ten, attached to the USS Intrepid (CV-11). He was awarded the Silver Star Medal, a Gold Star in lieu of the Fourth Air Medal and a Gold Star in lieu of the Second Distinguished Flying Cross. The citations follow in part:

Silver Star Medal: "For conspicuous gallantry and intrepidity as Air Coordinator of Fighter Planes attached to the USS INTREPID, in action against enemy Japanese forces on the Island of Honsu, Japan, March 19, 1945. Leading an attack against Kure Air Base in the face of intense and accurate antiaircraft fire, Commander Hyland scored a direct bomb hit on a large hangar and engaged and shot down an enemy plane. After directing his flight in the infliction of extensive damage on important hostile installations, including the destruction of ten planes on the ground and infliction of damage on twenty others, he retired from the target area and successfully strafed two enemy transports in the Inland Sea ..."

Gold Star in lieu of the Fourth Air Medal: "For meritorious achievement...during operations against enemy Japanese forces in the vicinity of the Island of Okinawa, April 7, 1945. Leading a flight over our invasion forces, Commander Hyland engaged and shot down a hostile plane before it could crash dive into our ships or our troops..."

Gold Star in lieu of the Second Distinguished Flying Cross: "For heroism and extraordinary achievement in aerial flight as Strike Leader of Fighter Bombers attached to the USS INTREPID, during operations against enemy Japanese forces on the Island of Kyushu, Japan, April 16, 1945. Encountering five enemy fighters while leading a flight against hostile Naval and air installations, Commander Hyland directed a determined attack in which all five of the planes were shot down. Then, proceeding to the target, he scored a direct bomb hit on the hangar area and strafed parked aircraft to contribute materially to the destruction by his flight of twelve enemy aircraft and the infliction of damage on ten others..."

His Air Medal and Gold Stars in lieu of the Second, Third and Fifth Air Medal and the Gold Star in lieu of the Third Distinguished Flying Cross were awarded for completing 25 strike missions during the period 18 March 1945 to 6 August 1945.

In January 1946, he reported as air officer on board the USS Lake Champlain (CV-39) and in August of that year returned to duty ashore as assistant director of flight test at the Naval Air Test Center, Patuxent River, Maryland. From June 1949 to January 1950 he was operations officer on board the USS Kearsarge (CV-33), after which he served on the staff of Commander Operational Development Force. Again assigned to the Naval Air Test Center, Patuxent River, he was director of the tactical test division from August 1951 to August 1953.

Completing instruction at the National War College, Washington, D.C., he reported in July 1954 as air operations officer on the staff of the Commander in Chief, U.S. Pacific Fleet. From August 1956 to July 1957 he commanded the USS Onslow (AVP-48) and in August became a member of the Atomic Energy Team, Joint Strategic Plans Group, Joint Chiefs of Staff, Washington, D.C. In September 1958 he assumed command of the USS Saratoga (CVA-60) and in November 1959 was detached for duty as Commander Airborne Early Warning Wing, Atlantic and Commander Fleet Air, Argentia, with headquarters at the Naval Air Station, Argentia, Newfoundland.

Assigned in September 1960 to the Joint Staff, Commander in Chief, Atlantic, he served as Commander in Chief Atlantic Representative, Joint Strategic Target Planning Staff, with headquarters at Offutt Air Force Base, Nebraska, until October 1962, when he became Commander Carrier Division Four. On 15 November 1963 he reported as Assistant Director of the Strategic Plans Division, Office of the Chief of Naval Operations, Navy Department, and in July 1965 assumed duty as director of that division.

In December 1965 he became Commander Seventh Fleet and "for exceptionally meritorious service...during the period December 1965 to November 1967..." was awarded the Distinguished Service Medal. The citation further states in part:

"During this critical period of continued intensification of combat operations and the concomitant buildup of forces and facilities in Southeast Asia, Vice Admiral Hyland has demonstrated outstanding leadership, astute judgment and foresight in directing the complex and manifold operations of the SEVENTH Fleet in support of our national objectives in the Western Pacific. Under his dynamic and personal leadership all of the forces assigned to his command have been molded into a most potent and effective fighting fleet which covers the entire spectrum of naval operations. In the past twenty-three months the SEVENTH Fleet has expanded from 175 ships and 72,000 men to 220 ships and 80,000 men; naval gunfire operations have been expanded from support of our forces in South Vietnam to include targets along a portion of the North Vietnamese coastline; amphibious assault operations have been conducted along the entire South Vietnamese coastline in order to search for and destroy enemy personnel and equipment; and air strike operations against heavily defended targets in North Vietnam have been greatly expanded. Many of the operations conducted by the SEVENTH Fleet were without precedent in modern naval history, requiring the development and employment of new tactics, techniques and equipment. Coordinated electronic and tactical measures have been successfully developed to counter the surface-to-air missile threat; new weapons and equipment have been introduced into combat operations; and a positive radar surveillance and indentification system has been established for all air operations over the Gulf of Tonkin and North Vietnam. These achievements are a direct result of [his] ability to master the complexities of integrating and employing new techniques, procedures, and equipment to meet the challenges posed by a fast changing combat environment. In addition to his deep involvement in and massive contribution to the advances mentioned above, Vice Admiral Hyland achieved that detailed and exacting coordination with other service commanders which was required in order to attain the maximum effectiveness and efficiency of combined operations against the common enemy. He continuously demonstrated the great tact and diplomacy which have been required to protect our vital national and naval interest in the Western Pacific. Through persuasive negotiation and personal leadership, he has served with distinction in nurturing effective channels for liaison and in furthering the United States goodwill and prestige with foreign nations..."

On 30 November 1967 he assumed duty as Commander in Chief, U.S. Pacific Fleet and was awarded a Gold Star in lieu of the Second Distinguished Service Medal "for exceptionally meritorious service..." in that capacity. The citation continues in part:

"Admiral Hyland provided dynamic leadership, outstanding executive ability, and exceptional foresight in directing the complex and manifold operations of the Pacific Fleet in the execution of United States national policy in the vast Pacific Ocean area. During this three-year tour of duty, United States combat operations against the enemy in Southeast Asia reached their peak intensity; United States military forces, with United States Navy craft and personnel in the lead, undertook combat operations in the IV Military Region of the Republic of Vietnam, which for years had been an enemy-controlled sanctuary, and, together with forces of the Republic of Vietnam, succeeded in large measure in pacifying that area; and an accelerated program to turn over in-country operations and craft to the Republic of Vietnam was begun and carried more than half-way to completion. Admiral Hyland's tour was characterized by dramatically increased involvement in and responsibility by the Fleet Commander in all areas of resources management for both the Fleet and its supporting shore establishment. During the latter half of his tour, budgetary constraints directed by national authorities made necessary a reduction in the order of one-third of the Pacific Fleet force levels and supporting base structure. That these severe reductions were accomplished with the minimum possible impact on combat operations in Southeast Asia, and without comparable reductions in Fleet commitments is a tribute to his inspirational leadership, management and foresight..."

He had temporary duty at headquarters of the Fourteenth Naval District, Pearl Harbor, Hawaii, from December 1970 until relieved of active duty pending his retirement, effective 1 January 1971.

In addition to the Distinguished Service Medal with Gold Star, the Silver Star Medal, Distinguished Flying Cross with two Gold Stars, the Air Medal with four Gold Stars and the Presidential Unit Citation, Admiral Hyland has the Navy Unit Commendation Ribbon, the China Service Medal, American Defense Service Medal, Asiatic-Pacific Campaign Medal with three stars, American Campaign Medal, World War II Victory Medal, Navy Occupation Service Medal, Asia Clasp, National Defense Service Medal with Bronze Star, Armed Forces Expeditionary Medal (Lebanon), the Vietnam Service Medal with three stars and Philippine Defense Ribbon. He has also been awarded the Order of the Bronze Cross by the government of the Netherlands, National Order of Vietnam, Third Class, Gallantry Cross with Palm (Vietnam), Order of the Rising Sun, Second Class (Japan), the Medal of Cloud and Banner (Republic of China), and the Order of National Security Medal, First Class (Republic of Korea), and the Republic of Vietnam Campaign Medal with Device. He received the Navy League's 1966 John Paul Jones Award for inspirational leadership. He also has the Army Presidential Unit Citation Ribbon and the Army Distinguished Unit Emblem.

Admiral Hyland is married to the former Florence Whiting of New Rochelle, New York, and they have four children: John III, Nancy, Pamela, and Whiting.

Authorization

The U. S. Naval Institute is hereby authorized to make available to individuals, libraries, and other repositories of its choosing the transcripts of five oral history interviews concerning the life and career of the undersigned. The interviews were recorded on 7 March 1972, 8 March 1972, 9 March 1972, 10 March 1972, and 29 May 1984 in collaboration with Dr. John T. Mason, Jr., and Paul Stillwell for the U.S. Naval Institute.

The undersigned does hereby release and assign to the U.S. Naval Institute all right, title, restrictions, and interest in the interviews. The copyright in both the oral and transcribed versions shall be the sole property of the U.S. Naval Institute. The tape recordings of the interviews are and will remain the property of the U.S. Naval Institute.

Signed and sealed this 26th day of June 1989.

Admiral John J. Hyland, Jr., USN (Ret.)

Hyland #1 - 1

Interview Number 1 with Admiral John J. Hyland, Jr.,
U.S. Navy (Retired)

Place: Admiral Hyland's home in Honolulu, Hawaii

Date: Tuesday, 7 March 1972

Interviewer: John T. Mason, Jr.

Q: It's certainly nice to meet you, Admiral. I've heard a great deal about you, and now I see you in the flesh. I'm looking forward to an account of your very exciting career. It's a notable career in the field of naval aviation. I wonder if you'd begin this oral biography in a very proper way by telling me the date and place of your birth, and a little bit perhaps about your family background.

Admiral Hyland: Well, Dr. Mason, I'd be delighted to. I was born on the first of September 1912. I was born in Philadelphia, and I'm told that I was born in what's called the Girard Estate. I wouldn't be able to find it for you if I went there now, but I know it's somewhere near the big football stadium. I've been told that I stayed in Philadelphia just a couple of weeks, and then my family went down to Atlantic City for the summer. After that, my father, who was also in the Navy, was reassigned, and I never did get back to Philadelphia except to go to Army-Navy games. And that's all I've gone to Philadelphia for over the next 59 years.

Q: What area of the Navy was your father in?

Admiral Hyland: He was a regular straight line officer.

Q: Was he on duty at the navy yard on that occasion?

Admiral Hyland: Actually, he was on duty then, I believe, in sort of a turbine experimental laboratory that was run there at the Philadelphia Navy Yard at the time. Shortly after that, he was sent somewhere else, and I can't remember just where that was. He was a naval officer. He was in the Academy class of 1900, so I grew up in the Navy.* We spent most of our time in New England, it seems to me. We spent five years in Newport, Rhode Island, quite a few years around Boston and various places. He did have a couple tours of duty out in California, where we lived in Long Beach, but by and large all my schooling was done around the Boston area.

Q: Then the family followed him as best they could?

Admiral Hyland: Yes.

---

*John Joseph Hyland (1878-1949) stood eighth among the 61 graduates in the class of 1900. He retired as a captain in 1935.

Q: How many children were there?

Admiral Hyland: Well, we're four youngsters in our family: two boys and two girls. My brother followed me into the Navy a year behind me, and he later turned out to be a supply officer.* He's been retired now about five years from the Navy and lives in California.

Q: Was it taken for granted that you boys were going into the Navy? Was no other career possible?

Admiral Hyland: Well, really, I don't recall my father ever pressuring me or my brother to go. I can remember that I always felt I wanted to go to the Naval Academy. I think we were a little bit conscious of the fact that around the 1930s it was pretty expensive to go to college, although I don't recall that being a really serious thought in my mind. I just wanted to go to the Naval Academy. I went to Brookline High School--which is a suburb of Boston--for the last two years of high school. That was an amazingly excellent public school in those days. It was the equivalent of what today would be a very, very expensive preparatory school. We had teachers in that school who wrote the textbooks that were commonly used in

---

*William Walker Hyland (1914-   ) stood 54th of 442 graduates in the Naval Academy class of 1935. He retired in 1966 as a captain in the Supply Corps.

the New England high schools and so on; it was very, very high quality. So when it came time to take the exams for the Naval Academy, I had no trouble at all.

Q: What sort of a scholastic record did you make at Brookline?

Admiral Hyland: I was one of the better students there, but I wasn't the best. I wasn't the brightest student by any means. I can remember our nickname was the "wealthy towners." Brookline is an incorporated town--still is, I believe--and it's known for the wealthy people who live there and, therefore, for the large amounts of money that are available from the taxes there. So the schools have always been very, very fine--better than they are in other areas right around Boston.

Q: Well, that was an exceptional advantage then.

Admiral Hyland: Yes. Well, my older sister was a couple of classes ahead of me. She later went on to Radcliffe, which was a difficult college to get into in those days. And, as I say, I went to the Naval Academy, and my brother followed me a year later. We certainly had good luck with the public schools there in Boston in those days.

Hyland #1 - 5

Q: As a navy family, and a family that did move around considerably, did you have any political connections which would enable you to get an appointment readily?

Admiral Hyland: Well, we didn't, except that I can remember so distinctly that when my father tried to get an appointment from a congressman in Boston, this fellow, who's long since gone, first told my dad that he couldn't have anything to do with appointing me or my brother, because we were not properly in his district. We were living in the Boston Navy Yard, and that was federal property.

Well, this led my father to go further with it, and I can remember he explored the political scene there and finally was able to get a meeting with an old fellow--I'll never forget his name--Martin M. Lomasney. He was a political boss in Boston, and I believe he was one of the earlier members of the group that's now thought of as the Kennedy machine there in Boston.* We went to see him; my father explained that his boys were fine students; they were good, solid Catholics, and he listened to that very carefully. And, lo and behold, about two or three days after we'd gone to see this old fellow, my father was called up by the congressman concerned, who said that he'd

---
*John F. Kennedy, from Boston, was President of the United States, 1961-63, and his brother, Edward M. Kennedy, has been a U.S. senator from Massachusetts since 1963.

Hyland #1 - 6

changed his mind and that he was going to give me a principal appointment to the Naval Academy.

Q: Who was this congressman?

Admiral Hyland: His name was Douglass.* He died a few years after I entered the Naval Academy. Well, I can remember going to take the examination to get into the Naval Academy, though, after I had been named as the principal.

Q: Was this the civil service exam?

Admiral Hyland: Yes. It was just a regular exam, and I'd say there were 20 people from that district, which was a very tough and poor district in Boston. And of the 20 people who went in to start the series of exams, I actually was the only one who even finished. All the rest of these youngsters, I guess, just simply weren't prepared for that sort of an examination. They left before the thing was even over, so I guess I could have been the tenth alternate in the case and I still would have been able to go to the Naval Academy. But it was a fact that I was the principal, and I still was able to pass the exam. So I've always remembered that sort of political setup, where a thing like

---
*John J. Douglass (Democrat--Massachusetts) served in the House of Representatives from 1925 to 1935.

that was possible. The next year, old Mr. Lomasney did exactly the same thing for my brother Bill, and that's how come he got to the Naval Academy.

Q: That's very fortunate, because some boys entering had a terrific time.

Admiral Hyland: Well, in those days an appointment to the Naval Academy or to West Point was very highly regarded and very much sought after because of the big Depression that was on right then. A lot of people just simply couldn't get to college unless they would go there, so there were many, many people trying to get these appointments. Now my old schoolmates there in Brookline, that was a different story with them. They were by and large from families that were well-to-do, and most of them went to Harvard or to MIT, or certainly went to one of the so-called prestige colleges.* I've lost track of most of them, but I can remember that none of them had any problem getting into college as far as the scholastic standards were concerned. It was all due to this absolutely excellent Brookline High School.

Q: So you really didn't have to do any special prepping,

---

*MIT--Massachusetts Institute of Technology in Cambridge, Massachusetts.

as so many of them did, going to some of the special schools.

Admiral Hyland: No. Quite a large number of my classmates at the Naval Academy had gone at least one year to one of the preparatory schools that were specialists in prepping youngsters for either West Point or Annapolis, but I didn't have to do that. I was 17 years old when I went in, which, of course, meant I was only 21 when I graduated. I wasn't the youngest man in my class, but I was on the younger side of the whole group.

Q: Was that a disadvantage in any way, going in so young?

Admiral Hyland: Well, yes, I think so. In looking back on it, as the men in the class went at that time, I was young, I was small, and I was somewhat immature. Later on, of course, that doesn't make any difference at all.

Q: You rapidly catch up.

Admiral Hyland: My own son went to the Naval Academy when he was 19, and he had relatively more success at the school than I did in that he was able to make a varsity athletic team, and he was a more mature person when he was there. And he actually did better scholastically than I was able to do when I was there.*

Q: Tell me about the academy in those days. I'd like to get a picture of it.

Admiral Hyland: I enjoyed it very much. There used to be a certain amount of hazing, which has since been outlawed. At least, they now no longer permit any physical fooling around--no physical hazing. I never experienced anything very serious. It was all sort of a game and I think in many cases it was a very effective way of straightening out a smart aleck type and so on. Since that time they don't permit any of the physical hazing. In fact, they're rigidly opposed to it, and if anybody's ever caught doing it or trying it, I think he's dismissed immediately right out of hand. Now, they give them a pretty rough plebe year just the same. They have this game of asking them professional questions, and there is, I think, a sort of a mental hazing that goes on. In my opinion, it's much tougher on the youngsters than any of the physical stuff that we had to put up with. It was pretty much of a joke. I saw a few cases of people overdoing it, and there were some men who apparently enjoyed swinging a broom on plebes' behinds.

---
*John J. Hyland, Jr., stood 57th of 464 graduates in the class of 1934; John J. Hyland III stood 100th of 789 graduates in the class of 1962.

Q: Was this upperclassmen who did this?

Admiral Hyland: Yes, but it really was relatively a rare thing. I think it was good for the discipline, and by and large we were well taken care of, I think.

Q: How did you take to the regimen? Of course, being a navy junior, you knew what you were getting into.*

Admiral Hyland: I didn't have any particular trouble with it. I had a certain amount of trouble with conduct at the Naval Academy, but I had to learn that I wasn't going to be able to get away with it. And that seemed to go with quite a few people who were navy juniors. Now whether some of the older upperclassmen found out that I was a navy junior and they thought I might be a special target for straightening out and so on, I don't know.

Q: Was this an infraction like smoking, where you weren't supposed to smoke or something like that?

Admiral Hyland: Oh, it was all just minor things, but I can remember having a certain amount of trouble with the demerits and having to do a lot of marching with the rifle,

---
*Navy juniors are the sons and daughters of career naval personnel.

Hyland #1 - 11

which was the standard penalty for these small regulations that you'd break. But I got straightened out after a while on that. I actually found the Naval Academy a very pleasant experience. I personally never suffered from the fact that we were behind the four walls, that we really didn't get out very much. Looking back on it years later, I certainly could see that when we did get out of the Naval Academy we were socially somewhat less mature and experienced than, we'll say, the fellow out of Harvard or Yale who had had a lot more freedom. But I've never had any regrets about going to the Naval Academy. I was very pleased when my son went there, but I made a special effort to lecture him against going there if he was doing it just because I'd gone there and my father had gone there. But I think he'd thought it out for himself.

Q: It must have been an interesting contrast in your own mind between your experiences there and your son's experiences. He was class of what?

Admiral Hyland: He was in the class of '62. He's now a submarine officer in the Navy. He didn't go into aviation. I've never been able to explain this, but it seems that more and more you see the sons of submariners all going into flying, and the sons of aviators in the Navy all going

Hyland #1 - 12

into submarines.

Q: I suppose this is self-expression.

Admiral Hyland: I guess so. But you really do see a surprisingly large amount of that going on.

Q: Tell me about the course of study. I mean, how did you react to it? What is your estimate of it as an adequate course?

Admiral Hyland: I thought it was, in the mathematics, and the physics, and the sciences, and the technical navy subjects, it was first class, and it did prepare you to just get started in the Navy. I think on the literary side of things it was mediocre. The cultural studies were just given a very superficial once-over. I suppose a certain type of fellow could do a lot of reading on his own, and so on.

Q: Were you encouraged to do that in the English Department?

Admiral Hyland: You were by the English professors, sure. But there really wasn't any time to do it. I think the general way things ran at the Naval Academy then, there was an awful lot of regimentation. A bell rang every so often, and you just did something right then and there. Your life was just planned for you, and there was no time for any deviations and so on. So perhaps, compared to a school where you're left on your own, you might graduate from the academy still expecting to have a bell ring at 2:00 o'clock so that you'd know that you were supposed to do something then. I think the training was good, though, and I always have thought that the bachelor of science degree was authentic.

Q: I'm sure it is. During a portion of your time, I guess Admiral Hart was there as Superintendent, wasn't he?*

Admiral Hyland: Yes, he was. He was there for the last three years that I was at the academy, as I remember it now. He was preceded by Admiral Robison.** Now in those days--and I don't think it's changed very much today--the individual midshipman doesn't really see much of the Superintendent. You see him on a few ceremonial occasions, and you listen to him as one of a large group, but as far as seeing him individually and really getting to know him as a person, it just is impossible.

---
*Rear Admiral Thomas C. Hart, USN, was Superintendent of the Naval Academy from 1931 to 1934.
**Rear Admiral Samuel S. Robison, USN, was Superintendent of the Naval Academy from 1928 to 1931.

Q: I can imagine, however, with Hart that you felt his influence permeating everywhere. He was a strict disciplinarian, wasn't he?

Admiral Hyland: Yes, he was. He was a very, very proper fellow. I can remember that he wore remarkably high collars; that would be everyone's memory of him, I think, of the way he looked. And he was, we thought at that time, quite stiff, extremely proper, absolutely tough as nails, never would permit any serious infringement and so on. And I was quite amazed later on, when I was him out there in the Philippines, to find out that he wasn't like that at all.*

Q: And in retirement he was quite different again.

Admiral Hyland: Well, I guess so. I saw him several times when he was retired and I was progressively going up in the Navy, and he always remembered me and was always very, very pleasant, and always seemed to be so pleased that I remembered him, of all things. But he would be genuinely pleased and almost touched if some younger person came up and told him that they remembered him and so on. It was really very nice to see him every time I did.

---

*As a four-star admiral, Hart served as Commander in Chief Asiatic Fleet from 1939 to 1942.

Hyland #1 - 15

Q: He told me once that his idea of proper training at the Naval Academy was to produce a naval officer, a man who was capable of leadership and whose secondary attribute was that he must be a gentleman.* Would you make that estimate?

Admiral Hyland: Yes, I think that sounds just about right. Then there was an awful lot of mention of the fact that now that we were in the Navy, we were young officers and we were gentlemen. Even though it was by act of Congress, we were gentlemen and, by gosh, we were going to have to act like gentlemen. A lot of people, of course, came from very homely and very rough backgrounds and had a lot to learn.

Q: Were you involved in athletics while you were there?

Admiral Hyland: Well, I tried mightily to be a varsity swimmer. When I was in high school, I was captain of the swimming team, and Brookline was one of the few areas where swimming at that time was a major sport in high schools--that and the New York area. A lot of the national champions came from around there in those days. Well, I was captain of the swimming team at Brookline and, as far as I can see now, I never really got very much better in

---
*Dr. Mason interviewed Admiral Hart for an oral history under the auspices of Columbia University.

all the four years of trying to get better at the Naval Academy.

I think now that that coach, whose name was Henry Ortland--he's still going; he lives in Annapolis and still watches the swimming scene. I think old Henry should have told me about the end of the second year that I really ought to go somewhere else. I think I might have been able to make the tennis team, but I never even went out for it. I spent a lot of time trying to make that swimming team, and was just on the verge of succeeding all the time, but I never actually was able to qualify for a varsity letter. My younger brother followed me at Brookline as the swimming team champion and swimming team captain, and later on he became a star immediately. And he was a star for every year he was at the Naval Academy--one of the very best. He got a great deal better, and why I didn't, I've never understood.

Q: Did you go in for any other sport in addition to that?

Admiral Hyland: We generally just played the field, other than the swimming season. I played a lot of tennis, but--I don't know why--at the time I didn't think I could possibly make the tennis team. I wish I had tried. Since then, I've been able to handle the fellows who used to play on the team without any trouble.

Q: It's become a very great passion with you now, hasn't it?

Admiral Hyland: Well, I wouldn't call it that, but I enjoy it very, very much.

Q: Tell me about the summer cruises.

Admiral Hyland: In those days, we used to go on one of two battleships, the Wyoming and the Arkansas.* You went on two cruises, one right after your plebe year and one right after your second class year. In the intermediate one, right after your youngster year at the academy, you stayed at the academy and had what they called aviation summer. The first cruise I went on, we had an elegant time. We went to Northern Europe and England, and to the Azores. Then the last cruise, which was the first class cruise, the money was not as available as it had been, so that summer we went on an abbreviated cruise, which didn't amount to very much. And we were given two months' leave. Instead

---

*Both were relatively old ships by the early 1930s. The Wyoming (BB-32) was commissioned 25 September 1912 and the Arkansas (BB-33) on 17 September of the same year. As a result of the London Naval Treaty of 1930, the Wyoming was "demilitarized" by removal of six of her 12 12-inch guns. She spent the remainder of her commissioned service as a training ship.

of one month's leave, in September, we were given two.

I think those cruises were one of the best things that happened to the youngsters growing up at the Naval Academy; they really were wonderful. You got a chance to see quite a few foreign countries and see a little bit of the world, and they were really fulfilling that recruiting slogan that if you'd just join the Navy you'd get to see the world. They could afford, then, to have these two battleships; every summer they were entirely pointed toward the middie cruise and did nothing but that. In later years, the Navy hasn't been able to afford that, and now they fly the youngsters to deployed fleets, and they go on cruises after they get there. It's not possible to assign a ship the sole job of taking the middies out.

Q: In retrospect, which system is best, do you think?

Admiral Hyland: Well, I think in that day it was very, very nice that we had such a chance, because you couldn't pick out any ship in the fleet that would go to all these places; nobody would have a schedule as wonderful as that. Now the problem is that when they send them over to the Sixth Fleet or out to the Seventh Fleet or out to one of the numbered fleets on the coasts, they try to do a little bit about getting them to romantic ports and so on, but it's just that the schedule for the Navy is so tight and

Hyland #1 - 19

it's an operational unit. So the midshipmen just have to go ahead and go where the ship is scheduled to go. Frequently, it won't be anyplace especially unique.

Q: I suppose now, under the present system, that they can't accommodate as large a number of boys on a single ship.

Admiral Hyland: Well, that's it. I think it's mainly that the active fleet is so darn busy that they have enough of a problem absorbing the middies at all. I think perhaps the older system was a little better, and I think we'd still do it if we could afford it. Now, of course, the Navy's become so much more sophisticated. There's now, very frankly, a lot of competition among the various elements of the Navy. The aviators are trying to capture the best of the crop and get them to go into flying. The submariners are singing a siren song about life in submarines. The amphibious people try to get their share of the top guys, and so it goes. There really is a lot of proselyting done to the midshipmen as a group to try and attract them.

Q: On those cruises on the battleships, did you have classes? How were you kept busy during them?

Admiral Hyland: On the first one of those cruises, the

scheme was to treat you as an enlisted man. You would spend the summer being assigned as a compartment cleaner or a cleaner of the head, doing the painting, doing the holystoning of the deck and all that business, the idea being to show you what the enlisted men go through as a way of life.* That also was combined with quite a number of formal classes; you went to several every day, and they would be pointed toward teaching you a little about gunnery, about navigation, and about seamanship and engineering.

Q: Did some of your instructors go along with you then?

Admiral Hyland: Yes, quite a few of the Naval Academy instructors went on the cruise with us, and, of course, they were augmented by the ship's company who knew the battleship well. On the second cruise, on the first class cruise, you were treated as a young officer, although there wasn't room enough really to do that. We slept in hammocks on both of these cruises, but your duties on the second one of these cruises were more actually navigating the ship and standing watches up on the bridge, and that sort of business, standing watches in the engineering plant, rather than the menial labor assignments that we had on the

---

*Holystoning is the use of stones and cleaning solution to clean and smooth wooden decks. It requires a good deal of vigorous physical activity.

Hyland #1 - 21

earlier one. I thought they had it pretty well organized, though, and it was good training.

Q: By that time you had enough knowledge and had enough theory in the background to begin to apply some of it, I suppose.

Admiral Hyland: Yes, sure.

Q: Were the cruises useful to the boys in making them more firmly resolved to have naval careers? Was this a factor with any of them?

Admiral Hyland: Well, I think in those days--and it may have been because the Depression was still on--a very, very high percentage of the people in my class did stay in the Navy. At that time, because of the Depression, for instance, the class ahead of me, the class of '33, only the upper half were given commissions; the other half were just released.* And in those years if anybody wanted to resign from the Navy on graduation, he was allowed to do it with no problem at all.

Q: Did he go into reserve automatically or what?

---
*The limit on commissions was intended as an economy measure and affected only the class of 1933. Some members were commissioned the following year, and most of the rest had returned by 1941.

Admiral Hyland: He could, but he wasn't required to, and only a relatively few fellows did that. I noticed that almost without exception they all came right back on active duty the minute the war started. Almost to a man they came back, but it was just a fact that in my time darn near everybody stayed in the Navy and did so willingly. Now, of course, it's different. They have to require they stay for, I think it's either four or five years, and in many cases that's not quite so willingly accepted.

Q: No, but if not a rule, they'd lose so many of them, I guess, today.

Admiral Hyland: Yes, sure.

Q: Tell me about your aviation summer, your introduction to naval aviation.

Admiral Hyland: It actually was very rudimentary, although we were given passenger flights in two different types of airplanes--one in a little two-seater seaplane and one in a patrol plane that could take about five or six of us up at a crack.

Hyland #1 - 23

Q: Was this at the Naval Academy?

Admiral Hyland: Yes, it was done right at the Naval Academy. It's not done there now, but then it was just done in seaplanes that were actually based there at the academy or were augmented by patrol squadrons from Norfolk, I think it was, that came up and were there for a few months in the summer just to be there to give us these flights. You'd have a flight and be able to shoot a machine gun from a gun position up in the bow, and you'd be able to watch the people fly it, and you'd be able to see landings and takeoffs made.

There was a particularly wonderful officer there at the time; old Admiral Artie Doyle was then a lieutenant.* He was the coach of the baseball team and just a simply terrific leader. He happened to be there the summer that I had my aviation summer, and he was such an enjoyable guy and such a marvelous officer, and we all knew him also because of the baseball business. He was one of the first people that made me begin to think that that was the place to be in the Navy.

Q: Well, how did you occupy your time when you were not

---
*Lieutenant Austin K. Doyle, USN. An oral history covering a portion of Admiral Doyle's career is in the Naval Institute collection.

flying in these planes?

Admiral Hyland: They had a certain number of formal classes, just the usual thing telling you about early airplanes and early types of engines and propellers, and some of the theory of flight and that sort of business--very, very rudimentary.

Q: Is there anything else about that period at the Naval Academy that occurs to you as you reminisce?

Admiral Hyland: Honestly, nothing right at the moment. One of my best friends is General Brute Krulak.* He was a classmate of mine, and, in fact, I guess we were the two shortest people in the Naval Academy. We were in the Eighth Company, which was the last of eight companies, and we were in the fourth platoon of that company and in the last squad of that platoon. So when the old regiment went into the football stadium, Brute and I were two of the last four people to walk in.

He was very fortunate in the Marines, and I was lucky in the Navy, and we've talked about that a great deal. I guess it was about three months before we graduated, we were suddenly confronted with a request for us to resign, because we weren't tall enough to be in the Navy. You had

---
*Lieutenant General Victor H. Krulak, USMC (Ret.)

to be five feet six. In those days, they'd let you into the Naval Academy when you were shorter than that and your age was such and such. You were expected to grow, and he and I didn't grow quite enough. He didn't grow nearly as much as I did, but I got up to five-five and three-quarters. But they did find out I was not five feet six. Brute was only about five-two, I guess.

So he and I and about four or five others were told that we weren't tall enough for a commission and we'd have to resign. And I can remember how frightened we all were about it, and scurrying around. I sent a telegram to my father, and he sent back the word to be sure not to sign anything until he could examine what it was, and so on. It was a lucky coincidence that, of these seven or eight people, we were all good students; we were all in the upper 10% of the class. So I can remember at the same time my dad told me, he rushed to talk to Admiral Leahy, who was then head of the Bureau of Navigation.* And so after evaluating the whole thing this way and that way, they decided to let us graduate and stay in the service.

Q: Krulak told me, I think, that he came by this awful

---

*Rear Admiral William D. Leahy, USN, was Chief of the Bureau of Navigation from 1933 to 1935. He later served as Chief of Naval Operations and chief of staff to the commander in chief, President Franklin D. Roosevelt. The Bureau of Navigation was renamed Bureau of Naval Personnel in 1942.

Hyland #1 - 26

nickname because he was rather cherubic-looking in those days. Is that true?

Admiral Hyland: Yes, he was. He was the coxswain of the crew. You know among his characteristics later on, he's always been extremely accomplished on his feet. He's a wonderfully articulate speaker. He's always been very confident; he's never had any trouble at all handling the big guys and so on. It all dates back to the time on the crew when he was telling these monsters what to do, I guess. But these talents that he shows now--this ability to speak and ability to be very, very quick witted--he had it all in those days. He really was an outstanding fellow. Everybody knew him, everybody knew about him, and I wasn't surprised that he did as well as he did in the Marines. He should have been the Commandant, but it just didn't work out. Well, I suppose it wasn't the right moment or something. He's certainly an impressive fellow.

Q: Well, sir. So you were allowed to graduate and get a commission. And, I notice from the record, that you did indeed represent a new school, because you went to an aircraft carrier, did you not?

Admiral Hyland: Yes. My first ship was the old Lexington, which had started out, I think, as a battle cruiser and never was finished. The two of them, the Lexington and the Saratoga, were converted from there.

Q: Because of the limitation of arms treaty?*

Admiral Hyland: Yes, I think it was. They were electric-driven ships and wonderful carriers for those days. I'll never forget, the skipper of the ship was A. B. Cook, who later became the Chief of the Bureau of Aeronautics.** He was a very, very handsome, very glamorous and personally very wealthy man in the Navy. While I was on board the ship for that one year, the squadrons would come out from time to time. It was really then that I got seriously interested in aviation, and I decided then and there that I did want to go to Pensacola and learn to be an aviator if I could.

In those days, there was a rule that after you graduated you had to do two years of sea duty, two years on ships, and you couldn't get married for those two years either. But there were no deviations from the fact that you had to do two years on board a seagoing ship. Looking back on it, I think it was a darn good idea. It helped me

---
*The Washington Naval Treaty of 1922 established a warship tonnage ratio for the major powers. Under the terms of the agreement, two partially constructed battle cruisers were permitted to be converted to aircraft carriers, the Lexington (CV-2) and the Saratoga (CV-3).
**Captain Arthur B. Cook, USN, was commanding officer of the Lexington from 1934 to 1936 and, as a rear admiral, Chief of the Bureau of Aeronautics from 1936 to 1939.

a great deal. I spent a year on the Lex and then a year on a four-stack destroyer, and then I was fortunate enough to be able to get into the very first class at Pensacola that my group was allowed to go to. And then, further than that, I was fortunate on the weather and some other things down there, and I was the first fellow to get wings in our class.

Q: Do you have any vivid recollections of your year on the Lex? You were fortunate in having a skipper whom you could look up to and learn from.

Admiral Hyland: He was a very impressive man, I thought. He was one of a number of men who, I guess, actually went down to Pensacola when they were in their early 40s and were put through the flight training then.

Q: Similar to Admiral King.*

Admiral Hyland: Very much the same, yes. In fact, he was only a little bit behind Admiral King at the Naval Academy, I believe, and then later on in flying.** Of course, I

---
*Admiral Ernest J. King, USN, was Commander in Chief U.S. Fleet and Chief of Naval Operations during World War II. King was a captain when he took flight training at Pensacola in the 1920s.
**King was graduated from the Naval Academy in 1901 and Cook, in 1905.

Hyland #1 - 29

was a junior officer there. They had a scheme where you'd spend a certain amount of time in each of the various departments; it was just a continuation of your education as a young officer. I can remember just as I got near the end of the year on board, the navigator asked me if I would be willing to come up and be his assistant. He had had one for a couple of years, and this fellow was going somewhere else. And I can remember being so pleased with that prospect, because assistant navigator was one of the best jobs you could have as an ensign. But I never did get it, because, lo and behold, orders came from Washington, and I was transferred to this little destroyer in San Diego.

Q: How many of your classmates were with you on the Lex?

Admiral Hyland: We had 25 on board.

Q: And you had a junior mess, did you?

Admiral Hyland: Yes, they had the usual junior officers' mess. It's funny, my recollections of that time, though, have sort of dimmed. I can remember a lot of fun flying with the air group that was on board. Whenever they would come, I made friends with one or two of the people, and I used to bum rides in the back seat of their airplanes. In those days even some of the fighters were two-seaters, and many of the enlisted men who normally rode around in the back seat were sick and tired of doing it anyway, so it was always easy to get a ride.

Q: And there was no restriction against that?

Admiral Hyland: Well, you'd have to get permission, but they never did turn us down. And it was then that I decided definitely that that would be much more enjoyable in the Navy, to be in aviation, and I was able to do it.

Q: What percentage of your classmates who were on the Lex with you decided similarly?

Admiral Hyland: Only a very few, strangely enough. I can only think of one offhand, a fellow named Tibbets who's still on active duty.* He's up at Quonset; his job is ComFAir Quonset. He and I went to flight training together. We were roommates on the Lexington, and then we were separated for a year. He stayed aboard the Lex. Then we found ourselves in the same flight class down in Pensacola, and we roomed together down there.

Q: Where did the Lexington operate, in the Pacific?

---

*Rear Admiral Joseph B. Tibbets, USN, Commander Fleet Air Quonset Point, Rhode Island at the time of the interview. He has since retired from active duty.

Admiral Hyland: When I joined her, she was in Norfolk. This was in '34, of course. Just a month or two later, she sailed around to Long Beach and spent the rest of the time in Long Beach that I was on board. There was a fleet problem; I forget the number of it, but the whole fleet came around from the Pacific and went through the canal and held maneuvers and war games and so on in the Atlantic and then turned around and went back out to the Pacific. I recall very vaguely that it was part of the idea of showing how flexible the U.S. Navy could be as long as they had the Panama Canal to get through.

Q: Well, so then you were relegated to a destroyer.

Admiral Hyland: Yes, I went to a ship called the Elliot, and she had been converted to tow high-speed targets. And that's what we did, really, for a year. We'd just go out to sea and stream these targets and tow them at various speeds for other ships to shoot at. When we weren't doing that, we operated as a standard four-stack destroyer.

Q: What kind of an assignment did you have on board her?

Admiral Hyland: To start with, I was the assistant engineering officer, and then, perhaps for the last six

Hyland #1 - 32

months I was on board, I got to be the chief engineer on the ship. We only had seven officers on board, including the captain, so there was a lot of duty to be stood. But in those days we really didn't work very hard. The ship spent a lot of time swinging around the buoy in San Diego Bay. There wasn't too much money available to operate, but I was able to get qualified as an officer of the deck. I remember having trouble with the rough seas; I used to get so seasick on that thing. Everybody else on board just was a cast-iron stomach type who, when everything was battened down, they loved to light up the big black cigars and to drink the black coffee and so on. And, boy, I had too tender a stomach for it. But I had a wonderful time.

Q: That's an ideal assignment, isn't it, on a destroyer where you get the chance to really exert some leadership?

Admiral Hyland: Yes. I think it was wonderful from that point of view, and that's why a whole lot of people just love destroyers, because relatively, whoever you are, whatever your rank is, you're going to be more important on that destroyer than you could possibly be on one of the big ships. I enjoyed the year ever so much, and I think later on, just all the things I learned about the power of the wind and sea--that you certainly learn on a destroyer a lot better than you do on a bigger ship. They really were good things to know about.

Q: There was certainly a lot of positive thinking back of these various assignments as you progressed along, wasn't there? The careful planning of the development of a young man's career.

Admiral Hyland: It was certainly done for you; I can remember that. I had no idea in the world of ever asking to go on a destroyer. I can remember being fascinated--along about 1935, there were occasional chances to go to China. Everybody heard a lot of the China sailors coming back with all their stories and so on. I've always wanted to go out there and be on a ship that went to Shanghai and Tsingtao. But at the time it was possible for me to do it, I had to make up my mind whether to try to get assigned out there to the Asiatic Fleet or whether to go to Pensacola. By that time my urge to get in flying was so strong that I didn't really think twice. But if I hadn't gone to Pensacola, or if I hadn't been able to pass the physical and so on, I certainly would have tried to get out to the China station because of all the great stories that would come back.

My skipper on the destroyer had a couple of tours in destroyers out in the Asiatic Fleet, and he used to just entertain us constantly with these stories of how well they lived, and how he had his own rickshaw boy with his own crest on his jacket.* And his wife would tell us wonderful stories about how nicely they lived and how good it was out there, but I never got to see it.

In those days, you know, I would call them perhaps the best, or the most successful officers in the Navy, would very, very strongly counsel you against going into aviation. They really thought it was just an offshoot of the big Navy, the principal Navy, and if they thought you had any talent or any promise they would go to quite some lengths to talk you out of doing it. And this skipper on the destroyer several times tried to get me to see that it really wasn't a good move--that it was by and large a kind of a reckless group, not with a very bright future, always going to be just an arm of the Navy in support of the other things. And they thought that just staying with the ships and working your way up was much the better course to take.

Q: This was, in a sense, the last stand of the so-called "gun club," wasn't it?**

Admiral Hyland: It seems to me it was, yes. Now, my

---
*The commanding officer of the USS Elliot (DD-146) during Ensign Hyland's time on board was Lieutenant Charles L. Hutton, USN.
**The "gun club" of the pre-World War II Navy comprised officers who specialized in ordnance and gunnery. Postgraduate education in ordnance was considered career-enhancing. Members of the "gun club" held the top billets within the Navy.

skipper on that destroyer, when I put in a letter requesting to go to Pensacola, he forwarded it. He tried to dissuade me from writing the letter or from mailing it, but he didn't do anything to hold it up. But there were several other cases of friends of mine, particularly on bigger ships, where they would just take their time with those requests, and they actually delayed some of the fellows as much as a year or two from going down to Pensacola when they really wanted to go just as soon as they could. They would either just simply hold the thing, or pronounce that they couldn't be spared at the moment, and work it that way. But you would really get rather serious advice not to go into flying.

Q: And this was true from the early Twenties on, apparently, until that time. I think shortly thereafter it ceased.

Admiral Hyland: Yes. I can remember going home and telling my parents--by that time, of course, my dad had retired the first time. He came back on active duty during World War II, but in a shore job up in Boston, and then he retired the second time. When I came home, he was pleased about my going down to Pensacola. He had been there on the old North Carolina in one of his earlier assignments. She was at Pensacola and was fitted with a catapult and did some of the early catapulting of airplanes down there in Pensacola.* And at that time he had some kind of a yen to get into flying, but I think my mother talked him out of it. Anyway, he didn't do it.

But when my mother heard that I was going to go down to Pensacola, she was not very happy. She was concerned about that, and I can remember her saying one time, "Johnny, you don't really want to be one of those naval aviators, do you?" What she was thinking of was that they were kind of a wild group. They were hard-drinking and hard-playing, and they weren't a group that she admired particularly; I remember that so distinctly. My wife's uncle, Ken Whiting, was a few years behind my father at the Naval Academy; he was one of the very earliest of the naval aviators, and he was a wild man way back.** There's a field, Whiting Field, down in Pensacola that's named for him, and there was a ship named for him. The Kenneth Whiting was one of the seaplane tenders, but she is out of commission now.***

---

*In the autumn of 1915, the armored cruiser North Carolina (ACR-12) became station ship at Pensacola. On 5 November of that year, she became the first ship to launch an aircraft by catapult while under way.
**Captain Kenneth Whiting, USN (1881-1943). As a commander, Whiting was executive officer of the USS Langley (CV-1) when she was commissioned as the Navy's first aircraft carrier in March 1922. He had a great deal to do with the development of carrier aviation.
***The USS Kenneth Whiting (AV-14) was commissioned in 1944, decommissioned for the last time in 1958, and sold for scrapping in 1962.

Hyland #1 - 37

Q: He's one of the greats in early naval aviation.

Admiral Hyland: He was a terrific guy. In fact, he was skipper on the Saratoga when I was on the Lexington, and, boy, if he wasn't something. He'd get tanked on the beach and so on. My mother thought they were all like that.

Q: Then there's an element of safety, too, that mothers would worry about, I suppose.

Admiral Hyland: Despite the fact those old airplanes were just ridiculously slow and really simple to fly, I guess the engines weren't especially reliable, and really the casualties in naval aviation were high in those days. In fact, the casualties in my group that went to Pensacola, in my Naval Academy class quite a few were lost in flying accidents. I wouldn't know what percentage, but someone had figured out it's a higher percentage than the flight pay accounted for, really, if the flight pay was earned just simply on the basis of the statistics. Because flight pay for a long time in the Navy was the bone of contention between the fliers and the non-fliers, I think.

Q: But the frequency of casualties didn't compare with what happened when Ballentine, for instance, went through.*

Admiral Hyland: Oh, no. Nothing at all like that. Well, anyway, my mother wasn't pleased, but I think she lived long enough to see that it was going to be all right.

Q: So they let you go to Pensacola. Tell me about Pensacola and the course of training there then.

Admiral Hyland: In those days you got training, of course, in a primary trainer--first a seaplane, and then a primary trainer in a land plane.

Q: No glider?

Admiral Hyland: No. That had been tried, I remember, a few years before I went there, and at one point they were rather sure that the best way to teach people to fly was to start them out in these gliders and give them that experience and that feel. But it was called off, and I have never yet had a ride in a glider; I've never been able to find one available when I could do it. We started right

---

*Lieutenant John J. Ballentine, USN, went through flight training in 1920-21. He later served as first commanding officer of the carrier Bunker Hill (CV-17) and as Commander Sixth Fleet. Ballentine retired in 1954 with a tombstone promotion to four-star admiral. His oral history is in the Columbia University collection.

Hyland #1 - 39

out in powered airplanes, first in seaplanes and then in land planes, and then we were sent over to a scouting type of airplane. There were five squadrons at the time, and the scouting airplane was the third phase of what you did. Then you went to the patrol planes that were the bigger, twin-engine airplanes, and then last you got in the little fighters, which were over in squadron five. So you got training in all types of airplanes, and then it was just a matter of luck when you graduated where you would go-- whether it would be to carrier planes, or whether it would be to cruiser-battleship airplanes, or whether it would be to patrol flying.

Q: How long was the course?

Admiral Hyland: It was nominally a year, although I finished in about 11 months. We started out in July, and most of us got our wings along about the following May or June. I remember I got mine in May, and at that time I think we had about 400 hours of flying, something like that.

Q: So when you got your wings depended largely upon your own initiative, did it?

Admiral Hyland: Well, no, I wouldn't put it that way.

Everybody took exactly the same training, and periodically you were given check flights. If you couldn't pass the first check, then you were given two more opportunities to pass. If you couldn't pass those, then they made a decision about whether to give you extra flying instruction or whether to wash you out. I never had any particular trouble when I was down there. I only got one so-called "down," and that was given to me because I had become very pleased with my own progress, and I got caught for a violation.*

The next thing I knew, I got a down from this fellow who was one of the terrors that we had down there. His name was Cloukey, and I later saw him at Patuxent; we were there together, and he was a wonderful man.** But whenever you got a ride with Cloukey, you were almost certain to get a down, and I got one. I can still remember so clearly flying two more flights, both of which I got an "up" on, and I didn't fly nearly as well on either one of them as I had on the one that I got a "down" on. But I was being shown something there, and I knew what was going on, and it just scared the dickens out of me that I could let myself get out this far on a limb.

---
*A "down" was an unfavorble grade on a particular check flight.
**Lieutenant Malcolm M. Cloukey, USNR. Patuxent River Naval Air Station, in southern Maryland, was the site of the Naval Air Test Center when Hyland served as a test pilot.

Hyland #1 - 41

I remember what finally prompted it was that we were supposed to muster every afternoon at 4:00 o'clock before we went home. I wanted to play tennis with a fellow who was quite good, and I thought to myself, "Oh, hell, they'll never even miss me." After my last flight, I just shoved off and went back, and we had this fine tennis game. The next morning, the squadron exec had me come in and wanted to know where I was on the muster, and so I told him I'd just shoved off and went to play tennis. He looked at me, and he said, "Johnny," he said, "I wouldn't do that again if I were you, and I'm not kidding." So a day or so later I had this check ride; it was the 25-hour check in that squadron. It was the principal check. And old Lieutenant Cloukey just took me to the cleaners. That was the only difficulty I had, and it was all my own doing.

Q: I've heard stories about a very famous character, a doctor, who was down at Pensacola. Was he there with you?

Admiral Hyland: Oh, yes. Dr. DeFoney was his name, yes.* He was a real character, and he remained one, too. I saw him a little bit later on in my time in the Navy, and he always was a very controversial guy. They were just beginning to fool around with psychological tests at that time. I don't think they knew what they were doing, but

---
*Lieutenant Commander Clinton G. DeFoney, MC, USN.

Dr. DeFoney had something to do with those early programs. I don't remember being a patient of his for that purpose, but some of the psychological tests were just outrageously funny and silly, and I don't think they ever came to anything very much.

A lot of people claimed that Dr. DeFoney, who supposedly had quite a reputation for being able to predict whether someone was going to complete the course successfully or not, that he would run this test and then he would just baldly put a slip in one envelope that said "This man will never finish," and in another envelope one that said, "This man will get through flight training without too much trouble." And he would keep these two envelopes and then produce the proper one whenever something happened.

Q: And say, "I told you so," right?

Admiral Hyland: Whether the fellow finished or the guy washed out, he'd be able to tell. I don't know whether that could be true or not, but he was a real character.

Q: Just a moment ago we talked about the glider program, which was there before you were there, and I believe that it had some bearing on this, too. I believe they felt that through the glider course they could discern what the aptitude was for a new cadet.

Admiral Hyland: Yes. The instruction, I thought, was absolutely excellent down there. They did have a corps of sort of old-time instructors who seemed to go back to Pensacola more and quite a few of them who just stayed at Pensacola. In many cases, they were reserve officers, and they were just professional instructors and stayed on. They provided quite a bit of continuity there. I remember having a number of them, and for that day and age they really knew how to teach people to fly. I think it was a little bit of a club.

There were some stories about people who could fly perfectly well but who had somehow or other alienated the aviation hierarchy, and they'd just get rid of them one way or another. I think they were getting over most of that, if there ever was any of it, when I was there. Since then they've learned so much more about how to instruct, and really I think they know that it's perfectly straightforward and simple to teach anybody to fly. Whether the fellow's going to have enough aptitude to later fly military airplanes is the question. Anybody can be taught to fly. It's just that some of the hot stuff we have nowadays, you've got to be able to think fairly quickly in order to handle some of the situations. You've got to have good control of yourself and be a somewhat superior person both physically and mentally, I think. But, really, they can teach anybody.

Q: It's a little bit like power steering in an automobile, isn't it? Things happen very fast. Was Charlie Mason down there when you were there?* He has a great reputation as one of the early chaps on the scene, training and teaching.

Admiral Hyland: No, I don't remember him. The one I remember the most--and he was sort of my mentor when I was down there--was a fellow named Fitzhugh Lee, who got way up in the Navy and who was just an absolutely wonderful officer.** He had just come back from duty on the China station, and he was an instructor down there when I was going through. I had a classmate who got married while we were going through the course down there, and who later was killed, and it's a coincidence that Fitz is now married to that guy's widow; Hal Lee was married to my classmate at one time. But all the time I was down there at Pensacola, Fitz was a bachelor, and he liked to play tennis, and he went on a few cross-country flights that he was able to do as an instructor. He took me along in the back seat, so I

---
*Commander Charles P. Mason, USN, was at the time executive officer of the USS Yorktown (CV-5). Dr. Mason had interviewed him for a Naval Institute oral history.
**Lieutenant Fitzhugh Lee, USN, later vice admiral, is the subject of a Naval Institute oral history.

got quite a bit of extra flying with him, and I got to know him very well. He is the outstanding single person I can remember from those days.

There was a very glamorous guy, Jack Tate, who was a famous naval aviator.* He was skipper of squadron five, which was the fighter outfit. He was a very flamboyant man, wore a colored scarf, and was just the epitome of a dashing pilot, and he was a very competent pilot. He has a son who's a naval aviator now, and I can remember him very well. Old Admiral Murray--he's gone now, but he was married to Mrs. Mustin. Mustin died and then Murray married his widow.** Admiral Blakely was the head of Pensacola then, and he was one of the senior officers who'd been put through the course late in his career, because they just realized they were going to need a certain amount of qualified naval aviators to command the carriers and go on to the other aviation jobs.***

Q: They needed status, too, didn't they?

Admiral Hyland: Yes. I don't know the real history of how

---

*Lieutenant Commander Jackson R. Tate, USN. Tate gained some notoriety as a retired rear admiral in the 1970s when it was revealed that he had fathered a child with a Russian actress while serving at the U.S. Embassy in Moscow during World War II.
**Captain George D. Murray, USN, married the widow of Captain Henry C. Mustin, USN.
***Rear Admiral Charles A. Blakely, USN, commandant of Naval Air Station Pensacola.

it got written into the law, but you couldn't command a carrier unless you were a naval aviator. So they just had to qualify a certain number to be able to have skippers for these ships. Of course, since then, they've had no problem at all with the numbers of people who've actually been flying ever since they were young people.

Q: Was Van Deurs there?*

Admiral Hyland: Yes, he was. I didn't see anything of him when we were down there, though. Joe Clifton was an instructor down there; he was one of the younger ones at the time.** My instructor when I was in squadron two, and that was the one in which I had the minor problem, because I'd gotten so pleased with myself--but I got a Marine warrant officer. He was a gunner whose name was Al Munsch, and everyone said you were really the luckiest man in the class if you got Al Munsch for an instructor because not only was he about the best instructor, but he also was the toughest check pilot.*** You never were checked by your own instructor; you were instructed by him, and then some other man would give you the check ride. But Al Munsch was famous as a killer down there. Hardly anybody could get an

---
*Lieutenant George Van Deurs, USN, whose oral history is in the Naval Institute collection.
**Lieutenant (junior grade) Joseph C. Clifton, USN, later a rear admiral.
***Warrant Officer Albert S. Munsch, USMC.

"up" from him. He was a famous Marine aviator. They didn't have very many of those flying warrant officers, but he was one, and he'd been through all sorts of things--the Nicaraguan experience and so on--and he was a rough, tough Marine.* But he sure showed me how to get by without any problem.

Q: Did you find the life there what it had been purported to be, a fast-moving, hard-drinking set?

Admiral Hyland: Well, it certainly could be if that's what you wanted to do, although that really wasn't the average pattern at all, when I was down there. Of course, Pensacola is known as the mother-in-law of naval aviation; there are a hell of a lot of gals from Pensacola that marry naval aviators. I survived that part of the course; I didn't get married until a little later on. Pensacola is a very pleasant town. It was a very small city in those days and absolutely wonderful for anything outdoors, particularly the swimming and the beaching; just a little old southern town, very, very partial to the Navy--as it's remained. And I found it just a simply wonderful year.

I never was really worried about getting through, after I learned that one lesson that I told you about. And

---

*The United States intervened in Nicaragua several times in the early 20th century. U.S. Marines operated in the country from 1926 to 1933.

Hyland #1 - 48

I never had anything happen in the flying that concerned me about whether I really wanted to do it. I found the more I did of it, the better I liked it and the more certain I felt that that's where I'd like to be in the Navy. I think some of the fellows occasionally would have a close call, of course, and some of the wives began to worry about them. Those were other considerations that I just never even thought about when I was down there.

Q: Did you have at Pensacola in those days the counterpart of the Blue Angels?*

Admiral Hyland: No. Although this fellow Jack Tate--one of the famous names in aviation is Charlie Crommelin, who was an instructor in squadron five at the same time Fitz Lee was.** And there was a fellow named Gehres who was a kind of a flamboyant officer, too. Leslie Gehres was captain on the Franklin when that disaster happened in World War II.*** But Jack Tate and Gehres and Charlie Crommelin had been members of demonstration teams that were just formed here and there in the Navy, and they were very well known pilots.

---
*The Blue Angels comprise the Navy's flight demonstration team that performs at public air shows.
**Lieutenant Charles L. Crommelin, USN.
***Lieutenant Commander Leslie E. Gehres, USN. Later, as a captain, he was commanding officer of the aircraft carrier Franklin (CV-13) when she survived after heavy bomb damage while participating in air strikes against the main islands of Japan on 19 March 1945.

They had the reputation of being very skilled in the stunting of airplanes and very skilled in aerial gunnery and all that sort of business. But they never actually put a team together when I was down there, you know, as a thing to give you a shot in the arm about how glamorous it might be if you stuck with it. If I recall correctly, the Blue Angels didn't start until shortly after World War II. I think that's been a very worthwhile enterprise, though. I think it's done a great deal of good. You know, every year it comes up for a real hard look, because it does cost some money, and it does take some fine airplanes, and it takes some absolutely excellent people. I think the net effect is very, very much worth it.

Q: What an impact it makes on the general public!

Admiral Hyland: Oh, boy. Last October I went back out to Japan, to the Nagoya air show. The Blue Angels flew for a couple of days out there, and then the local government requested that the Blue Angels not perform anymore. They were so absolutely sensational that they were drawing crowds from all over the area, and they had the worst traffic jam they'd ever had in the city of Nagoya. And they knew that if the Blues flew the next two days that they were scheduled to fly, they were going to have a simply impossible situation. So they officially asked that

Hyland #1 - 50

they not perform, and they put it on all the radios and all the TVs that, unfortunately, the Blue Angels would not be able to perform these next two days. And that's the only way they kept the crowd in line. It's sort of a reverse compliment.

Q: Is there anything else about Pensacola at that point which you might recall?

Admiral Hyland: Really, I honestly can't think of anything except it was just very pleasant. About half the fellows in the class were married, and about half of them weren't. It didn't seem to me that it made an awful lot of difference one way or the other. We had just a couple of cases, as I said, where the gals would begin to get anxious about this flying business and, one way or another, got the fellow out of there. But, by and large, the gals liked it fine, too, and most of the wives I'm thinking of now are still married to the same fellows, and so went through the whole time in naval aviation very happily.

Q: You got your wings, and then you went to Fighter Squadron Six.

Admiral Hyland: Yes. The squadron had been called Fighter Squadron One, and it was attached to the Langley out in San

Diego. But to make up the air group for the Enterprise, which was then being built and was going to be commissioned in a few months, that was one of the squadrons that was sent around to Norfolk to form Air Group Six. And Fighter Squadron Six was the one I went to. I spent three years in that squadron.

Q: So Enterprise hadn't been commissioned yet?

Admiral Hyland: No. When she was commissioned, she was sent on a shakedown cruise and went down to the Caribbean and then down to Rio de Janeiro.* She took about a six-week period in all to go down there and back. I can remember on that cruise they took the fighter squadron and the torpedo squadron; the bomber squadron and the scouting squadron were left back in Norfolk. So I was very lucky to be in the two squadrons that made the shakedown cruise.

Q: How much exercise did you get on that trip?

Admiral Hyland: Well, we did quite a lot of flying from the ship on the way down and while we were there, and, of course, on the way back. It's a long way to go, but in those days when a new ship would be commissioned, they always went on a shakedown cruise to some wonderful place.

---

*The USS Enterprise (CV-6) was commissioned on 12 May 1938.

Hyland #1 - 52

That certainly was a grand cruise that I'll just never, ever forget.

Q: Did you impress the Brazilian Navy?

Admiral Hyland: I think so. We did a lot of formation flying and that sort of business around there. I remember the social schedule being so absolutely terrific. We were there for ten days, in Rio, and we started out, of course with the old rule that everybody's going to make morning quarters at 9:00 o'clock, and then within a couple of days the exec changed it to 10:00 o'clock, and then I can remember he canceled quarters altogether. And the last admonition to everybody was that, by God, everyone would go to his share of the parties; there would be no shirking this responsibility. We just had a wonderful time. I've never been able to get back to Rio to see it again, but it was just a wonderful city in those days.

Q: Did we have a naval mission of any kind down there?

Admiral Hyland: Yes, we did, and I believe that's properly what it was called, too. I can remember a fellow named Eddie Ewen, who later got to be an admiral in the Navy; he

was the man in charge of the naval mission down there.*
We were told that the Brazilian Government duplicated his
salary; whatever the United States Navy was paying him,
they also paid him. So he just lived like a king. He had
a wonderful apartment there on that famous beach. I can
remember he was a marvelous man, telling all of us
youngsters that this was his one chance to live like a
millionaire, and they were sure doing it. But it took this
double pay in those days to be able to do it.

Q: Did they have any naval aviation, the Brazilians?

Admiral Hyland: Yes, I believe so. They didn't have any
carriers, but I can remember they had some naval officers
who came out and visited our carrier, and some of them were
aviators. I don't know just where they did their flying.
A little later on, of course, the Brazilians did get a
carrier. We were there for ten days. In the middle of the
visit, we went out to sea for just a day and put on a
demonstration. We took a bunch of Brazilian dignitaries
out to watch the operation. I can remember the president
of the country then brought his daughter with him, and it
was a very amazing thing that the U.S. Navy had consented
to let a gal go to sea. It was the first time I'd ever

---

*Lieutenant Commander Edward C. Ewen, USN. As a rear admiral, Ewen served as Commander Task Force 77 during the Korean War.

Hyland #1 - 54

seen it, and I didn't see it again for a long time, but she came out and watched the flying from the Enterprise.

Q: Did the Enterprise live up to expectations on this shakedown?

Admiral Hyland: Yes, I think so. She was built from the keel up as an aircraft carrier, and she was a very fine ship. There were two of them, the Enterprise and the Yorktown, and they were rivals all up and down the line for everything as long as they both were in active service in the Navy. They had arresting gear forward and aft.

Q: This was something new, wasn't it?

Admiral Hyland: Yes, I think it was. They could back down and take airplanes over the bow. I remember doing that a couple of times just to do it. Later on in the history of the ships they realized that just wasn't necessary, and all the weight of those arresting engines and all the rest of it up forward just was unnecessary, so they were removed. I remember that was the scheme. The idea at one point would be to land going in one direction and then just turn the planes around and launch in the other direction. It was so simple to just respot the deck that it wasn't a really good concept. They also had the idea that you might suffer damage aft and you'd still be able to recover your airplanes up forward, so we practiced it a few times, but it never was used as a routine.

Q: It was an evolving idea, wasn't it?

Admiral Hyland: Yes. Of course, they were straight-deck carriers. While I was in VF-6, we changed over from old F4Bs, which were Boeing fighters, little single-seat biplanes, to Grumman F3F-2 airplanes.* This was the first fighter in the Navy that had an engine rated at 1,000 horsepower. And I can remember we were the envy of everybody, having these hot little fighters that were so marvelous.

I remember one fellow describing the takeoff--he said, "My gosh, it's just like a catapult shot." That was an exaggeration, but it certainly had a remarkable takeoff performance compared to the airplane we'd had previously. When I first went to the squadron, we had these little Boeing airplanes, which were a little later version of the last airplane I flew down in Pensacola, so it wasn't much of a transition to go to a fleet squadron. In those days you went right to a fleet squadron and just simply had to get in the airplane that they had. There was no transition training squadron like we have now, where the pilot goes

---
*VF-6 was the official abbreviation for Fighting Squadron Six.

Hyland #1 - 56

there first and one step later goes to the fleet squadron.

Q: In the case of a plane like the F3F-2, this was a new plane. How long would it have been in the process of being turned out, being available to the fleet?

Admiral Hyland: If I remember correctly, it took about a year. Grumman had built a few airplanes for the Navy before. In fact, the one on the old Lexington that I used to bum rides in was a Grumman airplane. It was a two-seat fighter, and it was the first airplane in the Navy that had retractable landing gear.* That was one of the principal points of design that Grumman came out with that seemed to give them a step on the competition, because, of course, that reduced the drag so much. We were told when those new airplanes came along, those F3F-2s, that we really had to be careful with them, because they cost $25,000 apiece. And we were really impressed with that--the idea that this lovely little airplane was worth that much money. By God, you really would have to be extra careful with it until you got used to it.

About 35 years later, Grumman gave me a model of the F3F-2. When I first got to be a section leader, I relieved

---

*This was the FF-1, the first navy fighter to have a retractable undercarriage and the first fighter Grumman manufactured for the U.S. Navy. Deliveries of the FF-1 to the fleet began with squadron VF-5B of the Lexington in June 1933.

Tom Moorer as the leader of the sixth section.* A fighter squadron had 18 airplanes in those days, and the junior division of three planes was the sixth one, which had the yellow stripe around it, and that was my airplane. It's an absolutely lovely model of the airplane. It was made in the model shop up at Grumman by some fellow who is an absolute wizard at making the models that go into the wind tunnels and all that business, and it's a perfect model. It has my name on it, and it's exactly like it was when I was in that squadron. It's one of my most prized possessions. I got it a couple of years ago at the Tailhook reunion; they brought it out and gave it to me.**

Q: When you were flying these new planes on the Enterprise, did a Grumman man accompany you on this shakedown?

Admiral Hyland: I don't remember having any Grumman company people on at all. Now that picture has changed substantially. We wouldn't be able to get along without them now, particularly with a new airplane, and it's too

---
*Lieutenant Thomas H. Moorer, USN, a close personal friend of Admiral Hyland, is discussed throughout this oral history. He was in the Naval Academy class of 1933, later served as Chief of Naval Operations, 1967-70, and Chairman of the Joint Chiefs of Staff, 1970-74.
**The Tailhook Association is an organization of naval aviators and naval flight officers who have made carrier landings.

bad that the Navy has to have company technical representatives along. But with the turnover that we have and with the complexity of the airplane, it's absolutely essential that you have them, at least in the beginning. And the way it works out now, we pretty much have them throughout the active life of the airplane. They've got one fellow on every carrier that's deployed, and they have one or more at every air station where the airplane might be based ashore.

Q: I would think it would work both ways, though, in helping them with feedback on new models.

Admiral Hyland: It does. There's a move afoot right at the moment to do away with them and to replace them with civil servants who would become all-purpose airplane experts and would be able to work on more than one airplane. It's a very, very poor concept in my opinion, and all of the companies--Grumman and Vought and Douglas and the whole bunch--are really up in arms over that, because if that's done, they will lose their firsthand observer right on the scene, who's pumping stuff back to the company and telling them, if he's a good man, that they're doing poorly or they're doing well and what has to be done, and so on. So it is a two-way street. I think from the Navy's point of view, though, and just purely military excellence, it's too bad the Navy has to have them at all. We should be able to do it with our own people, but we just don't have the permanence to take care of it.

Q: What would be the advantage of a civil service man who is a jack-of-all-trades, so to speak?

Admiral Hyland: Well, there's a civil service empire that's headquartered in Philadelphia that claims it's cheaper. They claim that the companies kind of take the Navy to the cleaners by what they charge for those representatives. It's not true. We've had it exhaustively looked into. I'm a consultant with Vought now that I'm out of the Navy, and the company is very distressed about that statement that these guys are going to be much cheaper, because they could show you very easily that it wasn't that way. Now, how accountants can leave this or that out or put this or that in, makes a big difference in the picture, the way it's presented.

Q: Well, under the present system then, the company sends a representative, but the Navy pays for him, pays his salary?

Admiral Hyland: Well, the Navy just pays the company; the company pays his salary. The company signs a contract with the Navy to provide technical support, and this fellow's presence on board is the technical support that they provide. Some of the big carriers have two people for a certain type of airplane; it just depends on the kind of airplane and what the problems are. You very often have an electronic expert as well as an airplane expert. Those are the big systems now that are so difficult.

Once in a while, especially if you run into trouble, they'll rush out a fellow who's an expert on the engine, if that's the thing that's giving you the problem, but normally you wouldn't carry an engine man around with you. You just carry an all-purpose airplane man, and then if it's a very complex electronic airplane, you have to have a fellow who knows that system, too. But in those days, back in VF-6, there were no civilians attached to the squadrons or to the air groups. Whatever problems there were, and, of course, the airplanes were so simple that there wouldn't be really very many, they were handled mainly through the aeronautical engineering officers that we had through the local O & R shops.*

Q: I suppose all the bugs, for the most part, were ironed out at the test center, too, weren't they?

Admiral Hyland: Yes. Now in those days the test center

---
*O & R--overhaul and repair.

was up at Anacostia.* It was just a division of the Naval Air Station Anacostia. It wasn't until about 1942, when Patuxent was built, that they moved the flight testing down there, and it's stayed there ever since.**

Q: Well, now after you came back from her shakedown cruise, where did you go? What did you do in the Enterprise?

Admiral Hyland: We operated around the East Coast for about two years of the time that I was in that squadron, and then the Enterprise and the Yorktown were both transferred out to the West Coast. We were based in Coronado--based in San Diego--and I remember living in Coronado. During that time, the last year I was in the squadron, they formed what was called the Hawaiian Detachment, which was a special group that was sent out here and supposedly based that far forward and that much more ready. There were a couple of cruisers and a number of destroyers and the Enterprise. We based our planes then out here at Ford Island.

Q: You began to face up to the potential enemy?

---
*Naval Air Station Anacostia was in the District of Columbia.
**Naval Air Test Center, Patuxent River, Maryland.

Hyland #1 - 62

Admiral Hyland: Yes, although I'll have to say I wasn't really aware of it. I was just delighted that we were transferred out to Honolulu and we could take our families with us, and we operated from Ford Island. By that time, it was 1940, and I was almost at the end of my three-year tour of duty in the squadron. We just performed periodically aboard ship, most of the time based ashore, and did the regular gunnery training and navigation training and formation training.

It was a very, very pleasant life in those days. When we were aboard, we'd fly maybe an hour-and-a-half flight in the morning and one in the afternoon, but the second flight would be over by perhaps 3:30 in the afternoon, and everybody would rush down below, get in athletic clothes, come up on the flight deck, and fool around throwing the football or playing medicine ball and all that sort of business. We didn't fly at night very much, and when we did, we prepared very, very carefully for it. You only made a very few landings and that qualified you, and that's as far as they wanted to go with the risk.

Q: There was no great emphasis on night flying?

Admiral Hyland: No. They did want you to be able to launch or recover at night, but really as far as doing any useful military task at night, they didn't think much of

Hyland #1 - 63

it. Our squadron mainly practiced gunnery and dive-bombing during those three years that I was in the squadron.

Q: But speaking in terms of war games and potential enemies, there was knowledge of the fact that the Japs were doing night flying, wasn't there?

Admiral Hyland: Oh, yes. In those days I can remember that these Japanese ships then had started this procedure of just shadowing our carriers, and almost always there'd be a Japanese ship somewhere within sight.

Q: What, a merchant vessel?

Admiral Hyland: Usually they were, yes. Just a ship that would follow you around and that we knew was there for the purpose of observing the way we operated the carrier, because they were at the same time building up their carrier fleet, and most of the techniques that we had in the U.S. Navy were adopted by the Japanese. They did it the same way after watching us perform.

Q: And some of their planes were modeled after ours. Wasn't the Zero?

Admiral Hyland: I'm not sure about that. The Zero was a

very fine airplane for its time, and temporarily it had a big advantage over anything we had, but that was quickly overcome later in the war.* In these early days, though, when I was in that fighter squadron from '37 to '40, I don't recall any of the people seriously talking about a potential war with Japan and actually getting down to cases and preparing for it. I don't remember anyone ever studying a target folder or looking at the geography of Japan, or beginning to talk about where their strengths were and all that sort of business. We just weren't that close to any real trouble.

I can remember it as mainly a very pleasant and very interesting sort of military sport. A lot of the pilots wore colored scarves when they flew, and a lot of malarkey of that sort was the order of the day. It was just great fun. We would go out to sea on that Enterprise, and, as I say, we'd have these wonderful days where we'd fly a couple of times, but that wasn't too much, and then after our workout we'd have dinner, and then everybody'd go down on the hangar deck and go to the movies. The captain would come down just a minute before the movie started, and everybody would stand up. And he would smile at us, and we'd all sit down and watch the movie, and then we'd all go to bed. And the next day we'd do the same thing. Usually

---
*The Japanese Navy Mitsubishi Reisen (Zero) was a low-wing monoplane fighter that had a top speed of 317 miles per hour and was extremely maneuverable. It had the Allied code name of Zeke.

we'd be at sea for a week at the most, and some of us thought that was a long time.

Q: I remember an officer who was chief of staff to Admiral Yarnell at one point who was telling me that they sent back reports on Japanese night activities, target practice, and night flying.* They even sent pictures of Japanese landing craft, but nothing seemed to happen to all these things that came back.

Admiral Hyland: Not that I can recall. Later on in the war, the Japanese did fly a little bit at night, but I don't remember them doing very much that was effective at night. We worked very hard on the night business later on. It never in World War II really got beyond the point of being anything but a kind of a heckling operation, something to keep the enemy awake, something to keep him busy. But we never really had the machines or the delivery systems to do anything really very effective. It was all done in the daytime, and the night flying, for the most part, was simply defensive night fighter work, and that was done by a small corps of very excellent people who wanted to do it. Most people didn't enjoy the night flying and didn't do enough of it to become confident about it.

---
*Admiral Harry E. Yarnell, USN, was Commander in Chief Asiatic Fleet from 1937 to 1939.

I can remember it was always the most hairy thing that you ever had to do, and normally we only did it once or twice a year, and it was a very brief thing. It was just enough to get you qualified so that if you did come back from a flight, something happened and it got dark before they could get you aboard, you'd be able to get aboard. That was really all they were thinking of. Now, the senior officers in that squadron that I went to were all officers who had been flying all their naval careers. In other words, they'd gone to Pensacola when they were ensigns, just like I had done, and they were veteran navy pilots, and by and large were wonderful people, I always thought. There was just a great deal of squadron spirit in those days. We all had athletic teams of this kind or that kind. We'd have a game against Fighting Five, and there'd end up being fistfights between the competitors and the--oh, it was really just a great kind of a sporting life, a little on the military side.*

Q: Did you take part in any of the national air races or that kind of thing?

Admiral Hyland: I was after that, and when I was in the squadron the Navy didn't do any of that. Shortly before, I can remember one incident--it seems to me it was at

---

*Fighting Five is short for Fighting Squadron Five, which operated from the carrier Yorktown (CV-5).

Cleveland--one navy plane had plowed into the stands and killed a bunch of people, and that cooled this air show business off quite a bit.

Q: I think it was Herb Riley that told me that he did participate at Los Angeles or someplace like that, in those years sometime.*

Admiral Hyland: Yes. Jimmy Flatley is a famous name in navy flying.** He was in that squadron that I first went to, and he stayed for about the first year I was in the squadron. He was the hottest pilot in the squadron; he could fly better than anyone. He could shoot guns better than anyone, and he could do all the maneuvers better than anyone. He was a very small man, but he was just an absolutely marvelous aviator. They'd give you a position of advantage or disadvantage; it just didn't make a single bit of difference to him. About one or two minutes after a fight would start with him, you'd find him right behind you. How the devil he ever got there, you'd never really know for sure, but there he'd be. It was a great pleasure to get in with people like that right at the very outset.

Our big rival was Fighting Five. They had F3Fs also,

---

*Vice Admiral Herbert D. Riley, USN (Ret.), is the subject of a Naval Institute oral history.
**Lieutenant James H. Flatley, Jr., USN, was later one of the Navy's top fighter plane tacticians in World War II.

and they were on the Yorktown. We were normally each in half of the same hangar, and there was competition up and down the line in everything from the appearance of the airplanes, the appearance of the people, the appearance of the hangar, to actual performance in the air in gunnery and bombing and everything that went on in a squadron in those days.

I was very impressed with my first skipper and the people who followed him; they were all very fine with the younger people. They were just wonderful officers. It seems to me every one of them who lasted went on to very high places in the Navy. When I first joined up, it seemed to me I knew the name of every other naval aviator; I had heard about him, or I knew a little bit about him, and now it's changed.

Q: Well, this was pre-World War II. It was a small family, really, wasn't it?

Admiral Hyland: It really was. Now it's gotten so large that I remember in my last days in the Navy I'd be distressed because I'd be introduced to a fellow who was a wing commander on one of the carriers, one of the most select people in the whole Navy, and I would never have even heard of this fellow. I wouldn't know his name or know anything about him, and then I'd be told all the things that he'd done. And yet I had never heard of him until the time I'd happened to meet him because I was on board. That's how big it's become.

Hyland #2 - 70

Interview Number 2 with Admiral John J. Hyland, Jr.,
U.S. Navy (Retired)

Place: Admiral Hyland's home in Honolulu, Hawaii

Date: Tuesday, 8 March 1972

Interviewer: John T. Mason, Jr.

Q: It's good to see your smiling face again this morning, Admiral.

Admiral Hyland: Well, thank you.

Q: I think you assumed some duty with a patrol squadron out here in Hawaii, in the year 1940, was it?

Admiral Hyland: Yes. After I had finished three years in Fighting Squadron Six, I was transferred to Patrol Squadron 26, which at that time was based on Ford Island, right here in Pearl Harbor. I think I mentioned earlier, it was routine in those days to go from carrier flying--for instance, fighting squadron flying--to flying the big patrol planes, and at that time they were the old Consolidated PBY airplanes.*

---

*The PBY patrol bomber, built by the Consolidated Aircraft Corporation, had first reached a fleet squadron in late 1936. It was a two-engine flying boat with a wing span of 104 feet and length of 63 feet. Its maxium speed was approximately 175 miles per hour, cruising speed about 115.

Q: Good old reliables.

Admiral Hyland: I actually welcomed the change ever so much, because, naturally, of the opportunity to live in Hawaii and the opportunity to fly something else, and something entirely different. I spent about six months in that squadron at Ford Island, and then in December of that year, just almost a year to the day before World War II started, that squadron was suddenly transferred out to the Philippines, and its name was changed to Patrol Squadron 102.

Q: Before you make that leap to the Philippines, would you tell me about the policy of patrol planes, the using of patrol planes here in that time?

Admiral Hyland: At the time we were here in Honolulu, this was from July to December in the year 1940, it was mainly a training program to learn to operate the airplane, learn to make patrols, and there were a certain number of fixed patrols that were flown just for surveillance around the islands here. They didn't go very far, perhaps 500 or 600 miles out, and they weren't continuously flown at that time.

Q: They weren't daily flights?

Admiral Hyland: No, there was no such thing as a daily coverage of certain areas, just because at that time there was no particular threat to the Hawaiian Islands seen by anyone. It was mainly just a regular training program in the patrol wing that was out there. It seems to me we had four of the squadrons, and mine was skippered by the fellow who was junior among all the skippers, and we all thought when we were sent to the Philippines that that might have had something to do with it, but anyway our squadron was the one that was chosen to go out there just a year before the war.

Q: Now when you went to the Philippines, it was more in earnest, was it?

Admiral Hyland: It certainly was touted as such when we left, because at that time there was one other squadron based at Sangley Point in the Philippines. And we were told that that squadron was working so hard, and the situation was becoming more and more tense between us and the Japanese out there, that they needed the help of another squadron.

I can remember that the Navy, always the most conservative of the services, had been evacuating dependents from the Philippines, from the China station, for several months before we went out. I was newly married at that time--I guess I'd been married a year and a half or so--and we had one very small son. But I was not allowed to take my wife and my youngster out to the Philippines. She had to go back home and stay with her folks, and we all went out as bachelors. When we got to the Philippines, we found a few of the dependents still there, but they were evacuated just as rapidly as the Navy could do it or the Navy could induce the ones who didn't want to go to be sensible and go on home.

At that time, the Army and the Army Air Corps had their dependents on board in the Philippines and showed no signs whatever of sending them home.* And it wasn't until very, very late in the game, quite soon before the war started, that they did get those dependents out. They weren't able to get all of them out, and some who were there spent some very uncomfortable months, and I guess years, in that Santo Tomas prison in Manila. So at that time, of course, we felt good about the navy policy, but for the year that I spent in the Philippines as sort of an enforced bachelor, we all felt a little sorry for ourselves. Because here on the other side were the dependents all having a very fine life there, General MacArthur living in great splendor in a Manila hotel with

---

*In June 1941, the Army Air Corps was renamed the Army Air Forces. Admiral Hyland uses the same term to cover the branch both before and after the change.

his family, and so on, while we were forced to be single men.*

Q: This difference in policy between the two services indicates a much broader difference of opinion, too. Could you see this in terms of flying? I mean, the Army and Navy were not of the same mind.

Admiral Hyland: Oh, I should say they were not. The Navy was very conservative and very cautious, and I think the leadership could see what was coming, and some of them could see it a lot more clearly than I could. I'll say for the last six months before the war began, we experienced a series of sort of weekend alerts. People would have plans to go to Baguio or to go to Manila for a weekend, and late on Friday the word would come out that, sorry, no one could go. We had to assemble the squadron.** We had to be in a state of readiness, and so on. And it went on and on like that for months at a time.

Q: How did that affect your morale?

Admiral Hyland: In a way, we all thought it was crying wolf just once too often, because we got kind of sick and

---
*Lieutenant General Douglas MacArthur, USA, was commander U.S. Army Forces Far East, with headquarters in Manila before the start of World War II.
**Baguio is a resort area in the mountains of Luzon.

tired of having these alerts, and then nothing would happen. It would pass, and as younger people, we wouldn't be able to see why the alert was called and why we had to stay on the base.

Q: You weren't really convinced then as to the necessity?

Admiral Hyland: No. In fact, I as an individual--and I have several friends who were in my squadron that felt the same way--honestly right up until the day before the war started we were not convinced that anything was going to come of it. It just didn't seem to make sense to us that a relatively small country like Japan would ever attack the United States; it just wouldn't happen. We felt a little like political pawns in a sort of a game that was going on. But I'll say now, looking back on it, I can see that Admiral Hart very clearly saw the potential danger.*

    I can remember some cases where a fellow would be on patrol out there and would be intercepted by a Japanese airplane and would radio that information back to the base. And whenever something like that happened, Admiral Hart and his people would really jump on it and would want to know exactly what was going on, and wanted to be sure that we got continuous reports from that airplane. Because they

---
*Admiral Thomas C. Hart, USN, was Commander in Chief Asiatic Fleet from 1939 to 1942.

apparently were thinking that perhaps the Japanese airplane would shoot down our airplane, so there might be a fracas out there that would cause some trouble. They would take the incident very, very seriously. Most of us never really did.

Q: What was the purpose of these interceptions?

Admiral Hyland: By that time, we were making standard patrols from the base at Sangley Point and the one up in Subic Bay where my squadron was. And we were making just area surveillance, trying to find any Japanese ships or trying to just see what was there. Occasionally on flights up to the north, Japanese airplanes from Taiwan would cross our paths, and each airplane would look at the other one, and once in a while come a little closer than normal just to see what was up. Those were the incidents that always seemed to concern the senior people there in Manila.

Q: What kind of planes were the Japs using--seaplanes?

Admiral Hyland: They were in some cases, yes. But in most of the interceptions, it was a twin-engined land plane, and I can't think of the designation of the thing right at the moment. It was a much higher performing plane than a PBY, and I think for that reason our leaders felt that we were awfully vulnerable in such a situation. Later on, we found out that we certainly were, when the war began in earnest. But for almost that whole year, when we were flying out of Subic Bay, this regular and quite frequent calling of alerts and admonitions to be more ready--that something might happen and so on--went on so much that I think they lost their effect just a little bit.

Q: Who was the officer on Hart's staff who was in command of air activities?

Admiral Hyland: You know, I can't remember who he was. Admiral Hart and his staff were at that time based in downtown Manila, and we never saw any of them. My squadron was up at Subic Bay, up at Olongapo. The other squadron was at Sangley Point, across Manila Bay, and we simply got our directives from a wing commander who happened to be a Captain Wagner out there, Commander of Patrol Wing Ten.* We just did what we were told, but there was no direct liaison between the squadron and Admiral Hart's staff.

Q: What relationship did you have with the air people under MacArthur?

Admiral Hyland: We just had absolutely none. The Army Air

---
*Captain Frank D. Wagner, USN.

Hyland #2 - 78

Corps at that time had some P-40 fighters and some B-17 bombers, and they were based up at Clark Field and some over at old Nichols Field, which is a field right near Manila. We would occasionally see those fellows socially, perhaps if we had a chance to visit Baguio or perhaps see them in Manila at the Army-Navy Club, but we had absolutely no liaison with them on the military side at all. We just knew they were there, and we could see them flying occasionally, but what they were doing we had no knowledge and no part in and no partnership.

Q: Did they also experience the same series of alerts that you people did?

Admiral Hyland: Yes, I think so, but I'm really not sure about that.

Q: Tell me about some of your special operations. You've told me off tape yesterday about that mission you performed.

Admiral Hyland: Things really did get quite tense for perhaps a month before the war started. And about two weeks before it started, I was chosen to go on a special flight to go down and conduct a surveillance of the Spratly Islands. The whole thing was done very secretly. I was ordered to go to Manila and to talk personally with Admiral Hart. I wasn't told what this was going to be about or any such thing, but when I talked with him he explained that they wanted to have a look at the Spratly Islands. There were some rumors that the Spratly Islands had been transformed into a major Japanese naval base, but nobody knew whether that was so or not, and the point of the mission was to go out and get some pictures and see.

He told me that they didn't know at the time really whether I'd be intercepted by fighters or whether I'd be fired on with antiaircraft guns, but it had to be a secret mission. I could tell my crew where we were going, and I was going to take a very skilled chief photographer along on the trip. We were going to make one pass over the islands and try to get pictures of it so they could decide whether there was really a threat of this supposed base down there in the South China Sea.

I made the flight, and we found the Spratly Islands, and there was just absolutely nothing there at all. There was one little pier, with no boats alongside as far as I could tell. There were no people on the islands at all, but certainly if there were, there were very, very few. We made this one run, quite high for the old PBY, and this chief photographer got about 20 pictures in that one pass, and when I got back to Manila they rushed the pictures through the photo lab and so on. And I had to take them secretly back to Admiral Hart and show him what we'd found. I can remember he was very, very pleased, and I suppose he was relieved to find out that there really hadn't been any military buildup whatever on that little dot.

Q: How did you happen to get selected for that?

Admiral Hyland: I never really knew how it happened. I can just remember my skipper asking me if I would be interested in going on a very special flight, that I wouldn't be able to talk about until it was over, and that there might be some risk. And I said, "Sure, I'd like to do that." It kind of sounded exciting. So that's what happened on that particular flight. A couple of weeks later, the war started. I can remember just the night before the war we'd gone up to the little O-club in the naval base there at Olongapo, and we were all sitting around having some drinks, and I can remember getting warmed up to the occasion and we were joking.* I made a little speech that it was silly to imagine that Japan was going to attack the United States. They just wouldn't do it. It simply didn't make sense for a country with their strengths and so on to attack a huge country like the United States.

I really had to eat my words, because not more than

---
*O-club--officers' club.

Hyland #2 - 81

four hours later, after we'd gone to bed, we were waked up--it was 1:00 o'clock in the morning--and the information we were given was, by God, the war had started. They had attacked Pearl Harbor. And there we were. As I recall, the wording of one of the messages that came from Admiral Hart was, "We are at war. Conduct yourselves accordingly." And there was no one in the squadron, including the captain, who'd ever been at war. We had no idea what, really, we were going to do, or how you conducted yourself, and what that meant. Then gradually, as the days went on, we began to get a little more information on that.

Q: May we lap back for a second and let me ask, were there other specific missions of the sort that you performed to the Spratly Islands that you performed, or some of your colleagues?

Admiral Hyland: If there were any like that, I never knew about them myself, and I don't believe there were. Now, a little bit before that, I can recall a mission that I also was able to go on. We flew three of our airplanes from Olongapo over to Hong Kong, and the purpose of that mission was to take some Chinese officers who had been in the United States--we never knew what they'd been doing in the United States or how they got to Olongapo, but we took them up in our airplanes. They were Chinese Army officers and one or two civilian dignitaries, and I can't remember really who they were. But we took them to Hong Kong and stayed for about a day and a half and then flew back. That was an extremely interesting trip. That's the first time I ever got to Hong Kong in my life. We utilized the old Pan American seaplane facilities; the China Clippers went into Hong Kong in those days, and we camped on their facilities.

But about special missions like that one down to Spratly, I don't remember any. At that stage, there was quite a vigorous program of patrols going out into all the sectors to the north, to the east, and to the west of the island of Luzon. There were no patrols down to the south; I don't think they expected any trouble from that direction. We were mainly interested in what was going on in the more obvious threat areas.

Q: Were you interested in the Japanese merchant shipping, I mean, the bringing of raw supplies from the Netherlands East Indies?

Admiral Hyland: The orders on all of these patrols were simply to report whatever you saw, and we did the best we could with the kind of primitive tools we had to report what ships, and what they seemed to be doing, what their size was.

Q: Did you use photography?

Admiral Hyland: No, we didn't. One of the missions I can remember flying just about straight west, perhaps a little to the south. I went over to Camranh Bay, which, of course, has been a very important harbor and very important base here for us during the Vietnamese War. We had heard that the Japanese, in moving their fleet from north to south, were using the harbor at Camranh Bay. I remember on that particular flight we got over there, and there were no ships in the harbor at all.

But we did, on that flight, see a Japanese airplane, and we really didn't know where it came from. It was a land plane. The leader of the missions was my squadron exec, and he figured out that it must have come from a carrier. He was very alarmed over seeing it, and the minute that he did see it, he ordered us both to turn and head back for Manila as fast as we could go. Of course, after about 15 minutes we lost sight of him, and there wasn't any further danger. But I especially remember that flight, because we'd heard so much about Camranh Bay but yet really had no intelligence on it at all. There wasn't any information about whether it really was being used, or whether it wasn't.

Q: Did you have any active liaison with the Philippine

forces themselves?

Admiral Hyland: No, there was none at all on the part of the navy patrol squadrons.

Q: Admiral, tell me about your feelings on your level at that time about the seeming attitude of the military commander?

Admiral Hyland: Well, it was obvious that there was no real meeting of the minds between the top Army and the top Navy leaders out there. Going back again to our status in that year before the war as sort of enforced bachelors, all of us young pilots and the rest of us in the squadron were puzzled over the fact that we were unable to have our dependents there at the same time the Army and the Army Air Corps had theirs. General MacArthur, who, of course, was the top leader, lived in great splendor in a penthouse on a Manila hotel and had his family with him. We would ask ourselves, "How can it really be as serious as they sometimes say if he still has his family there and all these other dependents are still there, and there are no signs of them being asked to go home or ordered to go home?" So we were a little puzzled about it.

Looking back, it's rather clear that what the Navy was doing, it was doing entirely on its own and separately, and the Army and the Army Air Corps were doing the same thing. We really had hardly any knowledge, at least at my level, of what the other people were doing or where they were going. I never saw any B-17 bombers when I was on any of my patrols as we would pass over close to Clark Field and around the other smaller fields where the Army Air Corps had their fighters. We'd see them flying locally, but that would be all. As far as seeing the people in the other service, we'd only see them occasionally in social things at the Army-Navy Club in Manila or on a visit up to Clark Field or perhaps up to Baguio.

Q: Well, now that Pearl Harbor day has come and has had its repercussions in Manila, tell me about your activities.

Admiral Hyland: Of course, we then had to become entirely serious about the whole thing. Our squadron stayed in the Manila area for only about a week, and in that first week we lost more than half of our airplanes to attacks, either on the water or in the air from Japanese fighters that had come in and attacked in the Manila area. About the fourth or fifth day of the war, we were dispersed from Olongapo and sent over to an inland body of water which is right close to Manila. It's called Laguna de Bay; it's a very large lake. We were told to just go over to the lake and try to find a place to hide our airplanes and just wait for instructions.

Q: Did you resort to camouflage?

Admiral Hyland: Yes. I'll never forget--one long day I took my airplane over to Laguna de Bay and found this little cove. And right in the same area there was a bunch of trees and vines and foliage, and we actually completely covered up the PBY with greenery that we picked. Another fellow in my squadron told me that he taxied by in his airplane not very far away, and that he didn't even see my airplane--we'd done such an effective job of covering it up. It took us all day long to do this, and we spent all night long awake wondering what the dickens was going to come next. And early the next morning we were told to get out and head south. So that's what we did, but with all of our airplanes.

Q: How were these Japanese attacks on the squadron effected?

Admiral Hyland: For the most part, they were done by fighters, and they obviously came from carriers, which were somewhere up to the north of Manila and, we thought, to the west of Manila. I think it was about the third day--I was not present in Olongapo--but we had seven of our airplanes on the water right there at Olongapo tied up at buoys. And these two fighters came in and went around the bay and attacked and set fire and sank all seven of these airplanes that were just sitting there. In each one they had a caretaker or two, perhaps a young officer and maybe one enlisted man. They all jumped over the side. I can remember on that attack hearing that one man was killed out of perhaps 14 or 15 or so total that were on board the airplanes at the time. This was early in the morning, and they jumped over the side and swam ashore and all the airplanes were lost. So when we got the order to head south, I'd say we had lost perhaps half of our airplanes.

We'd been extremely lucky about losing the people, and that continued to be the picture as we went on down south and operated in the Dutch East Indies for several months. We would have an airplane attacked either on the water or in flight. The airplane would always be able to land straight ahead in the ocean, and the people would jump out. They would be missing for a week or so, and we would have to assume they were gone. And it got to the point in many cases where they notified the people at home that they were missing in action. And then, by gosh, another week later they would turn up. In all the places where they were knocked down in the Philippines or in the Dutch East Indies, the natives were very friendly and helped them. There are lots of islands down there. There's no place that you could go down without being reasonably close to land, so these people had some wild escapades, but they survived them.

Q: Already the system of watchers was beginning to develop.

Admiral Hyland: Yes, apparently. In several cases the fellows would be taken care of by the natives, who would either walk them to where they wanted to go or would take them in little dugout canoes--the little outrigger canoes that the Filipinos used--and these fellows would all turn up a little later on. The net result was we had an awful lot of people and very few airplanes as the campaign got to an end. I can remember when we finally got to Australia, we counted up the airplanes that we'd had on hand in Manila when the war started and added the ones that came out from Hawaii to take part--they joined us in the Dutch East Indies--and there were a total of 46 PBY airplanes that were involved in the whole of the action from the time we started until we got to Australia. And out of those 46 airplanes only two of them got to Australia. A few of them had gone to Australia on trips and then come back, and then they were later lost in some of the action. Yet we really didn't lose very many people. We perhaps lost a total of four or five crews out of all of those we had.

Q: You really did have surplus of pilots.

Admiral Hyland: We certainly did have that.

Q: What about servicing the planes, though? How was this done?

Admiral Hyland: When we left the Manila area and, of course, no longer had the fixed bases there at Olongapo and Sangley Point, all of the servicing was done from the seaplane tenders after that. We had three. We had the <u>Childs</u> and the <u>William B. Preston</u>, which were converted four-stack destroyers and were made into seaplane tenders, and we had one bird-class tender called the <u>Heron</u>. Now, of course, in many places in the Dutch East Indies, the Dutch had facilities. We operated principally from Surabaja, which was the headquarters in Java, and from a second naval base on the island of Ambon, which is about 1,000 miles north and east of Surabaja. Most of our operations were done from Ambon. It was quite a fine little seaplane base, but we were the only ones who had any airplanes at the time.

Q: The Dutch didn't have any?

Hyland #2 - 90

Admiral Hyland: The Dutch did have some, but I can remember at one point in the proceedings down in the Indies there, they transferred about 12 of their airplanes to us. These were late-model PBYs, and one of the interesting features about them was they all had the European instruments. They had been bought in the United States and flown out to the East Indies, but we had more trained people, and they had the airplanes, so we got the PBYs. I think there were about 12 of them, and they're included in that total of 46 that I'm telling you about. Most of them never got out of the Indies either. It was interesting to fly them, because they had altimeters that were in meters, and pressure was in centimeters of mercury rather than inches of mercury and that sort of business, but it was perfectly straightforward and easy to adapt to it. Really it was just a PBY with Dutch-European markings and gauges and so on.

Q: What was the attitude of the Dutch military at that point? How cooperative were they?

Admiral Hyland: Extremely cooperative. When we finally got down to Surabaja, which is where we went first, we went by way of Manila down to a big lake on the island of Mindanao which is called Lake Lanao. It was one of the most lovely lakes you'll ever see in your life, quite big, and we stayed there overnight. Then I can remember flying from there down to a port on the island of Celebes. It was called Menado, and then from Menado to Balikpapan, and from Balikpapan down to Surabaja.

On my flight from Menado to Balikpapan, one of the engines on my airplane failed, and that was the first time I'd ever had any problem in a twin-engine airplane with either one of the engines. This engine failed completely, and just ran itself out of oil because everything internally just came apart. In those days you could not feather propellers, so I had to go along windmilling, and the reason I went to Balikpapan was I couldn't fly all the way from Menado to Surabaja, which you could easily do in a PBY if everything went well.

I can remember going to Balikpapan, and there the Heron happened to be, this little bird-class tender, and by gosh they had a spare engine on this little ship. We changed the engine with the advance base gear that they had aboard and that we had in the airplane. And it was really quite a chore to get that failed engine off and get the new one on, because we really never had actually done that in the squadron. We'd thought about it, and we had the emergency gear to change the engines in other than prepared hangar arrangements, but it worked very well. The engine ran fine, and I can remember that airplane continued to operate for a lot longer.

Q: Were these tenders able to cannibalize any of the planes that were destroyed by the Japs at the shore base?

Admiral Hyland: No. There was absolutely no time to do anything like that. If the plane was shot down or forced down and damaged, holes in the bottom from running aground, or anything like that, we just simply had to leave them there. There was just no time. Most of our squadron flight personnel got out of the Manila area and got away in the airplanes. Almost all of the ground segment of the squadron was just simply left there at Olongapo and later fought with the Army down the Bataan peninsula, and they all ended up on Corregidor. Most of them spent the rest of the war in a prison camp, because they were there on Corregidor when the thing finally fell.

Q: This would include some of your communication men, too?

Admiral Hyland: Oh, yes. Mostly the squadron maintenance people and ground support people were the ones who were, unfortunately, left there. We got as many out as we could, but the fact of being separated here and there on this dispersal operation that I told you about and other reasons, you just couldn't get them. Now, a certain number of airplanes that were superficially damaged, they were able to work on, and perhaps a week or ten days after the majority of us flew south, one or two or three rejoined because they had been able to get patched up and bring some people out and rejoin us down there in Surabaja. Back to the reception by the Dutch, it was very, very cordial. We spent a couple of weeks in Surabaja, and then all of our squadron, which by that time had gotten down to substantially a single squadron, went up to this island of Ambon and operated there.

Q: Had the Japanese discovered you there?

Admiral Hyland: Oh, I think they had, yes, but it took another couple of months before they actually got around to invading Ambon, which they finally did, and had no difficulty landing on the island and capturing whatever was left. By that time, we had returned to Surabaja and had begun thinking about eventually going down to Australia. The Dutch were very cordial. They had fine bases there, both in Ambon and in Surabaja, and just simply gave us everything they had. They couldn't have been nicer.

Q: It must have been a major project to keep your squadron together under such circumstances, through communications, to coordinate things.

Admiral Hyland: The wing commander, Captain Wagner, had a very small staff, and they came with us. They would evacuate in one or another airplane, and they continued to direct the operation. They decided where the patrols were going to go. Of course, due to the number of airplanes available, which was not very large by that time, it was pretty easy to plan it, so we just continued to do what we were told.

Toward the end of our stay there in the Dutch East Indies, it, of course, became obvious that we really weren't doing any good. We were going on patrols, and occasionally someone wouldn't return. We never would know why, and in a few cases we never did find out what happened to these people; they just simply were lost on the patrol. We could see that even if we did intercept Japanese forces and we were able to warn that they were here, or they were there, and they were obviously headed on such and such a mission, there simply weren't any military forces anywhere that were going to be able to do anything about it; there was just nothing left.

The Air Corps had lost almost all of their equipment on the ground up in Manila. The fighters moved south sort of with us, and for a time they were flying out of Java, but those old P-40s were outperformed by the Japanese airplanes and certainly badly outnumbered, so they didn't last very long either. What I think you can say is that we

Hyland #2 - 95

just had a kind of fiasco there toward the end. The thing became a little more and more disorganized, and people began to be a little more concerned about what was going to happen to them and why thy were flying these patrols, and we had a certain amount of difficulty with people who tried to avoid going on patrols.

Q: Were you in constant communication with the commander in chief, with Admiral Hart? Was there communication?

Admiral Hyland: Yes, as far as I know, there was, but I never was privy to any of it and just have no idea what might have been said. While we were in Ambon, I was assigned to lead a six-plane attack on a port called Jolo. It's in the southern part of the Philippines, south and west a little bit from Zamboanga. We had information from somewhere that there was a concentration of Japanese ships there in the harbor at Jolo. And I was sent on this mission, which left at dusk in the evening, flew all night long, and arrived overhead in Jolo very early the next morning.*

Q: With the intention of dropping bombs?

Admiral Hyland: Yes. We were all loaded with 500-pound

---

*The PBY raid against Jolo took place was 27 December 1941.

bombs, as many as we could carry, and my instructions were to just see what was there, and if anything was there to attempt to attack it.

Q: Did you have any kind of a bombsight?

Admiral Hyland: Yes, we had the old Norden bombsight in the airplane, and it was a good piece of equipment.* Well, as we got very close to Jolo that morning, I was absolutely astonished to be attacked by fighters, and four of those six airplanes were shot down on that one mission. I, who was the section leader, and one other airplane that was in my section--all turned and ran when we started getting these fighter attacks; we had to turn around and beat it. I and this other fellow got away. All the other four were shot down; one of them landed on the water and was later rescued right there in the southern part of the Sulu Sea.

Q: You never did get over your target at all?

Admiral Hyland: No. I could see there was a cruiser there. These fighters came from a field that was there; that was what was so astonishing to us. There was no

---

*The first effective bombsight was developed by Carl L. Norden and Theodore H. Barth in 1930 and was used by the Navy throughout World War II.

aircraft carrier anywhere around that we could see. But as we approached, this cruiser had obviously seen us first, because it was under way, and it was making very high speed. We started the attack. We started to go in and make a run on this cruiser, but I could see that we just simply couldn't possibly do it--get away with it--so we turned around and ran. They chased us for a while, but they weren't very long-range airplanes, thank heavens, and so after a while they turned around and went back.

Q: Were you riddled with bullets?

Admiral Hyland: No. I can remember tracer bullets seemingly going all around me. You could see them under and out to the side and so on. Whoever the pilots were in those Japanese airplanes, they must have been the poorest gunners that you could find, because they never even touched my airplane or the other one that got away. But the other four were all shot down. They didn't do badly with them. I can remember flying back to Ambon, and we didn't get there until later that same day, and Captain Wagner was standing there on the pier when I came ashore.

I told him what had happened, that we had had no success at all, that there had been this Japanese cruiser, but the thing that foiled us was this fighter attack. I think there were about six fighters; it's hard to say.

Some of the people estimated numbers a lot higher than that, but I don't think there really were. But in a PBY there's just nothing you can do about a fighter attack. Any good fighter pilot ought to be able to get a PBY on one pass.

Q: What was Wagner's reaction to this?

Admiral Hyland: Well, of course, he was very dismayed about the loss of the four airplanes and was unhappy because we had had absolutely no indication at all that there might be fighters up there. If he had ever had any information like that, he never would have sent the PBYs into a place that was defended with any kind of fighters; it would be absolutely foolhardy to do it. So, of course, he was very unhappy. I can recall another incident after that flight up to Jolo.

Several days later, I was making a patrol up to the north again, and on my way home I heard someone talking on the radio, and they said that an Australian Hudson airplane had gone down, and they named the position. I put it on my little chart that I had there in the cockpit, and I noticed it was only about 35 or so miles away from where we were right then. So I headed over to see if we could see anything, and, sure enough, here was this wreckage of the bomber in the water. And all I could see down there on the surface of the ocean, in addition to the wreckage that was floating around here and there, was this one man waving his arms at us.

It was a very still day, and the ocean looked quite smooth. And I decided to go down and land and see if I couldn't pick up this man and maybe anyone else who happened to be there that I couldn't see from the air. I'll never forget that experience. It's the only time I've landed a PBY more or less in the open ocean, and what I wasn't prepared for was that however smooth and nice it looked from the air, it was really rough. They had big swells, and I can remember hitting like a ton of bricks on top of one of these swells, and it seemed to me, bouncing about a couple of hundred feet into the air.

But we finally got down on the surface of the ocean, and I taxied up, and we were able to pick up this Australian fellow who had a very, very badly broken leg. From him we learned that the plane had been shot down. It had attacked a Japanese ship, and in doing that it had been shot up and then later had to land in the water or crashed in the water. He was sure that no one else in the airplane could possibly have survived. He was a big fellow, and we had a dickens of a time getting him into the PBY, but we finally made it, and this is the part that I wanted to tell you about.

You talked from the cockpit back to the after station.

You couldn't see it from the cockpit. You had to talk on an interphone, and I said, "Now that he's aboard, are you all set for takeoff?" We wanted to get going and get him back to the hospital. I had a plane captain, a chief whose name was Schnitzer, and he was a fine fellow but in some ways not exactly the smartest guy in the world. When I asked the question, "Are you ready for takeoff?" the answer came back, "No, sir, we're not because Schnitzer is gone." I said, "What do you mean, gone?"

He said, "Well, he's in the water back there someplace." He went over the side to try and help this injured Australian into the airplane, and he finally succeeded in getting the fellow up enough so that they could grab him from inside the airplane and pull him aboard, but in so doing, he lost his foothold and drifted astern. So he was back there someplace. I thought to myself, "My God, what a decision I've made. I've landed in the water here, and I've almost lost my airplane because it's so rough and I didn't realize it would be that way. Now I've lost my plane captain, and I'm not sure I can even get off in this situation. So what have I done?"

By that time, the wind had picked up quite a bit. I turned around and went directly downwind and put men up on top of the wing to try and see if they could see the plane captain if he was back there. We went up and down over these swells, and when you were down in the trough you just couldn't see out of the trough at all, so they really couldn't see anybody more than about 50 feet away. Well, the good Lord was with me that day, I'll say, because it seemed an eternity, but I guess it couldn't have been more than ten minutes of taxiing straight downwind. I ran right into old Schnitzer, and there he was, floating in the water in his life jacket. He was completely unconcerned.

He was very good about getting himself on board; he knew how to do that. And when we got him, he had spent that time completely separated from our airplane and without the slightest worry in the world. I berated him and told him he shouldn't have risked himself; they should have done it some other way and so on, but there he was back aboard. So we took off and went back to Ambon, and I was later very, very happy to find out that this Australian had survived and had recovered and was okay.

Q: Did you have difficulty getting off the water?

Admiral Hyland: It was a very rough takeoff, but, of course, by that time we were on our way home, as I told you to start with, so we really didn't have too heavy a load, but it was awfully rough. I learned a lesson that you can't really learn without doing it. Landing in the open ocean with a plane that size--big for its day but really not big considering the magnitude of the average seas that you have in the open ocean--it's a very difficult thing to do, and it never should be done unless it's an absolute necessity. I thought there was, but I really didn't foresee how ticklish it was going to be to get away with it.

Q: Did you know the circumstances under which the Hudson had been shot down? Was there not danger that there might have been fighters somewhere near to get after you, too?

Admiral Hyland: I don't think so, no. Apparently, the airplane had made the attack on this Japanese ship some distance up to the north and then had gotten that far back. There was a land plane field at Ambon, and an Australian Hudson squadron was stationed there, and it was one of those airplanes that this fellow came from. Everyone else in the airplane was killed; I believe they had a crew of four or five men in those things at that time. It was that incident that got me recommended for a DFC.* I was one of the first fellows in the squadron to be recommended for a decoration, and that was a great thrill. I didn't get it for many months later, when I got back to Washington. Captain Wagner decided that since I'd gotten away with the whole thing, it was a legitimate effort.

I think it was perhaps another week after that that we

---

*DFC--Distinguished Flying Cross.

realized that we would not be able to operate from Ambon. The Japanese had taken islands to the north, and they were coming in, and there was just no sense in staying there. So what was left was all withdrawn to Surabaja, where we continued to operate for a little bit longer.

One other incident I can recall about the time--when we were there in Ambon, that was the time that VP-22, Patrol Squadron 22 in which Tom Moorer served and which was commanded by Frank O'Beirne, who later got to be a vice admiral in the Navy--well, his executive officer was a fellow named Ducky Donaho.* They had flown their airplanes all the way from Pearl Harbor out there to Ambon, and they'd gone by way of Australia. It seems to me they'd gone to Townsville and perhaps to Darwin, but anyway they finally made a flight to join the war and get with the rest of us who'd been fighting the war from Manila on down.

They finally joined us there in Ambon, and communications were terrible. This Lieutenant Commander Donaho landed his airplane on the water there in the harbor of Ambon. He was still on the step, still slowing down to stop and taxi in and go up on the ramp, when a Japanese fighter came down and strafed him and set his airplane on fire, and it burned up and sank in the harbor of Ambon. And this was at the end of his flight from Pearl Harbor to Ambon. Very luckily, again, not a single person in the

---
*Lieutenant Commander Frank O'Beirne, USN; Lieutenant Commander Doyle G. Donaho, USN.

plane was even touched; they all leaped over the side and swam ashore to the ramp. His question when he walked up the ramp soaking wet was something like, "My God, is this the way it is all the time out here?" He had been in the war for about 30 seconds, and his plane was lost.

That and some other incidents a little like it made it obvious that we weren't going to be able to operate from Ambon any longer. Because, from that time on, it was practically a daily occurrence that fighters would come in and go around strafing here and there and trying to find airplanes on the water; we would have gotten them all out before the sun came up in the morning.

Q: It must have called for tremendous courage on the part of individuals involved in this.

Admiral Hyland: I'm not so sure it was that. As I say, really right from the very outset we had no idea what you were supposed to do in a war. Nobody knew what the standards were. Later on in the war, when we started to take charge and march back across the Pacific from our retreat, some of the old "black cats," Catalina PBYs and so on, performed exploits that made anything we had done just look sick.* But by that time people had some measure of what was possible in an airplane, and what you were supposed to do rather than what you would do.

Q: This raises a question in my mind about the efficacy of all the months and years of training. Of course, it was an unusual situation even for wartime, but your training didn't prepare you for anything like this, did it?

Admiral Hyland: No, it just didn't at all. We should have paid more attention to some of our inter-type training. When I first got into this patrol squadron that later went out to the Philippines, one of our annual practices, for instance, was a camera gun practice where very briefly you were attacked by fighters. And you tried to shoot them down using regular guns on which you had a camera mounted, and later on you'd evaluate the film and decide whether you'd shot the fighter down or he'd shot you down. I had just come from Fighter Squadron Six, and I was very current in those airplanes. So when this yearly practice came along, I went back over to my old squadron and borrowed a fighter and made a number of runs on our own airplanes for the training and for the actual practice of the exercise.

---

*The PBY crews later in the war covered their planes with lampblack and soap to make them difficult to see during bombing missions at night. Patrol Squadron 22 is generally credited with creating the nickname "black cats." See Richard D. Knott, <u>Black Cat Raiders of World War II</u> (Annapolis: Nautical & Aviation Publishing Company, 1981).

When we looked those films over, I would say that the fighters had scored perhaps 2,000 hits to the PBYs' two or three hits. It was just so absolutely one-sided that it was just comical. From both of the waist positions in the PBY, you couldn't even point the gun to defend against a normal high-side fighter approach, which would be what you'd have to have. There was a gun sticking out the tunnel hatch, but nobody would go down underneath the PBY to try to come up under it. So, really, the PBY was essentially defenseless.

I can remember the gunnery officer in that squadron being concerned that the gunnery score achieved by the patrol planes was so terribly low that he would be criticized, and it would look like he hadn't done a good job. What we really should have done but didn't do was go just a little deeper into that and realize that the airplane was defenseless. Not that anyone was doing a poor job, because the same experience showed up again and again in all of the fighter versus patrol plane actions that we used to simulate. And it later turned out just about like that.

When Tom Moorer was shot down, he happened to be attacked by the wing commander of a Japanese air group that was on its way to attack Darwin, and he said that this fellow got him on the first pass.* He said it was the

---
*Admiral Moorer discussed this incident in his oral history.

most simple thing; he couldn't do a darn thing about it, except get down close to the water. And this fellow set him on fire on one run and then proceeded on into Darwin, where they did quite a bit of damage to the ships that were in the harbor and so on. But he can still talk about the fact that he just flew under this whole assembled group of airplanes coming in to attack Darwin and was just absolutely cornered there.

Q: He was just incidental to their mission, wasn't he?

Admiral Hyland: He certainly was. I'm sure that wing commander hollered to everybody else, "Don't touch it. It's mine!"

Q: Was Moorer a part of your group by that time?

Admiral Hyland: Yes. He came out in this squadron--I was just telling you about the exec who lasted about 30 seconds in the war zone--and he just continued to do regular patrols. On the incident when he was shot down, he was flying out of Darwin and was on a patrol up to the north just to see what he could find. And he unfortunately just flew right under this whole Japanese air group from one of the carriers and was shot down. And then from there on, he and his crew had a terrific escapade. Finally, all survived, but they really had a hard time of it and were missing in action for perhaps ten days. I can remember that they sent word back to Carrie Moorer that he was missing in action. We certainly never expected to hear from him again, but we did.

Q: Your tribulations were unending then. Where did you finally arrive?

Admiral Hyland: After this period in Ambon we went back to Surabaja and operated there. Fairly quickly, Surabaja started to suffer attacks on a twice-daily basis, so we had to disperse the airplanes that were available that were not going to go on patrol. We would disperse them down into the interior part of Java. A very interesting thing was done there. They would flood rice fields. They had a way of making these dikes or something, and they would be able to flood an area which would be big enough to land a PBY. The water would be perhaps three or four feet deep in this area, and landing a seaplane there looked like landing right on the ground. Because sticking up out of the water would be these rice plants and other things, and you'd just have to land so that you didn't run into a tree. Then we would taxi slowly up to the edge of the levee that they'd built to make this area, and that's where we would hide the airplanes during the day. Later in the day, just as the sun was going down, we'd take off and fly back to Surabaja, and they would decide during the night whether they were going to need the airplane the next day or not.

Q: That's certainly an example of cooperation with the Dutch, isn't it?

Admiral Hyland: Yes. We would go down and land on one of those artificial lakes, and we would be taken to a restaurant in the nearest little town. I can remember that every single day for lunch the Dutch had what they called rice stoffle, sort of rice and curry--a very, very heavy meal. And I can tell you that after you've had a midday Dutch meal--the rice stoffle with the beer and so on that went with it--there is absolutely nothing to do but have a nap. From about 1:00 o'clock to 3:00 o'clock, you just couldn't do anything but nap, and I recall so vividly doing that. It was really a great adventure.

I can recall only one other attack that was made. Again, we flew up to the north, in the neighborhood of Menado, which is on the island of Celebes, and attacked a large group of Japanese ships that were coming down on an invasion of one or the other of those islands. I can remember the attack was absolutely fruitless. We were

Hyland #2 - 110

flying at about 14,000 feet, which is as high as you could get.

Q: How many in the group?

Admiral Hyland: In that particular one just three. I had a good bomber. He was a fine youngster. We made individual attacks, and he sighted in on this ship, but they were smart about it. They just looked up, and the minute they saw the bombs released they'd make a radical turn. And he told me later that, doggone if the guy hadn't turned, he thinks he'd have hit him, but he didn't, and just ahead of what would have been the position where all our bombs dropped.

Q: Did they have fighter protection?

Admiral Hyland: No, they didn't. They shot at us a little bit with antiaircraft fire, but that was quite inaccurate and nobody was damaged at all. All three of us got back from that flight. That and the Jolo flight were just about the only offensive actions that we ever attempted. On a few other occasions we headed up north prepared to bomb, but we never found anything to bomb and just came back. I would say except for the information that we provided in part--about where the Japanese were, and how many ships, and roughly what kinds, and so on, and from that information the leaders could tell what they were obviously up to--I never felt we did any good at all. We were simply not equipped properly to be able to attack ships at sea, or to attack anything for that matter. It was really a patrol plane. If it got close to any good base or ship where they did have airplanes, why, it was a sitting duck.

Q: And yet, Admiral, under the circumstances, flying in the face of reason, you couldn't have just withdrawn completely, could you?

Admiral Hyland: I suppose not. We were there to do a job, and I think we stayed as long as we possibly could, and it didn't really do any good. It seems to me I made the final flight and went from Tjilatjap, which was on the south coast of Java, down to Broome, Australia, and it was in late March or early April. Corregidor had fallen, and the Japanese were imminently about to invade Java. In fact, they'd actually landed on the north coast of Java, and I'll say for perhaps a week before that we shuttled airplanes from Surabaja down to Australia. The plane would come back, and in some cases we had as many as 25 people in those old PBYs just evacuating people to get them down to Australia.

Hyland #2 - 112

Q: Were these military people?

Admiral Hyland: Our own squadron people, yes. We had nothing at all to do with evacuating any civilians. It was just my luck on one of those flights we came back from Australia and went to Tjilatjap, which was the final point of departure for the few people who did get out. Somehow or other, we still had some people there who had been able to get to Tjilatjap from Surabaja, and among them was Captain Wagner, who was the wing commander. I flew the last airplane out, and he was in the airplane. I vividly recall that because he was the boss. He was a captain then; we thought of him as an old guy. He later became a vice admiral in the Navy.

On that last flight from Tjilatjap down to Australia, we got about halfway down, and I experienced an electrical fire in the airplane. We were flying over the Indian Ocean then, and we were flying at low altitude, because it was known then that there was a Japanese carrier and there were some battleships that had gone down south of Java. They were there to try and intercept anybody who was going to try to escape, either through the Sunda Strait or through Makassar Strait or out of the south coast of Java. So I was flying low to make sure I'd be as inconspicuous as possible, and the wind was just blowing about 40 or so knots, it seemed to me, and I've never flown over an ocean that looked so rough to me.

It was almost solid whitecaps, and here about halfway down to Australia, we suddenly started to get the airplane full of smoke--this damned electrical fire. I thought, "Holy cats, what a time for this! And what are we going to do about it?" After some fooling around with the switches and so on, we were finally able to get it to stop, and it just went out. But I prepared to land; I thought we were going to have to land that darn thing with about 20 people on board and in the roughest ocean I've ever seen. We wouldn't have survived. We wouldn't have been able to make the landing successfully at all, but there wasn't anything else to do. So the darn fire went out, and we continued on down to Australia, and we got there.

The whole experience there toward the end was that sort of thing--living from hand to mouth, and just everything going wrong, no chance to really maintain the airplanes well, and about all we could do was fill them up with fuel and oil and get going again.

Q: Once you landed at Broome, did you discover what actually caused this short?

Admiral Hyland: No, I never did understand what caused it. They did renew some wiring in the airplane, and it never did reoccur. It was just one of those things where, in flight, you had no way of analyzing the thing. I was too worried to make a calm appraisal, and the plane captain didn't know what to do. So we got down to Australia and, as I say, only two out of the original 46 airplanes got down there from the campaign up north.

After we got to Australia, still another squadron of PBYs came out from Hawaii. They joined in Perth, and they stayed and operated out Perth most of the time. I can recall being sent home in July of 1942. Tom Moorer and I and a few other people went back on the USS West Point, which had been the liner America.* She'd been put into service as a troop transport and she sailed out of Melbourne. We flew over one day from Perth to Melbourne and got there about 10:00 o'clock at night and got on board the ship, which sailed at midnight, so we didn't see very much of Melbourne. From there we went on home.

Q: Did she sail with an escort, or did she rely on her speed?

Admiral Hyland: No. Because of the worry about Japanese submarines, she went around south of Tasmania and sailed at

---

*The USS West Point (AP-23), a 35,400-ton transport, had entered commercial service as the liner America, flagship of the United States Lines, in August 1940. She was commissioned 15 June 1941 as the USS West Point. She returned to merchant service in 1946.

Hyland #2 - 115

25 knots all the way to New York. I remember going through the Panama Canal on her.

Q: That was a fairly safe speed, wasn't it?

Admiral Hyland: Oh, yes. She zigzagged and so on. We just had a long sort of rest.

Q: I suppose there was a danger from raiders, however, was there not?

Admiral Hyland: No, not really where she went. If you look at the map, it was, I think, a pretty safe passage. And going that fast, we had no sightings and no alarms of any sort. There were some other military people on board. There were a bunch of army nurses who had been rescued from Corregidor by one of our submarines; they were on board the ship for the trip home. I can remember that Tom Moorer and a fellow named Emmet O'Beirne, who's a younger brother of Frank, and I were the principal passengers on the ship.*
They asked us to stand a few watches and that sort of business, but by and large it was just a long, uneventful trip home. It was great for me, though, because Floss was with her family in New Rochelle, New York, and we sailed right into New York when we finally got home.

---
*Lieutenant Emmet O'Beirne, USN, had been a member of Patrol Squadron 21.

Q: Well, did you have leave when you got back home?

Admiral Hyland: Yes, we had about a month's leave. I was ordered to another seaplane squadron which was down in Norfolk at the time. I didn't want to do that, and I was able to get my orders changed to go to duty at Anacostia, which is where I got into the so-called "admirals' airline" there. At Anacostia they had a bunch of transport planes which were used to take the secretaries and the top admirals and the top navy officials around, and I spent a couple of years doing that. It was during that time that I got to be the private pilot for Admiral King; that's how I ran into him.* Back to Australia, though. We got to Australia and finally assembled the squadron at Perth in about the middle of April. Very shortly after that, I was sent up to Geraldton, which is a little town on the west coast of Australia, perhaps 400 or so miles north of Perth.

Q: Rather desolate, isn't it?

Admiral Hyland: Oh, boy. There was an Australian primary training field there, an Australian Air Force base. I was put in charge of a contingent of three PBYs which ran

---
*Admiral Ernest J. King, USN, was Commander in Chief U.S. Fleet and Chief of Naval Operations during much of World War II.

patrols out of Geraldton.

Q: What was the objective of those patrols?

Admiral Hyland: Just surveillance of the west coast of Australia. They really were terrified of a Japanese invasion. They didn't seem to know where they might get it, but we didn't apparently expect it to come into Darwin. If someone did land in Darwin with military forces, they wouldn't be able to do very much in those days; it's so far from any other place. I think they were worried about an invasion right on the west coast and perhaps down in the more populated areas. We ran patrols--we used to have one flight a day that we had to provide from these three airplanes, and also continue a little bit of training there. It was a very interesting experience.

I've always thought that western Australia in those days must have been a little like our West when it was being opened up--almost no people, a very, very desolate area, very, very hardy and very friendly people but not many of them. Really, what honest good those patrols did I've always doubted and always wondered about. I spent from about the end of April to July in Geraldton, until I was sent home. I was the commanding officer of this little unit at Geraldton, and I've never forgotten that experience.

My number two was a fine young fellow, and he married the daughter of the town banker there in Geraldton, Australia. She was a lovely girl, and he took her home and was assigned down to Texas. Lo and behold, she hadn't been in the United States longer than about a month and he was killed in an accident. She was then pregnant. I was in Washington at the time, and we had the problem of trying to get her back to Australia. That's where she wanted to go, because she knew nobody in the United States. Her young husband had been lost in this accident, and there she was. We finally were able to get her home.

She had a boy, and I understand he's just an image of his father, who was a very good-looking Greek fellow named Jim Thanos.* Young Jim Thanos has turned out to be a first-class Australian citizen, I'm told, a very bright boy, a very handsome boy, and has been a real young success out there. This gal has since remarried a doctor out there. I corresponded with her a little bit, but not for many years now. I've never forgotten that courtship; it was really a whirlwind affair if I've ever seen one.

Q: I suppose that during your stay there in Australia there was beginning to be an infiltration of American military forces, was there not?

---
*Ensign James Thanos, USNR.

Admiral Hyland: Yes. While I was in Perth, I can remember one visit. The Queen Mary came in and had 10,000 troops on board.* They were all deposited there at Perth, and whatever happened to them I never really did know. But I remember flying out in a PBY on sort of an antisubmarine protective patrol and flying close to this magnificent big ship, just thousands of portholes, and out of every one of them a little head with a guy waving and so on. I think most of the military buildup there took part on the eastern part of Australia, which was, of course, the part they were worried about. MacArthur was in Melbourne when he came out of the Philippines, and they did some of the planning there and then to commence the march back up through the island chain from there.**

Q: Our submarines were beginning to operate down there, weren't they, out of Perth?

Admiral Hyland: Yes.

---

*The Queen Mary was a large passenger liner built for the British Cunard Line in the 1930s. She was put into service as a fast troop transport during World War II and then returned to commercial service following the war.
**Rather than have him captured on Corregidor, President Franklin D. Roosevelt ordered General MacArthur to be evacuated to safety. On 11 March 1942, he and his family left the Philippines by PT boat and went to Australia.

Hyland #2 - 120

Q: And were you any assistance to them, the PBYs?

Admiral Hyland: No, I don't remember any operations. I can remember one occasion where, fortunately, I wasn't involved, but one of our PBYs attacked one of our own submarines, and it did it in the vicinity of Geraldton. It wasn't one of my airplanes. By that time I had gone back to the States, but I later heard about it. This submarine was coming back from patrol and was on the surface just off Geraldton on its way back to Perth, and this youngster in a navy PBY saw it and decided it was a Japanese submarine and attacked it with bombs and damn near hit it. The story is that our wing commander went down to apologize when they got into Perth and just said, "Well, is there anything we can do for you? We're terribly sorry this happened," and so on.

And the submarine skipper just said, "Please leave us alone. That's all we want."

There weren't a lot, but there were some desertions from those submarines that came into Perth. Those patrols in the old S-boats must have been just simply awful.* I ran into a friend of mine up in Surabaya one time, and one of our submarines had been out as long as an S-boat can

---

*The U.S. S-boat submarines were constructed during the 1920s and incorporated World War I submarine technology. They were limited in range, endurance, and general capability. They were designated by numbers, such as USS S-1. Names were assigned to the later, larger fleet boats.

Hyland #2 - 121

stay out, and they had done several of these patrols before. This fellow had lost about 30 or 40 pounds, and he had developed a very unhappy skin condition. It was so hot and so humid and so difficult on those things, and this guy looked like a physical wreck to me. And I realized that as tough as we were having it, of course, in flying around there in the PBYs, the fellows on these submarines must have really had a wicked time of it. They weren't equipped to handle a long patrol. This guy looked like death warmed over to me. So when they would get to Perth, they had a certain problem with people going over the hill, and there's kind of an amusing story about it. These men would be caught within half a day. They would decide to desert, and they'd be gone. And once the Perth police were told about them, they would find them almost in no time at all.

Q: There wasn't much coverage was there, once they got inland?

Admiral Hyland: We asked this police fellow how it was done, and he said it was the simplest problem in the world. He said, "We just have our people go around and they look in the bars, and they go anywhere where people might foregather." And he said, "We just pick up anybody, one, who is wearing white socks, or who uses the phrase, 'Goddammit.' In every case, it's an American deserter from a submarine." So it was a simple problem for them apparently.

Q: What happened to these boys once they were caught?

Admiral Hyland: They wouldn't want them to go back on patrol, because they'd just simply had it. They would get the usual discipline; I don't think they were too tough on them. They would punish them and send them off to some other duty. I never really knew much about what was done. Old Admiral Lockwood was the boss down there then.*

That's about all I can remember about the Australian stay. Several of our people married Australian girls, all of whom came from Perth, except for this one gal who came from Geraldton. By and large, those gals have been very fine navy wives. I've noticed one thing about them: about every two or three years they get this irresistible homing instinct, and they absolutely have to go back to Australia and check in. In all cases they're American citizens, because, of course, it's a big advantage to them to be American citizens, but they just have got to get back to Australia and see how the family's doing and so on. Except for that, they've just been wonderful women in the Navy, most of them quite good-looking.

---
*Rear Admiral Charles A. Lockwood, Jr., USN, a submarine officer, was Commander Task Force 51 and commander of all Allied naval forces in western Australia. In 1943 he became Commander Submarines Pacific Fleet.

Q: Shall we then go on to Anacostia?

Admiral Hyland: When I first got back, I was ordered to a PBM squadron down in Norfolk.* At the same time, on our way back from Australia, we were told that the reason we were being sent home was because, by coincidence, all of us had had carrier flying before, and in particular fighter experience. We were being sent back because we were needed to be brand-new skippers of brand-new fighter squadrons. So I went home with a great deal of anticipation over that. I had decided I didn't want to be in patrol planes any longer if I could do anything about it, and this prospect of going to a fighter squadron was terrific.

When I got home and finally went down to Washington, it turned out there was absolutely nothing to that rumor at all. They didn't think they needed anybody for the fighter program, and since we had this recent experience in patrol flying, they wanted us to stay in it. And despite a fairly vigorous protest, I simply got orders to Norfolk to go to a PBM squadron. On my way down there, I went through Anacostia.

There were a couple of old friends there, and just sort of jokingly one afternoon I said, "Say, why don't you

---

*The PBM was a two-engine patrol bomber built by Glenn L. Martin Company. It was more modern the than the Conslidated PBY.

fellows fix me up with a job over here? I'm going down to those PBMs, which I don't want to do, and I sure wish I could get a job here." In those days they had a list of people--some sort of a preferred list, and I never knew who made it up--that had names on it of people they thought were good, reliable pilots and who might be suitable people to fly these dignitaries around. And, by gosh, I never even knew it, but I was on that list. When I said that just jokingly and informally one afternoon, that set part of the machine in motion, and the next thing I knew, I got orders to Anacostia.

Q: Was our friend Jocko there at that time?*

Admiral Hyland: No, Harry Sears was the operations officer there at the time, and he had the most to do with this procedure.** But I found myself at Anacostia flying various kinds of transport planes, and after I'd been there about a year, the fellow who had been flying Admiral King around, as his sort of private and personal pilot--in that job you did a lot of other flying, too, but you were always available whenever he was going to make a flight. This fellow was due to transfer and went back to fight the war, and I was selected to be the replacement for him. I really

---
*Captain Joseph J. Clark, USN, whom Dr. Mason interviewed for the Columbia University oral history program.
**Lieutenant Commander Harry E. Sears, USN.

didn't want to do it, since Admiral King had such a terrifying reputation that nobody wanted to be his pilot. They were afraid that he would be so difficult and that it would be an unhappy experience. But, anyway, I got the job.

Q: How frequently were you employed in flying him?

Admiral Hyland: Not really very frequently--perhaps a couple of times a month. Normally, he would make a flight from Anacostia and he would fly out to San Francisco. We would leave Anacostia perhaps 6:00 or 7:00 o'clock in the evening, fly all night long, and get to Alameda or San Francisco the next morning. There he would immediately go into meetings with Admiral Nimitz, who was there in San Francisco, and they would talk about things.* Then at the end of the third or the fourth day, late in the day, we'd get in the airplane and fly back during the night to Washington. That was what I did for him more than anything else.

Q: These frequent conferences with Nimitz, who came from Pearl?

---

*Admiral Chester W. Nimitz, USN, was Commander in Chief Pacific Fleet and Commander in Chief Pacific Ocean Areas during World War II.

Admiral Hyland: Yes. They would meet in San Francisco.

Q: What sort of a party did King take with him to these conferences?

Admiral Hyland: We had a Lockheed Lodestar, which could carry about six or seven people.* The airplane was, for that day and age, a very plush, twin-engine airplane, beautifully equipped with radio gear and everything you'd need. It was just the latest thing; it was a real treat to fly it. On one side of the airplane was a sofa long enough for him to stretch out, and he was able to sleep at night, so that when we would get to San Francisco the next morning, he would be reasonably fresh.

I noticed one of the people who always went with him was Admiral Savvy Cooke; he was one of the chief planners.** Another one who went along on many of the trips was Ruthven Libby, who now is in San Diego and writes for the Copley Press.*** These men would have to sit up during the night. And when we would get to the West Coast--we had to fly high often, to get over the mountains,

---

*The Lodestar, which had the U.S. Navy designation of R5O, was an executive transport plane with four to seven passenger seats. It had a wing span of 65 feet and a maximum speed of 250 miles per hour.
**Rear Admiral Charles M. Cooke, USN.
***Captain Ruthven E. Libby, USN. Libby, who retired as a vice admiral, is the subject of a Naval Institute oral history.

and the plane was not pressurized--these men would be absolutely fractured. They would be so fatigued that they could hardly handle themselves, and old Admiral King would just be fresh as a daisy and go right into a full day's work.

Q: But he'd slept all night, hadn't he?

Admiral Hyland: He was able to sleep. If they could sleep sitting up, which not many people can do, it would have been fine. But they just simply weren't in the same class with him as far as having that energy and ability to take a flight like that. It seemed to be particularly hard on old Admiral Cooke. He was a frail man to begin with, apparently one of the most brilliant minds we've ever had in the Navy and a wonderful officer. But, boy, those trips were hard. We would just have a pilot and a copilot; we'd usually go to Memphis to El Paso to Alameda, just landing and refueling as rapidly as it could be done.

Q: And what was the total hours of the flight?

Admiral Hyland: It would be a total flight time of about 16 hours. We'd leave at 7:00 or thereabouts in the evening and get in the next morning about 9:00 o'clock.

Q: What was King like as a passenger?

Admiral Hyland: At first, he was quite difficult. He had a set of earphones at his desk in the back part of the airplane, and he had a set of charts. And if he didn't have anything else to do, he sort of liked to navigate himself. He would keep track of where you were going, and he knew enough about flying radio ranges and so on to know whether you were doing it right or not. I'll say he kibitzed fairly actively. The first several flights I had good luck, and we had some low weather to handle and so on, and he became satisfied that I was reliable, and from that point on he left me entirely alone.

You know, he was just a class behind my father at the Naval Academy, and they knew one another.* And I don't think they liked one another particularly well. After I'd been his pilot for about six months, he suddenly wrote a fairly long letter to my dad and praised my performance and so on, so my dad then decided Admiral King was just the finest fellow in the whole world! But it really was a very nice thing for him to do. He didn't have to do it. He was busy as hell; he was running the whole Navy, and he did run a kind of one-man show. So it was a very thoughtful thing for him to do, and from that time on we got on very, very well.

---
*John J. Hyland was in the class of 1900, and Ernest J. King was in the class of 1901.

He could be terribly unpleasant. Once in a while, we would have to change our expected flight plan and maybe go somewhere else, and we would land at an Army Air Corps field perhaps. I would send word to the field just as far ahead as we could talk to the field that we were coming and we had on board Admiral King, the head of the Navy, and for God's sake to tell the commanding officer and tell anybody else there who felt they ought to meet such a dignitary, to be there.

Q: Was this done in code?

Admiral Hyland: No, just in plain language. A few times we would land right in the middle of the night, and we wouldn't have been able to give them very much notice. And after we were on the ground, Admiral King would get out of the airplane and just walk up and down sort of nervously and watch the fueling and make damn sure there was no way you could fuel the plane any faster and service it any faster than was being done. And in all cases, they were just busting their buttons at these stops. That was one of the great joys of flying that airplane around; when we came in anyplace, we really got the first-class treatment, because his reputation preceded him everywhere.

In a few cases, the skipper of the base wouldn't be

there when we pulled up at the line and stopped and they got out of the airplane, because he was still struggling to get his pants on back at the quarters. He'd come tearing down and salute, and, on a few occasions, Admiral King wasn't apparently in a good mood, and he would just be terribly unpleasant and rude to the officer. He'd say, "Where the hell were you when I arrived?" And this young officer would do his best to apologize, saying he simply didn't have notice at all, and I would try to confirm that he'd had perhaps only 10 or 12 minutes' time and he was home and sound asleep and just couldn't have made it on time. Yet King would be very unreasonable and very unpleasant once in a while.

On another occasion, almost the same thing might happen, and he would just be the soul of courtesy and consideration, and tell the fellow, "Of course, you couldn't get down here. In fact, there really isn't any reason for you to come down at all." But, oh boy, if they didn't come down, he would really be tough. I found him, actually, a very fine, very warm fellow. His reputation before the war started, he was a real party man. He liked to drink, and he liked to party and so on, and he completely swore off during the war. I never saw him take anything to drink, and that must have been a real sacrifice for him.

Q: Maybe that had some bearing on his disposition, too.

Admiral Hyland: It could have had. I flew him around a lot, and frequently he would loan that airplane to other people. I took Mr. Forrestal on a trip one time.* I can remember taking many of the lesser navy secretaries and quite a few of the higher admirals on separate trips that he didn't go along on but he wanted them to make, and his airplane wasn't going to be used. I had explained to him that it would be very much better for me if I could do other flying than just flying for him, because I'd get that much more experience and be that much more current, so he was very, very good about that.

All I did was check with the aide, who was a fellow named Charlie Lanman, who's dead now, class of '32.** And then after him, Kirkpatrick, who is retired.*** He comes from San Angelo, Texas; I know that. At one time he was slated to be Chief of the Bureau of Personnel, but he had a heart attack and had to get out. He was the Superintendent at the Naval Academy at one point; that's the Kirkpatrick I'm talking about. I would just check with Kirk whether there was any prospect at all of a trip, and if there

---
*James V. Forrestal was Under Secretary of the Navy from 1940 to 1944 and then Secretary of the Navy from 1944 to 1947. He was later the first Secretary of Defense from 1947 to 1949.
**Lieutenant Commander Charles B. Lanman, USN.
***Commander Charles C. Kirkpatrick, USN. Later, as a rear admiral, Kirkpatrick was Superintendent of the Naval Academy from 1962 to 1964.

wasn't, I could go away for a couple of weeks at a time on an extended trip, and they wouldn't worry about it.

Q: Sir, tell me that story you related off tape about your predecessor as King's pilot, because it's a colorful incident.

Admiral Hyland: Well, Dr. Mason, if you think it's good enough, I will. When I first got the word that I was going to be Admiral King's pilot, I asked this fellow what it was like. I'd heard stories about Admiral King being difficult to handle and difficult to get along with, so I asked him how did the flights normally go? And this is the story of what he said to me. He said, "Well, a typical flight will be one where you'll leave in the late afternoon or early evening and head west. The last time we made a flight, we took off and headed for Memphis and it was still light, and we droned on for an hour or so and then it got dark."

He said, "I just sensed a presence over my shoulder, and I looked around, and there was Admiral King looking over our shoulders into the cockpit. I looked at him inquiringly and he sort of snarled, 'Turn on the Goddamn cabin light! How do you expect anybody to be able to read back here without any light?' So I turned on the cabin lights and we continued on west. Several hours later, I again felt this presence of someone looking into the cockpit, and there was Admiral King again. This time he was in the same mood, and he snarled 'Turn out the Goddamn cabin lights! How do you expect anybody to sleep back here with the lights on?"

Then this fellow said, "Well, Johnny, it's just like that all the time. That's about the way you can expect to find it." Of course, later on, in flying him quite a few times, I didn't find him that way at all. He was never difficult with me, except on one or two occasions, and they would just normally be occasions where I would feel the weather wasn't good enough to fly, and we would be waiting for things to change and he would become very impatient. He would rather fly a long way around and keep moving than he would to wait at Point A and go straight to Point B. He'd much rather go to B, to C, to D, to E, to F, and then go to the destination than he would to sit there and wait. He wouldn't tolerate just sitting there.

Q: A very nervous, restless kind of person.

Admiral Hyland: Yes, he was. Now, he wouldn't order you to fly into thunderstorms, if you really thought there was a dangerous flight in prospect. But whenever there was any doubtful situation, he wanted to make sure that you had thought of all the possibilities. Any alternative that let the airplane continue to move and make some progress toward the destination was what he wanted, and that's what we would normally do.

Q: What was his attitude toward his staff with whom he travelled?

Admiral Hyland: With this group who travelled with him regularly, they very clearly had his complete confidence. They weren't the least bit worried about him, and they had their ways of weathering any of the storms that might come up. They just simply were not concerned about him at all. They respected him; I think they really loved him. And all of them, just like I was, were distressed sometimes when he would be so intolerant of other people, and sometimes for things that they had no control over. They were all very hard-working, they were all extremely able, and they all were absolutely top-notch people, and he had long since decided that they were the people he wanted to be doing work to help him get the job done. So it was a very, very close, very, very fine little team that he had.

Q: During the intervals when you weren't with him on trips, what kind of duty did you have? What did you do?

Admiral Hyland: In that unit in the operations department

there at Anacostia, quite a bit of steady training went on--just instrument flying and preparations to be able to take those transports almost any time they'd have to go, and to fly them within whatever limits were prescribed. Also, I did a lot of other flying on other trips, sometimes in the airplane that was assigned to Admiral King, but, of course, he would have to personally say it was all right to take the trip.

I can remember one time a fellow on Mr. Forrestal's staff called up and wanted to know if Admiral King's plane was available. When the answer was given to him that yes, it was, the plane was in an "up" status and could go on a trip, he then went to Admiral King and told Admiral King that he knew the airplane was available and wanted to know if he could take it. Well, this displeased Admiral King very, very much. We got the word back at the air station that, after that, when inquiries about the airplane came, we were not to answer them. We were to call up Kirkpatrick, tell him that we'd been asked questions about the airplane but that we hadn't answered them, and let him handle it from there. He didn't want anybody maneuvering to get hold of his airplane, which was a very plush airplane and one of the faster ones we had. He just didn't like the idea of this underling on Forrestal's staff setting him up where he couldn't say no. I don't think Mr. Forrestal had anything to do with it, but this other guy

Hyland #2 - 136

did. Then, on the other hand, he would want somebody to make a trip and would tell them that he would call up and say he'd like to have us take him in his airplane, and so that's the way a lot of the trips were set up.

Q: Were there any of those trips that were significant, as you recall?

Admiral Hyland: No, they were just simply straightforward trips to various places. Several times I can remember old Admiral Emory Land--I think he was head of the Maritime Commission--and he would go here and there where ceremonies were performed when numbers of ships were finished.* We went to various places where Kaiser was building ships and other locations such as that.** It was a very interesting tour of duty. Because of all these dignitaries who went along on these trips, by and large, my copilot and I were beautifully taken care of. Wherever we stopped, we were always included in the top official party, and the men in the airplane were always very nicely taken care of. And in all cases the airplane was given priority about servicing and so on. It was a very pleasant tour of duty.

The best part of it was that when it finally ended--

---
*Rear Admiral Emory S. Land, USN (Ret.) was chairman of the U.S. Maritime Commission, coordinator of shipping for the National Defense Commission, and administrator of the War Shipping Administration. He was a 1902 graduate of the Naval Academy, a year behind King. In July 1944 he was promoted to vice admiral.
**Henry J. Kaiser was an industrialist who set up shipyards in World War II to build both merchant ships and warships as part of the nation's defense effort.

Hyland #2 - 137

I'd had the job for a little over a year, and by that time I'd been on shore duty in the middle of the war, in Washington, and it was time for me to go back to sea. And at that time, I'll never forget that Kirkpatrick talked to me one day and he said, "Where do you want to go?" And for me then, a commander in the Navy, there were several possibilities, but I thought the very best one was command of an air group on one of the carriers. I was by then too senior to be a squadron commander. And, lo and behold, within a week I got orders to command Air Group Ten, which assembled up at Atlantic City in New Jersey. So we went out to the war in January of 1945, and I had that command for the rest of the war and then for several months after the war.

Q: May I ask you one question about your period as a pilot for King? Do you have any recollections of that occasion when Nimitz's plane coming into San Francisco flopped or turned over or something in the bay? Were you present on that occasion?

Admiral Hyland: No, I wasn't there when that happened.*
When he would go to San Francisco to meet with Admiral

---

*Admiral Nimitz and several members of his staff were injured in the crash, which occurred 30 June 1942 at Alameda. For further details see E. B. Potter, <u>Nimitz</u> (Annapolis: Naval Institute Press, 1976), pages 107-109.

Nimitz, I only saw the admiral when the plane arrived and when the plane departed, although we were quartered right in the St. Francis Hotel where they stayed and where they had their meetings, if I remember correctly. I know that old Mr. London, the famous manager of that hotel, was always very proud to have that group there, and Admiral King's flag would fly over the entrance to the St. Francis Hotel, which is right on the square there in San Francisco--an elegant place to stay.* We were always put up there; that's how nice it was for the pilots on the trip.

One of the more glamorous events we attended was the Quebec Conference.** We flew up to Quebec for that. I can remember getting weather information as we passed over Montreal that we would not be able to get into Quebec; it was too bad. General Arnold was en route in his private airplane, and General Marshall was in still another airplane going to Quebec.*** So I sent word back to Admiral King in the airplane that we probably weren't going to be able to land, because it was zero-zero or some such thing up at Quebec. As always, he said, "Well, we've got

---
*Dan London was for many years manager of the St. Francis Hotel.
**This conference of Allied leaders met in Canada in August 1943 for the purpose of planning strategy for subsequent stages of the war, including the invasion of Europe. For details see Thomas B. Buell, <u>Master of Sea Power: A Biography of Fleet Admiral Ernest J. King</u> (Boston: Little, Brown, 1980), pages 389-400.
***General George C. Marshall, USA, Chief of Staff of the Army; General Henry H. Arnold, USA, Chief of the Army Air Forces.

plenty of fuel to go up and give it a go, haven't we? Then we can come back and land at Montreal if we have to."

I said, "Sure, we can do that." We went up there, and it actually wasn't a very difficult letdown at all, and we were able to get in. Then it did shut down a little bit more after that, and it had been worse than that before, because all the rest of these dignitaries didn't make it to Quebec that day. They went back and landed at Montreal, and they came in the next day.

We were in the Chateau Frontenac, staying there, and Admiral King very nicely one time had this group of men standing around, all of whom had been delayed, and he introduced me as his pilot. He said, "You know, we got here yesterday." He was pleased about the fact that his airplane was the only one that had been able to get in. Really, it wasn't all that difficult at all; it was just lucky.

On another occasion, I remember we landed in Boston, and it was absolutely the lowest it could possibly be and still get in. I had told him down in Washington that I didn't think we ought to even try it, the forecast was so forbidding. But we got in all right and landed, and he was chatting with me outside the airplane, and I said, "Boy, we're lucky to get in, Admiral. I'm not sure it was really the smartest thing to try that, but here we are."

And he smiled at me and said, "Well, if we hadn't started we'd never be here now, would we?" His philosophy was he'd rather take a crack at going to Boston and turn around and fly all the way back to Washington than not try it. He couldn't stand the idea of staying there and thinking about it.

Q: You could carry this on. I mean, his sense of frustration of the war must have been very great at times.

Admiral Hyland: Yes. That tour of duty was very, very instructive for me. I ended up my naval career with quite a bit of flying, and all types of flying: the patrol planes, the carrier planes, the transport planes, and many other things. So it was a very fortunate period, and, as I say, the best part of it was that when I finished doing the job for him, he made sure that I got the best job that I could have. You could have either an air group command, or command of one of the big four-engine PB4Y squadrons, or you could get command of a little seaplane tender.* Those were the three sort of coequal assignments that were available, and of all of them I thought that by far the best one was to get back on the carriers.

Q: It didn't do you any harm to make the contacts at that level either, did it, in terms of career advancement?

Admiral Hyland: Oh, no. It sure didn't. I would say that for almost all the rest of my naval career, when some of

---
*PB4Y was the designation for the Consolidated Liberator bombers that were built for the Navy. The Army Air Forces designation was B-24.

those older officers were still around, they always remembered me, because they'd been in the airplane with Admiral King. And they just happened to remember the name of the pilot and had seen me a couple of times, and so it was a very helpful thing. Every young officer in the Navy should work for the CNO if he can.*

Q: So you went to the <u>Intrepid</u>.

Admiral Hyland: Yes, I went to command Air Group Ten. I trained with the fighters, because I'd had the previous experience in fighters; we trained at Atlantic City. I actually went to that job in August of '44, and a little later on we assembled the entire air group up at Groton, Connecticut, which is across the river from the sub base there.** It was a very nice little field which had at one time been an Army Air Corps field; they'd improved it, and then they'd moved out and my group went there. It was an

---

*CNO--Chief of Naval Operations.
**The Navy's submarine base at New London, Connecticut, is also the site of submarine school training.

outlying field under the direction of Quonset Point.* We finished our training there and ferried all the airplanes across the country, were put on board the Intrepid, and went out on board her.

In those days, when you got to Honolulu you normally took off the air group that was on board the carrier coming out. You normally took them off in the Hawaiian Islands and embarked an air group that had been here in the Hawaiian Islands for a few months doing advanced training. Then they would go out with the carrier, and you would get the next arriving carrier. I've never understood how this happened, and at the time no one had any idea that the war would be over as soon as it was, within a year. It looked like it would go on for at least another three or four years, but in any case Air Group Ten was not taken off the Intrepid. We were left on board. I was delighted, and so was everybody else. Of course, it was very pleasant to get off and fool around here on the Hawaiian Islands, but we stayed on board and went right out to the war. We got out there in January of '45. During the time we were on board, the ship was kamikazied when we were operating off Okinawa and went back to San Francisco to get repaired.**

Q: How badly was she damaged? Tell me about that attack.

---
*Quonset Point was the site of a naval air station near Newport, Rhode Island.
**The Japanese suicide plane attack on the carrier was on 16 April 1945.

Hyland #2 - 143

Admiral Hyland: I didn't personally see it. I was in the air on a flight at the time, but she was just attacked by a number of Japanese. One kamikaze airplane crashed right into the flight deck a little bit toward the forward end and made a hole in the flight deck about 10 or 15 feet in diameter. A bomb went off and started a big fire down in the hangar deck, and this crash also damaged one of the elevators. They finally got the thing under control, and an hour or so later I came back from my flight and landed on board with no problem. But here was this ship with all this major damage. So we went back to Ulithi, and there a ship repair expert came aboard and made the judgment that they could patch the flight deck up, of course, with no trouble there.* But they wouldn't be able to fix that elevator, so the decision was made to sail back to San Francisco. We went back and were there for about a month.

Q: All your planes went back, too?

Admiral Hyland: Yes. In fact, on this kamikaze attack, of course, they turned on all the sprinklers, and most of the airplanes that were not flying were so soaked with salt water from the sprinkling system that they were inoperable, and they were just pushed over the side. Then we went out again and had only a very, very few operations in July and August, and you'll remember the atomic bomb was dropped

---

*Ulithi is an atoll in the western Caroline Islands. It was used as a fleet anchorage by the U.S. Navy in 1944-45.

then.* None of us knew anything about that, but it was dropped and very suddenly and unexpectedly the Japanese surrendered.

Q: Where were you then, in Okinawa waters?

Admiral Hyland: Actually, when the bomb went off, the ship was again in Ulithi. So we just waited there.

Q: That was R & R area, wasn't it?**

Admiral Hyland: Yes. The operations that were going on principally then were attacks on the Japanese home islands, and we participated in quite a few of those, mainly against the island of Kyushu, although one or two attacks were in the vicinity of Kure, right close to Hiroshima.

Q: Were you under orders not to attack Hiroshima at that point?

---

*B-29s from the U.S. Army Air Forces dropped the first atomic bomb on Hiroshima, Japan, on 6 August 1945 and the second on Nagasaki on 9 August.
**R & R--rest and recreation.

Hyland #2 - 145

Admiral Hyland: No, there were no such orders. Actually all the targets at that time for us were military airfields, hangars, repair facilities, and any Japanese ships that you could find, particularly military ships. We took part in quite a few of those strikes against the Japanese home islands, and then all of a sudden the war was over.

Q: What sort of opposition did you meet with, air-wise?

Admiral Hyland: Not very severe, really. I'd say that last year of the war you could describe the whole thing as a great big steamroller, just mowing them down. We outnumbered them, we had airplanes that outperformed them, and really the principal hazard to the ships were those kamikazes. And if you could just find them and get to them in time before they dove into the ships, they were very easy targets in the air. I never was able to become an ace; I only shot down two airplanes, and they were both the most simple thing in the world to do.

Q: Were those kamikazes?

Admiral Hyland: Yes, I think so. One of them was for sure, and the other one didn't really do very much to defend himself--seemed to be just intent in boring straight in on our task force.

Q: They weren't particularly able pilots, were they?

Admiral Hyland: No. I remember in one case, one of our young pilots, who was an undisciplined youngster and a poor pilot and generally speaking a problem in the air because he was relatively inept--that youngster, by himself, ran into a group of seven kamikazes.* They were just droning along, and he got in behind them and shot down six Nates and a Val.** He shot down the last two when he had only one gun left in the airplane out of the four; only one gun would fire. And he got the last two of them with that one gun. These seven pilots never made any evasive effort whatever. They simply stayed in straight and level flight and continued on. Apparently their attitude was that if they didn't get to where they could see something to dive into, they'd just keep on going, and if they were knocked down, okay. But this very poor pilot got seven airplanes in one flight. And it always just burned me up and burned everybody else up that they weren't lucky like that, to be able to run into such a situation. It was just like

---
*The pilot was Ensign Alfred Lerch, USNR, of VF-10. His feat is described in Barrett Tillman, Corsair: The F4U in World War II and Korea (Annapolis: Naval Institute Press, 1979), page 145.
**Nate was the Allied code name for the Nakajima Type 97 monoplane fighter, which had a maximum speed of 286 miles per hour. Val was the code name for the Aichi Type 99 carrier dive-bomber.

shooting fish in a bucket. We just mowed them down.

One time I was leading a flight of 16 airplanes--they were all fighters, all F4Us--and we were headed up for a target on the island of Kyushu.* We got a couple of hundred miles up to the north of where the carrier was and here, below us, on an opposite course, came this single Japanese airplane. He made a 180-degree turn and started to run back up north. We sort of spread out in a line of 16 airplanes, and I can recall that I never even had to take the engine out of automatic lean; we were in a cruising situation. We just nosed over and pulled up behind him without even increasing power, and we then proceeded to get rid of him. I think I must have hit him with a couple of hundred bullets, and he kept on flying.

I stopped for just a second, and my wingman, who was over here on the right and a wonderful young pilot--his name was Brooks, and he realized that I had stopped firing, so he took aim and he gave one little blip, which I think probably fired ten rounds, and that enemy airplane just blew up into 1,000 pieces.** So this youngster got that airplane after I had just filled it full of bullets and it wouldn't explode. We never have understood that. We were

---

*The Vought F4U Corsair was one of the most successful fighter planes of World War II. It had a wing span of 41 feet and a top speed of more than 400 miles per hour. For details see Barrett Tillman's book mentioned above; the book mentions Hyland's Air Group Ten several times.
**Ensign Eldon E. Brooks, USNR.

pretty close to him, and it blew up and pieces went into the water, and we darn near got damaged from the flying parts of the airplane.

Q: Was he a kamikaze type?

Admiral Hyland: Well, I think so. He was all alone, and he did turn and run. But he just simply couldn't do anything. If he turned left, these fellows were out there on that side, and the other end of the line was over here. And here we were, 16 to 1, and in an airplane where our performance was so superior. He was going, I assume, at full speed for him, and we were cruising, for us, and that was generally the situation. In those later months it was very hard to find anything in the air; people were trying to steal them from one another and so on.

You could listen to the fighter directors and you could realize that there were some Japanese airplanes over here, and you'd run over there, and maybe you'd be lucky and you could get a crack at them before the fellow who was being directed to them would be able to get there. All that sort of silly business was going on. So militarily the name of the game became attacks on airplanes on the ground and attacks on the fixed installations, and that's what we did for the last month or so that we were involved out there. It was pretty one-sided there toward the end, just absolutely the opposite of how it had all started when we were thundering south in those darn PBYs.

Q: Just as a kind of a footnote, what was your code name at that point?

Admiral Hyland: You know, it's funny, I simply don't recall it. I don't know. They changed from time to time. We stayed on board the <u>Intrepid</u> for the rest of the war, and then for a couple of months after the war we operated in and out of Okinawa. A couple of times the ship went up into the Yellow Sea, and we put on an aerial show of force during which we flew over Peking, Tientsin, Tsingtao, Shanghai--all the fabled Chinese cities that I'd never been able to see--but we were never able to land at any of them. We'd just fly around in large numbers and in parade formation, and the idea seemed to be to convince the people on the ground that the war truly was over, that they could believe it; the Japanese had surrendered.

We even flew over the port of Darien, and the Russians were highly indignant about it. And on another occasion--you know, we gave the Russians a whole bunch of PBYs, and when the war was over and we were up in that area, one of my youngsters in the air group was just on a flight and recognized a PBY. So he flew over to the PBY to sort of waggle his wings at it, see who it was and say hello.

Because it was known that nobody in the air there could possibly be anybody but a friend, and darned if this Russian PBY didn't fire on him. They had their guns trained, and they shot at him as he came close. He, of course, veered off. We then got just a little initial taste of how unreasonable the Russians were going to be. The Cold War had started already, and we were just baffled by it. I wondered, what did they do that for?

I can remember one time going back to the ship and landing after we'd flown around Darien. We got this extremely heated protest from the general in charge there, who said that they had almost ordered their antiaircraft batteries to open up on us, because they'd had no word about us coming. We were just flying around being friendly. It was hard to believe that they had any real worries, because the Japanese hadn't been able to attack them for months, and months, and months, and there was no hazard from us at all. We were flying around in parade formation. But they were just as indignant as they could be about it, and from then on, of course, we went through those long Cold War years. They were established there, and they certainly weren't going to tolerate any sort of an intrusion. The idea of putting anybody ashore, of course, would have been refused absolutely.

Q: After your mission up in the northern part, around

Hyland #2 - 151

Darien, what then did you do?

Admiral Hyland: We just continued this show of force business, and along about December the <u>Intrepid</u> went back to Saipan. My air group was taken off, and we were shore-based there in Saipan waiting to go home. Another air group, Air Group 14, which was commanded by a classmate of mine, Sam Brown, got on board, and the <u>Intrepid</u> went back up and continued this postwar operation.*

Q: She didn't become part of the Magic Carpet then?**

Admiral Hyland: No, I don't think she ever did. I think she was kept up there doing that sort of business, just being a ship in readiness. And a few months later Sam and his group were back in the States. I had to stay there on Saipan for perhaps two or three weeks, just waiting to get transportation for the air group to go back to the States. We went back to Alameda and disestablished the air group then.

At the time, Floss's uncle, Red Whiting, was the "king" of Saipan.*** He was the reigning officer, had a quonset hut up on the bluff there in Saipan. He had gone

---
*Commander Samuel R. Brown, Jr., USN.
**Magic Carpet was the name for the postwar operation in which navy ships brought home the military personnel that had been serving overseas during World War II.
***Rear Admiral Francis E. M. Whiting, USN, was the uncle of Hyland's wife, whose maiden name was Florence Whiting.

down to Marcus Island to receive the Japanese surrender of that island; that was one thing he got to do after the war was over. When he was there on Saipan, it had upwards of 100,000 troops on it at that time--from Saipan, from Guam, from Tinian they'd done all the B-29 flying, and it was a very, very busy place--and I can remember joining up with him there.* He was very nice to me.

We finally got on board a jeep carrier, and I was very fortunate to get the whole air group on board the USS Barnes, and we went back to Alameda.** The Barnes went up to Tokyo and picked up a load of captured Japanese airplanes. They got as many as they could and of all the various types. Some of them were destined for museums, and others--some of their very late airplanes--we were very interested in getting a firsthand look at to examine the technology that they may have had. So we just loaded up this little jeep carrier with captured airplanes and then went over the northern route straight to Alameda. It was rough as the devil; I can remember that. Nothing much to do, but it was very nice to be able to get the air group all the way back to the States as a unit.

Q: Were there ever any reunions of the air group?

---

*B-29s were long-range Army Air Forces bombers used for bombing and mining of the Japanese home islands.
**Designated CVE for escort carrier, the "jeep carrier" or "baby flattop" was a small, slow aircraft carrier used mainly for transport work and combat support.

Admiral Hyland: No, there haven't been any of Air Group Ten. A lot of people are still around, and we kind of keep in touch, but, of course, now we're all getting to be pretty old. A fairly large number of the pilots in that group were just kids; they were high school graduates. As the air group commander I led a division of four planes. My other three youngsters with me were all under 21; one guy was only 18 years old. That's Brooks, the kid that got the Japanese plane that I couldn't seem to set fire to. We could just see the bullets winging off every part of him, but he wouldn't blow up, and young Brooks got him; he was only 18 years old.

A lot of those men went back and went to college. Whenever they asked me about staying in the Navy, I told them that if they could do it and if they would do it, they'd be very well advised to go get that college education, and then they could come back to the Navy. Quite a few of them were regular naval officers at that time, and they are all my age to perhaps eight or nine years younger, and a few of them are still going.

Q: They weren't particularly afflicted then with the disease that so many had, I mean, "Let's get out, the war is over."

Admiral Hyland: From about the time we started the operations up there in the Yellow Sea, doing this show of force, they did start demobilizing, and it was done on a system of points. All the people with me had an awful lot of points; they had enough points to get out right away. We could keep the pilots, because we needed them for this operation, and, if I remember correctly, nobody objected to it especially. Nobody seemed to be wild to get back home. But quite a number of the administrative types and people who were businessmen and were going to go back didn't want to miss any time from the competition, so they got out as soon as they could. I always felt very sad about the fact that they chose to go home rather than to wait and go home with us as a group, but I certainly couldn't blame them. I was sorry they did, but I didn't hold it against them. A lot of those young people were probably in their 30s then, and they felt that, by God, there was a great killing to be made back home, and they were going to get in on it.

Q: Having returned to the continent, what did you do next?

Admiral Hyland: After I disestablished Air Group Ten, I was ordered as air officer on the Lake Champlain, and I joined her in Staten Island in New York.* She had just

---
*The USS Lake Champlain (CV-39) was a new Essex-class aircraft carrier that had gone into commission 3 June 1945.

finished a few Magic Carpet runs back and forth to Europe, and at the time I joined her, she was ordered down to the Norfolk area and from there over to Newport News to be decommissioned and preserved. So I was on board that ship for only a very short time. The ship didn't operate at all, and only lasted a very few months. It was after that that I was ordered up to Patuxent River and had duty up there in the flight test division. I didn't spend any time or do anything of note at all on board the Lake Champlain except worry about the fact that I might have to stay on board while we went through the mothballing process. Nobody wanted to put up with that if he didn't have to, because it was just pure drudgery.

Patuxent was a very active place. By that time, it had been built, and the flight test division had come down from Anacostia and been established, and there were several other testing divisions established there at the same time. We had quite a number of new airplanes, including the very first of the jets, which was there in 1946 when I first went there. I spent a three-year tour of duty there that time and got to fly all of the early jet airplanes and all of the very early helicopters that the Navy got. It was one of the most busy, and one of the most enjoyable, and one of the most fruitful tours of duty I ever had.

Q: Was this your first experience as a test pilot?

Admiral Hyland: Yes.

Q: You weren't tempted while you were at Anacostia?

Admiral Hyland: Well, when I was there and flying Admiral King around, the testing division was right next door, but it had its own pilots and its own projects. There just was no way to cross over from what we were doing to what they were doing. Admiral Trapnell--he was a captain then--was the head of the flight test division then, and it was shortly after he went back to sea early in the war that the unit moved down to Patuxent.* Well, a few years passed, and by the time I got to Patuxent in 1946 it was a fairly well established community. I was able to get a very nice set of quarters for my family.

We had a number of Japanese airplanes, we had British Spitfires, and we had some German airplanes. And we had all sorts of new airplane types that were being expedited to get into World War II. And suddenly, of course, the Japanese surrendered, and the war ended, but these projects were very, very active.

Q: This was a period, then, of digesting all the things

---
*Captain Frederick M. Trapnell, USN.

that came from our enemies and friends?

Admiral Hyland: Of course, the big new things were those German jets, because they had appeared very, very late in the war. And thank goodness it wasn't any sooner, because they were so remarkably high performing over anything we had that they might very well have been significant if they'd had any number of them. Fortunately, they didn't.

Q: Along with those German jets did you have German scientists?

Admiral Hyland: No, there were none at Patuxent when I was there, and by the time I got there most of the German airplanes had already been flown and been tested by people who were there earlier and had run into one trouble or another for spare parts, which were difficult to get. They were sort of in a preservation status, and just being readied to put into museums here and there. They'd already flown them and found out what they could do: the Me 262 and Focke-Wulf 190.* Anyway, the latest and best German fighters were represented there, and fellows got to fly

---

*The Me 262, built by Messerschmitt, was the first turbojet fighter to become operational in World War II; it had a maximum speed of 540 miles per hour at 23,000 feet. The Focke-Wulf 190 was a fighter-bomber used in large numbers during the war; it had a top speed of 402 miles per hour.

them. I never did get to fly any of the German planes.

Q: I take it that the British newest models weren't comparable to the Germans?

Admiral Hyland: No, not comparable to the jet airplanes. You see, the jet performance is just an order of magnitude superior to anything you can get from a propeller.

Q: And the British hadn't moved on into that echelon?

Admiral Hyland: No. The interesting feature of the business down there at Patuxent in those days was that perhaps two or three, or in some cases even four, companies would be competing for a contract to build a large number of fighter airplanes, attack airplanes, special airplanes for one thing or another. You'd have the hardware, the actual airplanes, from each of the companies, and you could fly all of these prototypes and actually try them out against one another in the air. You could fly them all and see which one had good characteristics for this and not so good for that, and the Navy could make a decision about which one was best and which one you would go on to produce in quantity.

Now in the aerospace industry things cost so much that quite often we have to decide on the drawing board which one is best, and just go ahead and build it. And we have, occasionally, fiascoes such as the F-111 where you don't get a satisfactory airplane from it.* It's very nice to see nowadays that they may be able to go back to the idea of having at least two prototypes, and fly them off against one another and see which one is really the better one before you have to make the decision that you'll produce number one and not produce number two.

But Patuxent in those days was just thriving on all sorts of projects, on new engines, both reciprocating engines and turbine engines; all kinds of airplanes for various purposes; and all sorts of aeronautical equipment. It was very, very busy. In a very short time you'd get experience in multiple types of airplanes that you just simply couldn't get anywhere else. It was just a marvelous tour of duty.

Q: Was Patuxent an entity unto itself, or was it allied with various test centers throughout the States?

Admiral Hyland: It was called the Naval Air Test Center. It came under the Bureau of Aeronautics, and it was set up to test the airplanes and the equipment they had in them. Now there was duplication. We had another testing place

---
*In the 1960s, Secretary of Defense Robert S. McNamara created a great deal of controversy by trying to get both the Air Force and Navy to use different versions of the F-111.

mainly leaning toward the armament side over at Chincoteague, which is right near there. There were still some airplanes flying from Dahlgren, where they were interested in the bomb performance--you know, the shape of a bomb, and the flight characteristics of a bomb, and bombsights and all that kind of business.* We would get the latest article, with all this equipment in it, and would try to evaluate it at Patuxent just as a service airplane, and actually conducted the trials on the airplane to see whether or not it would pass the specifications against which it was built.

Q: What I meant was that there are various--I suppose they're not all called test centers, but Point Mugu, Lakehurst, and various other places today where things are carried on and they're all sort of coordinated with Patuxent. Was this true in that time?

Admiral Hyland: Not to the same extent that it is now, no. Some of the testing the Navy does now in the really hot airplanes is done out at Edwards Air Force Base, out there at Muroc Dry Lake.** As far back as 1947, we sometimes would take airplanes out to Muroc to fly them there,

---
*The Naval Proving Ground at Dahlgren, Virginia, tested ordnance equipment.
**Edwards Air Force Base is in the California desert. It has been involved in the space shuttle program as a landing site.

because it was much safer to do it than to do some of the things at Patuxent. For instance, there's a huge lake there, and you can have a complete power plant failure and have no problem at all getting down and landing, because the thing is about seven miles in diameter, and anybody could land on that.

Q: Is that different from China Lake?

Admiral Hyland: Oh, yes. China Lake is not far away. China Lake was beginning in those days, and, of course, it also worked on the late armament developments like the Sidewinder missile and all sorts of things that go into the aviation inventory, but they never actually tested airplanes as such there.* In all these things there is a tendency to overlap a little bit; there is some duplication. I've never worried about it. Personally, I think it tends to sometimes promote competition, and I can see that it sometimes spends a little extra money, but I've always thought that having several points of view about something was well worth the cost. Those who are thinking only of the dollars are earnestly trying to cut down any of this overlap that they possibly can, but it's not really all bad. In my opinion, it's mostly good.

---
*Developed by the Naval Weapons Center at China Lake, California, the Sidewinder air-to-air missile went into service in 1956 and is still in service today. It was widely used by U.S. aircraft in the Vietnam War.

Hyland #2 - 162

We had excellent liaison between the Naval Air Test Center and the Flight Test Center at Wright Field.* By that time, the Air Force had become separate, and we saw quite a lot of them.** When it came to the business of writing up specifications for the flying qualities of airplanes, we got together with the Air Force people on that and had no difficulty at all getting the specification written for what sort of stability you really ought to have, and what were the characteristics that were good and bad, and so on. It was very friendly and very good. We always worried in the Navy about the Air Force because of its size. We always felt they might swallow us up if we went too far with the liaison, but cooperation between the two technical centers was very good.

Q: That's interesting, because at one time they did try to, didn't they, swallow up the Navy?

Admiral Hyland: Yes.

There were two wonderful aviators down at Patuxent when I was first there; Admiral Trapnell was one, and Admiral Bill Davis was another.*** They were sort of our

---
*Now Wright-Patterson Air Force Base, Dayton, Ohio.
**In 1947, while Commander Hyland was serving at Patuxent River, the National Security Act became law, setting up a Department of Defense and creating the U.S. Air Force as a separate service in place of the former Army Air Forces.
***Captain William V. Davis, Jr., USN.

old mentors. They were super aviators; they were highly respected people. Both of them were part of a very, very small group that was qualified in heavier-than-air, they were qualified in lighter-than-air, and they had even been in the unit that had the little airplanes that based aboard the dirigibles, so they were qualified in heavier-than-air based on lighter-than-air. It was a very select little club in naval aviation; only a very few of them had ever had a chance to do it.

Later on, when the Air Force got going on some of their big bombers and they were interested in the possibility of a bomber carrying along its own fighters to defend itself, they went up to Lakehurst and they copied the trapeze apparatus that was used up there to take the little fighters aboard the Los Angeles.* They used exactly the same thing and put it on a big bomber and designed a small fighter that could hook up and go with the bomber, and it worked all right. It never was a practicable concept, really, but they looked into it, and that old stuff from the dirigible days was what they went to.

Q: I take it that the lighter-than-air wasn't completely rejected at this point that you're talking about.

---

*Naval Air Station, Lakehurst, New Jersey, was the East Coast headquarters for navy lighter-than-air programs. The USS Los Angeles (ZR-3) was a rigid airship operated by the Navy in the 1920s and 1930s.

Admiral Hyland: No. In fact, I guess it still isn't, really. As long as old Admiral Rosendahl is still alive, we're going to have at least one voice crying in the wilderness.* I begin to read a little bit in the aerospace magazines now about what they might do with the dirigible, and how the one you'd build now would have helium, and would be better constructed, and would be able to handle the weather. And it has its attractive features. I don't honestly think we're going to see any of them because it's a lot of money, but in theory it's got some very nice advantages. You go very much faster than a ship, but you don't really have to go across the Atlantic and the Pacific at jet speeds when you're trying to just carry cargo; you really don't.

---
*During World War II, Rear Admiral Charles E. Rosendahl, USN, served as the first Chief of Naval Airship Training. He retired as a vice admiral and lived until 14 May 1977, some five years after this interview was conducted.

Interview Number 3 with Admiral John J. Hyland, Jr.,
U.S. Navy (Retired)

Place: Admiral Hyland's home in Honolulu, Hawaii

Date: Thursday, 9 March 1972

Interviewer: John T. Mason, Jr.

Q: It's awfully nice to see you again today, sir, and to resume this fascinating account of your naval career. You were at Patuxent when we left off last time--your first tour of duty at Patuxent, and I realize you have a great deal more to say about that. You just told me that this was the most rewarding tour of duty you thought you ever had.

Admiral Hyland: Well, it was. I mentioned earlier in talking that I'd had a job during the war as a group commander on a carrier. Normally in the Navy, that would make the end of your active flying career. You might be engaged in proficiency flying for some years afterwards, but normally that would really be the last active and intensive flying that an officer would do in the Navy. I was still very, very fond of flying and enjoyed it ever so much, so the tour of duty at Patuxent gave me an additional three years of flying that I never would have been able to have any other way.

I think when I finished the tour there I really had

Hyland #3 - 166

the practical, the usable part of a master's degree in aeronautical engineering, and I was able to get it during those three years of flying there without having to go to a formal college somewhere for the same length of time in order to get it. Of course, I didn't have an advanced degree, but I think my understanding of the theory of flight, and what goes on in the various kinds of engines, and why we have all the various devices on airplane wings and in the fuselages and so on--all of those practical aspects of what goes into an airplane--I was able to learn there at Patuxent.

Q: I imagine that the professionals and industry recognized it as such, too, did they not?

Admiral Hyland: Oh, yes. In fact, while I was there, the test pilot school was formed. I can recall the first skipper was S. S. Sherby.* He was the engineer at flight test when I first went to that division, and before the test pilot school was formally set up, Syd Sherby used to conduct classes in the hangar at flight test. Many of us attended them, and he went through the basic things that are actually taught in a course in aeronautical engineering. So those of us who went to those pre-TPT classes have always said that we went to TPT, but we were

---
*Commander Sydney S. Sherby, USN.

Hyland #3 - 167

in class "minus one."* I was very fortunate to be able to do that, because he was a very gifted instructor and a very fine teacher. He got the TPT school off to a very, very good start.

Q: May I ask, as graduates of class "minus one," are you entitled to go to the annual reunions?

Admiral Hyland: Yes, we certainly are, and they always treat us very, very nicely. I haven't been able to get to one now for several years, but I hope I'll get to another one or many more before it's all over. When I first went to Patuxent, the jets were just then coming along. I can recall there was a Ryan airplane that had a reciprocating engine in front and a jet engine in the tail, and that airplane had actually gone out and landed aboard ship; it was called an FR-1.** I never was able to fly that particular airplane.

The first jet the United States built was called the P-59.*** It was built by Bell, and we had one of them

---
*TPT--test pilot training.
**The first Ryan FR-1 Fireball was delivered to newly created Fighter Squadron 66 in March 1945, but the squadron was decommissioned in October 1945 without going to sea. The piston engine was used because of the need for short takeoff runs and long endurance for carrier operations.
***The Bell Air Corporation's XP-59 Airacomet first flew on 1 October 1942. Its performance was disappointing, a top speed of 359.5 knots at 30,000 feet, which was slower than the propeller-driven P-47 and P-51. The P-59 developed into the XP-83, which did not go into production.

there at flight test at Patuxent. Of course, everyone who came there was very, very anxious to get a ride in this one airplane, which was quite underpowered as far as jets are concerned that we see today. But it was a jet airplane, it did have remarkable performance, and, naturally, was one we'll always remember because it was the very first. Shortly after that, the Navy started ordering numbers of jet airplanes, and I was fortunate enough to be able to get in on the early testing of all those early models that came along.

It was a coincidence that helicopters at that time had just come into being, and old Mr. Sikorsky, who built the very first one that we had in the United States, had brought his machine down there.* It was practically the same one that he had built and tested himself, which he had tied to the ground up there in Bridgeport, Connecticut. The one we first got down there at Patuxent was hardly any more advanced than that very first machine that he built. I can remember being taught to fly helicopters down there by another pilot, who had been able to do it by getting a company pilot to show him how.

Q: It was exceedingly hazardous, wasn't it?

---

*Igor I. Sikorsky (1889-1972) was a Russian-born aeronautical engineer who came to the United States in 1919. He developed the first multimotor airplane (1913), first commercial amphibian (1928), and first helo (1939).

Admiral Hyland: Well, it wasn't really hazardous, but there's a novel feature to flying a helicopter; they're actually just a little bit more difficult to fly than a fixed-wing airplane. One fellow would learn to do it, and then he would pass the skill along to the next fellow, and that's the way we learned. It wasn't until a couple of years later that the Navy ordered helicopters in such numbers that they actually started a training school for helicopter pilots, and finally a rule was passed that unless you went to the school and graduated from the full course, you weren't permitted to fly.

At the time that rule came along, there were five or six of us down there at Patuxent who had already gotten as much time in various helicopters as you got in that first helicopter school, and we had been able to perform all of the maneuvers that would be taught to a student at the school, so we all applied to be recognized as graduate helicopter pilots just from our own flying that we'd done at Patuxent. That was approved by the Bureau of Aeronautics, and we were all then designated helicopter pilot number so-and-so. I'm helicopter pilot number 75.

Q: This was an area, was it not, where the Coast Guard stole a march on the Navy, because the Coast Guard recognized the merits of helicopters long before?*

Admiral Hyland: Yes. One of the very early Coast Guard aviators was a fellow named Gershowitz, and Gershowitz was stationed there at Patuxent prior to the time that I'd gotten there.** He was one of the early instructors. In fact, he taught Admiral Tom Connolly to fly helicopters, and it was Connolly who checked me out in flying them just a little bit later on.*** I've never gotten to know Gershowitz, but I can recall that he had almost a famous name in helicopters at that time because the Coast Guard had become interested in them very early.

Q: During World War II, I believe.

Admiral Hyland: Yes, I think so. All the time I was at Patuxent, both in that flight test tour and then later on for a couple more years when I was skipper of the tactical test division, the Coast Guard always had two or three aviators down there, and in all cases these fellows were checked out in helicopters. That was one of the areas of

---
*See Captain Frank A. Erickson, USCG (Ret.), "The First Coast Guard Helicopters," U.S. Naval Institute Proceedings, July 1981, pages 62-66.
**Lieutenant (junior grade) David Gershowitz, USCG. Gershowitz eventually retired as a captain.
***Commander Thomas F. Connolly, USN. Connolly, who retired as a vice admiral, has been interviewed by the Naval Institute's oral history program.

greatest interest to the Coast Guard, just because of their function in supplying remote places and also in rescue work.

Q: Was there anything that pertained to antisubmarine warfare? Were there flights of that sort?

Admiral Hyland: We didn't do anything in the flight test division specifically for ASW.* While I was there, one or more of the early patrol plane models--versions of the P2V airplane--were there and were fully equipped, and were flown.** But the business of the flight test division was really to check the actual performance as far as landing run, takeoff distance, rate of climb, ceiling, handling qualities, and all that sort of thing--to make sure the airplane would actually pass the specifications under which it was built and which the contractor guaranteed to perform. It was very technical work, and not really directly associated with the tactical operation of an airplane at all.

Of course, all of the test pilots there were men who were experienced in one or more areas of tactical work in naval aviation. When one would test an airplane, it's

---
*ASW--antisubmarine warfare.
**The Lockheed P2V Neptune was the primary aircraft used in U.S. Navy land-based patrol squadrons from the late 1940s to the early 1960s. The P2V-1 had a maximum speed of 303 miles per hour at 15,300 feet, a cruise speed of 176 miles per hour at 1,500 feet, and a range of 4,110 miles.

pretty hard to get away from what you think of it or how you think it would perform in its intended mission, and so on. It was far and away the most rewarding tour of duty I've ever had, because I was able to fly so many different kinds of planes. I was able to make quite a wide acquaintanceship in the aerospace industry, as we call it today, among the various aircraft manufacturers, and I was able to make friends with a large number of the very well known military test pilots in the country. The quality of the people down at Patuxent was quite high. We had people such as General Marion Carl, one of the finest military aviators who's ever flown.* A number of well known people in all phases of naval and marine aviation were there from time to time, and it was just a great pleasure to be able to work with such wonderful men as they were.

Q: You certainly were on top of your profession when you left there, weren't you?

Admiral Hyland: You felt like you were, and certainly professionally it helped a very great deal. You got to be known. I think your personal reputation in the Navy, if you did even a halfway good job down there at Patuxent, was

---

*Lieutenant Colonel Marion E. Carl, USMC. During World War II, Carl tied for seventh place on the list of Marine Corps fighter aces; he was credited with shooting down 18½ enemy planes. He retired in 1973 as a major general.

enhanced a very great deal. There was one incident in which I figured down there that I think, temporarily, made me really quite well known, and I couldn't help but observe for the next 15 years in the Navy after that that all sorts of people would remember this single incident.

It was simply an occasion when I was flying one of the fairly early jet airplanes, the F2H made by the McDonnell Company, in an air show and inadvertently ran right into a big bird that I couldn't get out of the way of.* I was making over 500 knots and ran into this bird, and it completely cleaned the vertical tail right off the airplane. Very fortunately for me, the airplane flew straight and properly as long as I was flying fast, but I pulled up and, a little later on, decided to try at altitude the same maneuver that I'd have to make to come down and land. And when I got the airplane slowed down and put down the gear and flaps, the airplane went completely out of control and went into a spin. I wasn't able to get the airplane out of it, so I had to bail out and landed in the water off Patuxent.

Q: Did you realize the extent of the damage when it happened?

---

*This incident, in an XF2H-1, occurred 28 May 1948. The McDonnell F2H Banshee was used as a carrier-based fighter in the Korean War. The prototype was first flown in January 1947. The F2H had a maximum speed of 532 miles per hour at 10,000 feet and a cruising speed of 501 miles per hour.

Admiral Hyland: All I can remember when I struck the bird was a very, very loud and heavy thud. I knew that I had hit the bird because it was right in front of the windshield, and I can recall ducking in the cockpit because I thought it was going to hit me. It missed the canopy and went right over the top of it and hit the vertical tail. Observers on the ground said that it sounded about like a five-inch gun being fired, but in the airplane I didn't hear anything that was nearly that loud. The point of the incident, as far it seemed to make me quite a well known person at the time, was that there was a very large crowd of dignitaries. Admiral Radford was there; the Chief of the Bureau of Aeronautics was there; there were all sorts of flag officers and generals, and a lot of highly placed civilians, and they had all come down to Patuxent to watch this air show.*

The principal point of this part of the air show was to show these men that if we were going to be able to cope with airplanes with that sort of performance and shoot at them from our ships, that we had to improve the performance of the guns at least an order of magnitude. The airplane would come by at such a terrific pace that it would become

---

*Vice Admiral Arthur W. Radford, USN, Deputy Chief of Naval Operations (Air). He later served as Vice Chief of Naval Operations, Commander in Chief Pacific Fleet, and Chairman of the Joint Chiefs of Staff.

obvious then to an observer that our guns couldn't possibly train at anything nearly the rate that they'd have to if they were going to stay up with an airplane flying that fast. The point of flying low and flying right by this crowd, most of whom were ordnance experts, was to convince them that airplanes were now performing orders of magnitude far superior to anything that they had ever seen before.

I was making a high-speed pass over the field when I had this accident and ran into the bird, and all these men were right there on the field and saw it and heard it. Then about an hour later I was standing in front of them telling them about it, because I'd been picked up out of the bay and rushed back to the field, only bruised. I was able to get back into a dry uniform, and stood up in front of them and told them what had happened. Just that one thing, naturally, would stick in all of their minds. For years afterward, I'd meet people that I really didn't know well at all, and it got to be kind of a common thing that they would say, "You know, I was in that crowd down at Patuxent when you ran into that bird." They remembered my name from that from then on out.

Q: Was the poor bird ever identified?

Admiral Hyland: Yes, it was a bird called an osprey, which is a little like a buzzard, not exactly. It's a fishing bird. They're available in quite some numbers down at Patuxent. As a result of my accident, they went to quite some lengths to try and scare all these birds away as they realized what a really serious hazard they were to an airplane flying that fast. It still is one of the principal worries that pilots have who, for one reason or another, fly a jet airplane down near the ground where these birds are flying. There was just nothing that I could do. The bird saw the airplane coming, and it did its best to get out of the way, but in doing that it flew right into the path of the airplane. I hadn't seen it in nearly enough time to do anything about trying to move the controls. It just suddenly loomed up, and the next microsecond later I hit it.

For all the three years that I was in the flight test division, it was just one very pleasurable, very instructive, and very interesting project after another. I was the exec of the division, so I was able to get in on all of the projects without being the project officer on any particular one, and therefore being sort of stuck with that project all of the time until it was finished. I could kind of sample all of them across the board, just like my skipper did. He was the well known aviator Bill Davis--"Little Bill Davis"--an old stunt pilot and a very, very well known aviator in the Navy, and one of the greatest guys I've ever been associated with.*

Q: Incidentally quite a humorist, did you know?

Admiral Hyland: Yes, that's true.

Another distinguished officer who was down there then was Admiral Fred Trapnell, who perhaps was the most distinguished test pilot in the Navy--very, very much a perfectionist, marvelous pilot, and set the standards for all of us at a very high level.** He was just the sort of a leader you'd like best to have around you. It was just a fine tour of duty, and, one of my youngsters was born there at Patuxent while I was on duty that time. My daughter Pamela was born in the dispensary at Naval Air Station Patuxent River, and it's sort of a funny thing when she tells people, because not many people have ever heard of Patuxent River, Maryland.

I think that's about all I can recall about that time. It was just a very fine tour of duty. It got me, as I say, those three more years of very, very active flying in the very latest equipment, and I was doing what I enjoyed the very most. After it was over, I finally was cornered by the detail officer and sent back to sea on a ship, where I think he believed I should have been long since, but I hadn't done it.

---
*Captain William V. Davis, USN.
**Captain Frederick M. Trapnell, USN.

Q: That was the Kearsarge, wasn't it?*

Admiral Hyland: Yes. I went to the Kearsarge as air officer, and very shortly after that the Navy changed the setup on large ships and formed the job of operations officer, which is the third senior job in a big ship. It was actually started mainly because of the requirement for it in these big aircraft carriers that we had. I was the first ops officer on the Kearsarge. When it was first tried, the operations officer was head of, naturally, what was called the operations department, and he had under him the navigator and the air officer. That didn't turn out to be a very workable setup really, because of the fact that traditionally in the Navy forever the navigator has been an independent officer who worked solely for the captain and answered solely to the captain. To put him under this new job of operations officer just simply didn't work. He normally gets enough kibitzing from the skipper himself, and he does have to satisfy the skipper, and he just can't do the job properly and work for two bosses on a ship like that. It's been changed back, and the navigator is head of his own department and is an independent officer, and it's the way it ought to be. I was only on board the Kearsarge

___
*The USS Kearsarge (CV-33) was an Essex-class carrier, a sister of the Intrepid and Lake Champlain in which Commander Hyland had previously served.

for about six months.

Q: What fleet did she operate with?

Admiral Hyland: She was in the Atlantic. When I went aboard, she happened to be up in Boston, Massachusetts, going through an overhaul. Very shortly after that she was sent around to Puget Sound to be inactivated.* It was sort of an ironical thing; the decision was made to put her in mothballs and I was ordered elsewhere. The ship did go around and was mothballed there in Bremerton, and it seems to me it was within a month after that that the Korean War started. Of course, everyone then wished she wasn't completely mothballed and all locked up the way she was, because she could very well have been used in those early Korean War days.**

Q: How long does it take to de-mothball a ship of that nature?

Admiral Hyland: I'm not absolutely sure, but certainly four or five months, unless there would be an absolutely

---
*She was put in mothballs at the Puget Sound Naval Shipyard in Bremerton, Washington.
**The Kearsarge was decommissioned 16 June 1950; the Korean War began on 25 June. She was recommissioned 15 February 1952 after a modernization overhaul that enabled her to operate jet aircraft. She joined Task Force 77 off Korea in September of that year.

emergency 24-hour-a-day effort. Normally if you're taking a ship out of mothballs, you wouldn't do it that way because it would be so expensive. But I think when she did come out of mothballs for other purposes it was done in about six months.

Q: I suppose her consignment to Bremerton was part of the last gasp of the Louis Johnson economy program, was it?*

Admiral Hyland: Yes. That was just about the reason why it happened, and it was at that time that this was done.

Q: So you lost your ship from underneath you. What did you do then?

Admiral Hyland: I was sent then down to the staff of what was called the Operational Development Force. It was a staff based in Norfolk. I was sent down to be the air officer, which meant that I was the officer in charge of all the various air projects. At that time, the Operational Development Force was part of the Atlantic Fleet, but it was an independent part of it, devoted solely to research and development projects. In OpDevFor, which

---

*Louis A. Johnson was Secretary of Defense in 1949 and 1950. He instituted a dramatic cutting of Department of Defense budgets but was soon replaced when the beginning of the Korean War revealed how unprepared the country's fighting forces were. He was replaced by George C. Marshall.

was the short term, we had four squadrons of airplanes; each one of them was engaged in R & D projects in various areas of interest in the Navy.* For instance, VX-1 was an antisubmarine warfare squadron based down in Key West, Florida, and that squadron is still there and still is a specialty squadron in service tests of the lastest ASW equipment or the latest ASW airplane, or the latest anything you have that's concerned with antisubmarine warfare.

Some of the other squadrons have been disestablished since that time, but when I was there OpDevFor was quite a sizable independently operating segment of the Atlantic Fleet, which was given, in the case of aviation projects, all the brand-new airplanes to operate them and test them as tactical units in the fleet. While I was a staff officer, I was able to go around to these various squadrons, and because I'd been at Patuxent immediately before that, I was current in all the airplanes so I could then, in that capacity, continue to do even more flying and take part in the various projects that they ran. That was a fine tour of duty also. Our skipper was an admiral named Entwistle, who was a very, very well-known ordnance expert and a really brilliant fellow in the Navy.**

---

*R & D--research and development.
**Rear Admiral Frederick I. Entwistle, USN, Commander Operational Development Force, October 1950-February 1954.

Hyland #3 - 182

Q: Was Waters there then?

Admiral Hyland: Yes. Muddy Waters was the surface warfare man, and I was the air warfare officer.*

Q: And the old battleship Mississippi was there, was she not?

Admiral Hyland: Yes, she was owned and operated by OpDevFor. I remember the aft turret on the Mississippi had been removed, and a regular aviation omni-range had been put on the fantail of that ship. This was the forerunner of the tacan that we have now, a device that enables the plane to tell what bearing he is from the parent ship and how far away he is, and so on.**

Q: The whole program was the outgrowth of a World War II effort which really paid off in the last months of the war.

Admiral Hyland: Well, OpDevFor still exists in a slightly different form, and it now has units in both the Pacific and in the Atlantic, and they still do these projects on late model equipment of all sorts. It's still a very

---
*Commander Odale D. Waters, Jr., USN. Waters, who retired as a rear admiral, has been interviewed as part of the Naval Institute's oral history program.
**Tacan--tactical air navigation system.

Hyland #3 - 183

valuable part of the Navy, but we no longer can afford a very large number of airplanes and ships that formerly were simply assigned to OpDevFor and were used in the project work and for nothing else. Now they have to take the equipment, or the gadget, whatever it might be, and put it on a regular operating ship and, one way or another, get the tests done while the ship continues to do her regular job.

Q: Under that former system, the people testing them out were men who'd been with the fleet quite recently, were they not?

Admiral Hyland: Yes.

Q: They were operational people?

Admiral Hyland: The idea, of course, was to give all these pieces of equipment a real hard service test under the conditions that it would actually have to live in when it went aboard ship, which is a little different than how something operates when company technicians and experts can hover over it and keep it in top tune and keep it in top form all the time. When you turn it over to the Navy and you have to maintain it with the sailors that you have, and it has to live the life of a regular navy environment, it sometimes doesn't work quite the same way.

OpDevFor's job would really be to decide whether this sonar equipment or this radar equipment or this gun or this airplane really was ready in its present state for dispersal to the entire Navy. They would say yes or no. If they said no, there were procedures that the company, or the Navy, or the technical bureau would have to go through in order to improve the equipment or change it so that it was considered adequate for service life. It was very interesting work. I think I would have enjoyed it even more if I had been in one of the specialty squadrons, because I still, at that relatively late stage, was very fond of flying and wanted to do as much of it as I could.

Q: Your rank was catching up with you, though, wasn't it?

Admiral Hyland: Yes, it certainly was. I was a senior commander at the time, and there were really no active flying jobs available except for these few squadrons that we had. The commanding officer's job in one of them was always filled by a senior commander, but I was never lucky enough to be able to get assigned to one of them. I was just the air officer on the staff. One of the more colorful characters in the Navy that I've been with ever was Admiral Dan Gallery.* He was the number two man on the staff of OpDevFor when I was there.

After that tour of duty on OpDevFor, which was really very pleasurable, I went back to Patuxent as skipper of what was called the tactical test division, and that afforded me another two years of flying up there in that division.

Q: Was this something you requested?

Admiral Hyland: Yes, it was. And there were some occasions a little later on where I think if I hadn't been so anxious to get back to Patuxent as soon as possible--if I had, so to speak, played my cards a little more carefully--I might have been able to go back a little bit later and have been head of the flight test division, which is really the most prestigious job there. But this opportunity to go to tactical test as the skipper just happened to come up, and when I was asked if I'd like to do it, I just grabbed it. That meant just another couple of years of flying, very much like I'd done before in the flight test division, but a little more pointed toward the tactics of the airplane. It was not directly concerned

---
*Rear Admiral Daniel V. Gallery, Jr., USN. As a captain in 1944, Gallery was the commanding officer of the USS Guadalcanal when she captured the German submarine U-505. He later became even more well known as the author of a series of popular books. His oral history is in the Naval Institute collection.

with finding out whether the airplane met specifications or not but to devise tactics that would make it most effective when it was sent to the fleet. We also were assigned a number of R & D projects.

During those years, the Navy was just getting into the business of refueling airplanes in the air. I can remember my little division, tactical test, was given the project to explore the problems, if there were any, of approaching the tanker, and getting the airplane refueled while it was in the air. We conducted a lot of tests on the early jet airplanes to establish safe fuel loads and reasonable ranges to which you could send the airplane, and so on. So that the ordinary fleet pilot could read our report and get himself prepped about the airplane by just reading simple English, whereas that same pilot might not be able to read the highly technical report that was turned out by the flight test division and which really needed a graduate aeronautical engineer in order to interpret the thing. But it was another two years of duty in my favorite place. While I was at tactical test, I was selected for captain. It was pretty obvious that my flying days were pretty rapidly coming to an end then.

Q: Any repercussions from the Korean Conflict which were felt at Patuxent?

Admiral Hyland: No. Prior to that, when I was at OpDevFor, I did go out to Korea for one trip. Of course, the Navy paid a great deal of attention to what was going on out there and tried to make all the moves to make sure our equipment was going to be as good as it could be. As you recall, there was no particular opposition to the carrier operation out there in Korea; they more or less operated in a sanctuary and just flew in support of the troops ashore. There were no attacks made on any of the ships out at sea, either by airplanes or submarines.

Q: The danger was from mines actually, wasn't it?

Admiral Hyland: Yes, I think so, more than anything else. Of course, they were always worried about these other possibilities, but none of them ever came to pass. In some of those early jet airplanes we didn't have absolutely reliable engines. One of the more interesting projects I had there at tactical test was just to explore, in various jet airplanes that we had, the technique that a pilot could best use if he did have an engine failure and was flying at a decent altitude and would be able to make a dead-stick landing on the field.

We took some airplanes out to Edwards Air Force Base in California and flew them up to high altitudes and then deliberately shut the engines off, then maneuvered without the engine down to a landing on Muroc Dry Lake and gradually worked our way up to being able to land on a regular airfield with confidence. We were able to write parts of the pilots' manual that would tell a new pilot what he should do, the technique to use, in case he had to come down without any power at all. In those early jets it was feasible. For the most part now, the airplanes are so heavy and they're so hot that it really isn't feasible to make a dead-stick landing. It has been done, and it can be done, but in most cases, because of circumstances, when a complete engine failure is experienced the pilot usually has the only option of ejecting and forgetting about the airplane, because it just isn't feasible to bring it down without any power.*

Q: It's a great loss of money, though, isn't it?

Admiral Hyland: Well, yes, I'll say.

Q: You had another interesting tour of duty immediately following that, I would think, and this had great significance for your future career when you went to the National War College.

---

*Admiral Hyland discusses the dead-stick landing tests further in interview number 5, pages 293-294.

Hyland #3 - 189

Admiral Hyland: Yes. I was one of the younger people in that class.

Q: Was this a surprise to you?

Admiral Hyland: Well, yes. I was very pleased when I was sent up there. The National War College had a sort of reputation of excellence and prestige that was perhaps a little higher than the standard service war college--the Naval War College or the Army War College or the one down in Maxwell that the Air Force runs. I don't really think that it was any better than what you get at one of the service colleges.

It was interesting that most of my classmates from the other services had already been to their own war college before they came to the National War College. Now the Navy has hardly ever done that. An officer is either sent to the Naval War College or the Air Force War College. When I was there, the navy people just went there; they hadn't been to their own service war college, but all of our classmates had been. The most interesting part of it really was to get to know a few people from the State Department and from other civilian bureaucracies there in Washington, but mostly from the State Department, and to realize that they were human, too, and that they were as impressive a group as they actually turned out to be.

It was a very easygoing year, very, very interesting. We listened to some of the top people lecture there, from all walks of life and all the disciplines in the United States. And on that side of it, it could hardly be more interesting. We didn't have rigid hours. We weren't scheduled every minute of the day to do something. You were more or less left on your own, and I really believe that if there had been a completely lazy and indifferent member of the class who didn't choose to work regularly, I don't believe it would have been noticed.

Q: You don't think social pressure would have been involved?

Admiral Hyland: Of course, nobody did that.

Q: These were all the promising men for all the services included in this class.

Admiral Hyland: Of course. We were assigned professional reading and were given time to do reading beyond that, but the quantity of the professional reading that we were assigned was so large that no one could possibly do it. So there were unwritten rules that we came up with fairly early in the game, and we'd gotten them from officers who'd gone to the National War College earlier. It was sort of agreed that nobody would work beyond midnight at night, because we all had to be at work at 8:00 o'clock in the morning, and it just wasn't reasonable to try and get through all of this material. I thought everyone worked reasonably hard, but we were not tied to a rigid schedule, and it was the first time in my career that I really had a setup like that.

Right next door we had the Industrial College. It was being run at that time by an admiral. He was a very fine officer, but he was the type of officer who simply couldn't bear the idea of a bunch of military people sitting there with nothing scheduled.* So they were scheduled for as many as four or five lectures a day, or in between lectures for discussion meetings, or one thing or another. Our daily schedule was to just go to one lecture in the morning, and perhaps one discussion group in the afternoon, and otherwise we'd keep ourselves busy by doing some of the reading of things that we'd always wanted to read but never had the time, or doing the reading and the work on the occasional papers that we'd have to write and then later show to the class.

Q: Admiral, I understand from a number of men who did

---

*The Commandant of the Industrial College of the Armed Forces from June 1952 to July 1955 was Rear Admiral Wesley M. Hague, USN.

attend there that one of the really valuable things--a side effect, I suppose, or side benefit--was the fact that the men there usually formed car pools for coming in in the morning, and they had a chance to really exchange ideas in an intimate way day after day. Did you have this experience?

Admiral Hyland: Yes, exactly that happened to me, too. In my car pool there were myself and one other navy fellow, John Tyree--who's also an admiral now and a submarine officer--and then we had a fellow from the State Department and an army type.* So going back and forth to school five days a week, we really had wonderful opportunities to find out about the other fellow and talk about all these problems. It was really one of the nicest parts of the whole course.

Q: And then the other thing which I have noted in talking with so many men who went on to high command after that-- the friendships, the contacts which were made, which paid off in innumerable ways later as the career expanded and so forth. Did you have that experience?

Admiral Hyland: Yes, exactly that. All through the rest of my naval career--and then, of course, I began to become

---

*Captain John A. Tyree, Jr., USN, later vice admiral.

a more and more senior officer--as I traveled around in ships, and as I went here and there, I would run into classmates who had gone up in their services. And we would perhaps go into ports, and there the consul-general would be a fellow who'd been my classmate at the National War College, and that continued to happen all the rest of my time in the Navy. Several of the State Department people got to pretty high places in the State Department; one or two were ambassadors. Quite a few of the military people in the class went up to very high places in the Army and the Air Force, and also in the Marines.

Q: Of course, you were all the cream of the crop, so this was an inevitable thing, I suppose.

Admiral Hyland: Well, I can recall it was certainly considered to be a very lucky break if you were assigned to the National War College, and I think other people who weren't sent there envied our good luck in being sent there.

Q: When you were there, did they still have the system which Admiral Hill had originally inaugurated of having outstanding professors from various universities throughout the country who would spend a semester there, on leave from their alma mater?*

Admiral Hyland: Yes, that was the procedure that was followed. It's been so long, and I haven't been thinking about it. I can't recall many of the names, but they were very fine people. One fellow who was there as generally the head of the political science studies for the National War College had been the head of the department at Ohio State. There was another fellow, whose name was Walsh, who was a very, very distinguished scholar and fine person. The military faculty at the National War College was very high class also; there were really good officers assigned there. Always the articulate and very scholarly type of officer that you don't see all throughout the Navy, but people who were just gifted in that way were sent to jobs like that.

Q: Having graduated from there, without a degree, you went on to command the Onslow?

Admiral Hyland: Actually, I went from the National War College out to the Pacific Fleet staff. I was assigned as air operations officer on that staff for a couple of years. Admiral Stump was both CinCPac and CinCPacFlt at that

---
*Vice Admiral Harry W. Hill, USN, was appointed in 1946 the first Commandant of the National War College in Washington, D.C. He held that position until 1949, when he became president of the General Board.

time.*

Q: So you got a view of what you were going to do eventually?

Admiral Hyland: Well, I certainly didn't know it at the time. Of course, Admiral Stump was one of the great characters that the Navy's ever produced. I think really it's a controversial subject about how he got where he got, but he certainly was an effective commander of the Pacific Command when he finally got there. He was a very explosive person, sometimes quite moody, but such a colorful boss that if you ever worked on his staff you'd just never forget it. I know that on many occasions he would throw a fit of temper and conduct a terrifying tirade of abuse on people, and he would be doing it quite deliberately, just to make sure they remembered who was boss and just to make sure they were putting forth their best efforts.

Q: Was that necessary to repeat more than once?

Admiral Hyland: Well, he did repeat it more than once. He did it regularly. If you weren't personally involved but could see it from the sidelines while one of your staff

---

*Admiral Felix B. Stump, USN, was Commander in Chief Pacific and Commander in Chief Pacific Fleet from 1953 to 1958, when the commands were separated.

Hyland #3 - 196

mates was taking the heat, it was very funny. But it wasn't particularly amusing if you were getting it yourself. I had known Admiral Stump a little bit before, because when I was in that patrol squadron out in the Far East he was the skipper of the Langley, which was our big seaplane tender out there. So he knew who I was, and I certainly knew who he was.

But there the tour of duty, again, was very, very pleasant, very, very instructive, because there, of course, you see how a big staff operates. Really, you begin to find out how the Navy is run. Professionally it was a very good assignment. I have never really enjoyed staff duty nearly as much as operational duty, but at the same time there's no denying that staff duty can be rewarding. It has to be done by relatively good people, or the direction of the Navy just isn't going to be what it should be. So on those high staffs, normally there are procedures for screening people, and when an officer is assigned to one of them he should understand that it's a very high compliment.

I can recall that in those days, no one would be assigned to the Pacific Fleet staff without Admiral Stump being told about it ahead of time and without getting his stamp of approval for the fellow coming in the first place. Now the pace of things is so much higher, and the availability of quality people to go here and there isn't as lavish as it used to be, I guess you could say, so now they don't have time or don't consult the fleet commander to the extent that they used to. When I became commander in chief of the fleet, that used to bother me occasionally, but I could understand that there were reasons for it, and I was never seriously let down as far as the quality of the people who were sent.

Q: Stump was the kind of a man who would insist upon having to pass on each and every one.

Admiral Hyland: Yes. As I say, he was both CinCPac and CinCPacFlt, and it was a little later, after I left, that the Joint Chiefs of Staff directed that the command be split and that there be a separate CinCPac and a separate Commander in Chief of the Pacific Fleet. In other words, the CinCPac officer could not be his own naval component commander.* I think it's obvious that there were some things about the old setup that were very nice to have, as far as the officer who was CinCPac was concerned. If he could be his own component commander, a lot of things worked very nicely for the Navy, and worked very well for him.

---

*The Pacific Command, headed by CinCPac, is a joint command involving all the armed services; the Pacific Fleet is a Navy job, although it does include Marines as part of the Fleet Marine Force.

Q: He had two staffs, didn't he?

Admiral Hyland: Yes, he did have separate staffs, although there was very good liaison. But, of course, because of pressure from the other services, and for many good reasons, it wasn't best to have that setup, and it has been an improvement in organization to have the three coequal service component commanders under the one and separate CinCPac, and that's the way we have it now.

Q: In the mid-Fifties, the worries and the obligations of that joint job were not anything like what they came to be.

Admiral Hyland: No. I think perhaps that was one reason why it was set up the way it was. If they had held to the old setup, I don't believe it would be unworkable at all, except it would put a very heavy burden on one individual. However, people being the way they are, there are plenty of individuals who'd be delighted to accept the burden. They'd be able to handle it.

Q: What happened of interest to you? What were some of your interesting assignments in that two-year period?

Admiral Hyland: It was really mostly regular staff planning and staff operations work. Admiral Stump did a good bit of traveling in an airplane that he had assigned for his own personal use, and I had to plan all of the trips that he made in that airplane.

Q: Did you go with him ever?

Admiral Hyland: I went with him on one or two, but generally speaking he only took a very small group on those trips. We took part in all sorts of future plans for facilities in the Western Pacific that we thought were going to be needed to back up the fleet. I can recall the Navy worrying--and it still is worried--that we haven't really got an adequate airfield on Okinawa. Now that whole matter is coming to an end because we're going to turn Okinawa back to the Japanese.* But right after World War II, the Navy had tenancy of Naha Airfield, and a few of those extremely tough typhoons happened to come along about that time, and the Navy made an official judgment that Okinawa was simply an untenable place to have a base. They gave up tenancy of Naha; they gave it to the Air Force. Then, within a matter of a few years, they tried desperately for 20 years to get it back and never were able to do it.

---

*On 15 May 1972, shortly after this interview, the Ryukyus Islands, including Okinawa, were returned to Japanese control. The United States has been permitted to continue to maintain military bases on the island.

The air force view on the other hand, was simply that these typhoons--and I think they were correct--did come, and you could expect a certain number of them every year, and there was that problem. But because of the location of Okinawa and the need for bases there, they would simply build structures so that they would be typhoon-proof. That's exactly what they've done, and you see in Naha and in Kadena Air Force Base there some of the most marvelous facilities that have been built anywhere in the world. The typhoons come and go, but they don't blow those houses down; they're just marvelous for that purpose. Of course, those typhoons are so bad that navy ships in port in Okinawa all have to go to sea. There's no way to stay in port and weather those storms, because they just are terribly strong.

Q: But then the weather forecasting is so much more available now.

Admiral Hyland: I think nowadays, of course, they know when they're coming, and they know generally where to go to be the surest of avoiding them. It's not anything like the problem it used to be, because they would just appear practically out of the blue. You might remember right after the war we had some substantial damage on a few of our carriers.

Q: In that time, the Formosa Strait problem and the offshore islands was a hot subject, was it not?

Admiral Hyland: Oh, yes. As air operations officer, I was Admiral Stump's advisor, if you could call it that, on things that were going to concern air operations. We flew some reconnaissance flights from Taiwan over China, and, of course, he would be intimately involved in those and very, very interested in them. Part of my job was to make sure he was informed, to make sure that the plans for doing these covert operations were sound.

Q: These were associated with the CIA, were they?

Admiral Hyland: In part, yes. At the time they were very, very sensitive. They would be photo reconnaissance flights. I can remember one time Marion Carl was in a marine fighter squadron, photo squadron, that was based in Korea, and that outfit was sent down to Taiwan to get some up-to-date coverage of the area of China directly across the Formosa Strait.* There were rumors about military buildups, and there was concern about an invasion of

---

*Lieutenant Colonel Marion E. Carl, USMC, was commanding officer of a photo reconnaissance squadron, VMJ-1, based in Korea, from 27 November 1954 to 24 June 1955.

Taiwan, and this was part of the business of finding out really what was up. On one flight, Carl was over there with his wingman, over China, and ran into some jet fighters that they hadn't really expected to see and had potentially a very, very dangerous situation for a few minutes. Of course, a thing like that would interest Admiral Stump very, very much.

The Navy was just getting started in the nuclear business. We were working very hard to get our airplanes nuclear capable. We were working very hard to get the AEC to design smaller weapons and lighter weapons that could be carried on the tactical airplanes as well as on the bigger airplanes.* We also finally got in the very sensitive national plan for nuclear warfare if it ever came, and part of my assignment was to do that nuclear strike planning for CinCPacFlt.

Q: This was part of that overall idea of massive retaliation?

Admiral Hyland: Yes. I was the head of this little section, and I had three other officers--one Marine and two navy fellows--working directly for me, and we used to do all the nuclear strike planning for the fleet at that time. Of course, now all of that planning is centralized and is

---

*AEC--Atomic Energy Commission.

done at Omaha, Nebraska, by the Joint Strategic Target Planning Staff. But in those days the services planned separately and did the best job they could with what they had, but planned it themselves and had very little, if any, liaison with the other services.

Q: Was there any deep-seated conviction that, in case of an emergency, resort would be made to the use of these atomic weapons?

Admiral Hyland: We certainly took the subject very, very seriously in those days, and we went to very, very great lengths to train pilots and have them ready, and to conduct realistic tests, and to make sure that if the button was ever pushed we would be able to do what we were supposed to do. Now nuclear weapons had been used, of course, on two occasions in Japan. I think at that time, by and large, that we really believed that we would use them if certain things came to pass. But as the years went by, and as the scene evolved, it seems to me there's been more and more doubt come forth that they ever really will be used. Now one of the weaknesses of perhaps our posture is that I don't believe that people seriously think now that tactical nuclear weapons ever will be used.

At the same time, we have to be very careful about the strategic posture. We have to be very careful to do our best to find out what the other fellow has. We have to have a certain number of missiles on the land and at sea, and all of that, and we just don't dare to be unprotected in that respect. The effects of ever engaging in this nuclear exchange are so simply terrible to contemplate that I would think that the average point of view is that only a maniac would ever start it. But at the same time, we have to be prepared to be able to do it, just as part of the deterrent posture that I think we have to keep.

Now the use of tactical nuclear weapons here, or there, or anywhere is potentially so close to pulling the string on total nuclear exchange that I personally doubt they'll use them. But, again, not only would it be absolute folly to throw them away now that we have them and they are so developed and we have airplanes that are capable of doing it, we have the facilities in our ships--both in carriers and in others--to carry them and to use them if we are called on to do it. It seems to be absolute folly to deliberately get rid of them, unless we can have an arrangement with the potential enemies and be absolutely sure they're going to fulfill it that neither will have these things. But they're developed, and there's no question about the ability of our people to deliver them if they ever had to do it.

There have been certain situations here and there where, solely from the military point of view, the use of a nuclear weapon or two or three would have been a very simple and effective way of doing the job, but we have never found civilian leadership that was willing to take a risk. Because we have always been able to handle the problem without their use. I'm only saying that here and there, there have been occasions when it would be cheaper and more effective to have used them.

Q: I suppose the outstanding illustration is that in Korea, when General MacArthur asked for permission to use them and was refused.*

Admiral Hyland: I'm not well informed about that. I do understand that really did happen, and that he really did make such a request. But I wasn't involved anywhere where I could authenticate it. There were recommendations when the French were having their trouble down in Dien Bien Phu to use a nuclear weapon, but that also was refused.** I honestly don't personally know any more than that about it. I really think that whole subject is similar to the one concerning the biological and chemical weapons. As long as

---
*General of the Army Douglas MacArthur, USA, was Supreme Commander of United Nations Forces in Korea in 1950 and 1951, until relieved by President Harry Truman for insubordination.
**The defeat of French forces by the Vietnamese revolutionary army came at the end of the siege of Dien Bien Phu. The siege lasted from 13 March to 7 May 1954 and generally marked the end of French rule in what was then French Indochina and soon became North and South Vietnam.

you feel the other fellow has them and might use them, you have to have some deterrent to his doing that. So we do have to keep these horrible developments, in my opinion. You cannot afford to let one of them go as long as you can't absolutely be sure that the other fellow is going to also give them up.

Q: In other words, a Gandhi-esque policy doesn't go in this world, does it?*

Admiral Hyland: Not in my opinion, it doesn't.

Q: What was your opinion of the Nationalist Chinese Air Force in those days?

Admiral Hyland: From what I knew of them--and it certainly wasn't very much--they performed very well. I forget what airplanes we'd given them at that time and what they really were able to do, but by and large they did well with what they had. I know of a few cases where they had people assigned to fly some of our very highest performing airplanes that were used in some of this covert work, and there you would see they were more suited to it, because one of them might go down in China, and his chances were

---

*Mohandas Gandhi (1869-1948) was a Hindu nationalist and spiritual leader who espoused a campaign of "passive resistance" to British rule in India.

far better than an occidental caught in the same situation.

Q: And it was more nearly their problem anyway, wasn't it?

Admiral Hyland: Yes, and it really was more their problem. Those men were first class. That phase of things really was not navy business, and I wasn't really very well informed about it.

Q: Were you involved at all in the Vietnamese picture in the middle Fifties?

Admiral Hyland: Only to the extent that at the time, you remember, they moved quite a large number of people from the north down to the south. It seems to me they were mostly Catholics who were moved from North Vietnam to South Vietnam when the partition took place, and U.S. amphibious ships provided that lift for all of those people. Late in my tour on CinCPacFlt I can remember making a trip with Admiral Sharp; he was then a captain and had come to the fleet staff for a new job which put him in charge of both operations and plans.*

It's the O-2 job on the staff now, and it's still set up that way. He was the first officer that had that job,

---

*Captain Ulysses S. Grant Sharp, Jr., USN, deputy chief of staff (operations and plans). Sharp later served as CinCPacFlt and CinCPac himself. His oral history is in the Naval Institute collection.

and the point of it was--and it may have been particularly true under Admiral Stump--that the chief of staff was virtually worked to death, and this was a device to try to take some of the load off the chief of staff. It hasn't worked that way, because, if you know as much as I do about staff work, there's just no way to relieve the chief of staff of anything. He still has to handle all the details, see the big picture, satisfy the admiral, and run the show. Of course, he's going to be assisted one way or another by the good people you have, but it's not possible to start up a new position--sort of call him an assistant chief of staff--and really take any of the load off the chief of staff. It hasn't come out that way. But anyway, Admiral Sharp had just come to the staff, and he was making a makee-learn trip around the area, and I was fortunate enough to be able to go on that trip with him. We went to Saigon.

Q: That was something rare, was it not, with Admiral Stump because he didn't have his staff travel very much?

Admiral Hyland: No, but, of course, Admiral Sharp had worked for him a couple of times before and had made a tremendous impression on Admiral Stump. Admiral Stump had a number of people working for him who had worked for him before. I can remember the aide had been his aide twice before, and in those days that sort of the old team setup was more common than it is now. Anyway, we went to Saigon on that trip, and this lift of people had just recently been completed.* I can remember old Vice Admiral Sabin, who was in charge of that lift, was there in Saigon, and there were a few U.S. Navy amphibious ships that had been involved that were tied up there in Saigon just for a port visit when we happened to arrive there, too.**

One of my most vivid recollections of that visit to Saigon was that the official rate of exchange was such and such, and the black market exchange rate was tremendously higher and, therefore, for the visitor more favorable. I was dumbfounded to be advised directly, in the presence of then-Captain Sharp, later to be admiral, advised by the naval attaché there where to go and how best to get the black market rate of exchange rather than the official rate of exchange. I'd never even dreamed of that happening before, because elsewhere the military visitor was rigidly required to stay with the official rate of exchange and have nothing to do with the black market. Now, of course, that's been changed, too, but at that time the difference between the two was so completely unreasonable that apparently there was nothing wrong with it, and it was not

---
*See Edwin B. Hooper, Dean C. Allard, and Oscar P. Fitzgerald, <u>The United States Navy and the Vietnam Conflict</u>, Volume I (Washington, D.C.: Naval History Division, 1976), pages 270-299.
**Rear Admiral Lorenzo S. Sabin, USN, Commander Amphibious Force Western Pacific. Sabin, who retired as a vice admiral, is the subject of a Naval Institute oral history.

frowned upon to go ahead and get the best exchange that you could get.

Saigon was then very, very strongly French influenced, and it was pretty obvious that the French who'd been there and who were running the show really had a wonderful life: beautiful homes, lots of servants, really a rather pleasant climate, a little too hot for some people, but they had a simply wonderful tropical life there. There had been some violence in Saigon at that time. I can't remember what the provocation for it was, or who was involved, but nothing happened during the three days that we spent in Saigon.

Q: I think at that point the violence had to do with internal politics, didn't it, one faction against another rather than guerrillas?

Admiral Hyland: There was a certain amount of bomb-throwing into the lobbies of hotels and that sort of business, and we thought about it when we were there as some few incidents that happened within the week, but nothing happened when we were there that time. I don't recall Admiral Sharp visiting with anyone there except the U.S. Navy people: Admiral Sabin, for instance, who was there. I don't remember any liaison with any of the Vietnamese people, and I personally wasn't taken along if he did go on such visits while he was there. That was a

Hyland #3 - 211

grand trip. We not only went there, we stopped in places in the Philippines where we had interests, and then we proceeded throughout the WestPac area--went to several places in Japan, went to quite a few places in Japan, went to quite a few places in Guam and Marianas chain, as well as Chichi Jima, which is an unusual place to get to and hard to get to.*

Q: What was the reason for going there?

Admiral Hyland: It had been a stronghold of the Japanese during World War II, and there is a very fine harbor there, and I think we had ideas that perhaps we could operate submarines out of Chichi Jima. We did have potential nuclear storage there, because there are a number of caves that the Japanese had prepared and which would be very suitable for that sort of thing. Admiral Radford, I recall, then the chairman, was interested in Chichi Jima, and it was under CinCPac, CinCPacFlt, and was just a place that Admiral Sharp in his new job was going to have to sort of administer and monitor. He had a naval officer as the sort of resident person in charge at the time.**

Q: Was it a part of the mandated islands?

---
*WestPac--Western Pacific.
**Admiral Arthur W. Radford, USN, was Chairman of the Joint Chiefs of Staff, 1953-57.

Admiral Hyland: Yes. So he felt that it would be well for him to actually go there and see it. The way you had to do it was to take a little seaplane from Iwo Jima and fly up to this little island and land in the water, and taxi up the old Japanese ramp and make your visit that way. The airfield was not suitable for landing and never had been renovated from the days when we damaged it in World War II. It was a very short, very small field anyway. Chichi Jima had really been a sort of a Japanese Bermuda before the war, and there was one fairly nice hotel on the island, but it had been completely flattened by the navy carrier strikes during the war. It was a very unique visit. I've never forgotten going up there, and I've never managed to get back; I'd enjoy going there again.

Q: It doesn't seem to be on the beaten track.

Admiral Hyland: It's been returned to Japan now. One of the unique things about Chichi Jima is that all the names of the people, who all look very oriental now, are all English. They are descendants of English whalers who came there long, long ago, and they've been very, very inbred and so on. It's almost like the colony where the Bounty mutineers went.*

The time on Admiral Stump's staff was a very interesting and very instructive period for me. I got to work intimately with Oley Sharp during that last year I was on the staff and he was the O-2. As far as I can tell, I made a good impression on him. I enjoyed working for him. He's tough, he's smart as the dickens, and has really high standards, but he's a really nice guy to work for. And I guess as long as you're doing a good job, you're going to have a pleasant time of it. Of course, later on, he must have had something to do with the very, very good jobs I got. But I got to know him; I got to admire him very much, and nothing but good for me came from that tour of duty.

Q: That's one of the virtues of staff work, you know, as I view it from afar.

Admiral Hyland: Yes, it is. There were other very fine people who were working for Admiral Stump while I was there. Admiral Curts, who later got to be CinCPacFlt, was the chief of staff part of the time.**

---
*The mutiny on the British ship Bounty occurred in 1789. Some of the mutineers settled on Pitcairn Island, where their descendents still live.
**Vice Admiral Maurice E. Curts, USN. When the Pacific Fleet became an independent command in mid-January 1958, Admiral Curts served temporarily as commander in chief until relieved at the beginning of February.

Q: Was that Germany Curts?

Admiral Hyland: Yes, Germany Curts. He was after Admiral Hopwood.* Both of them later succeeded to the job of the commander in chief of the fleet out there. Putt Storrs was the chief of staff on the CinCPac side, and later George Anderson was there.**

Q: He was chief of staff?

Admiral Hyland: Yes, on the CinCPac side of the house. This was before the split came, it seems to me.

Q: Putt Storrs was one of the early stunt fliers, too, along with Art Davis.***

Admiral Hyland: Yes, he was. He had a very, very attractive oriental wife--Chinese-Hawaiian gal, Eve--who was a great beauty in her day and was quite a gal.

Q: After I left that job was when I went to the Onslow, which was a little seaplane tender. Then you had a job

---
*Vice Admiral Herbert G. Hopwood, USN, who was later Commander in Chief Pacific Fleet, 1958-60.
**Vice Admiral Aaron P. Storrs III, USN; Vice Admiral George W. Anderson, Jr., USN, later Chief of Naval Operations, 1961-63. Anderson is the subject of a two-volume Naval Institute oral history.
***Lieutenant Commander Arthur C. Davis, USN, who was later a flag officer.

Hyland #3 - 215

like that for just a year. It was interesting that there I'd gotten to the point where I was a young captain, and one of the major questions in your professional career was whether or not you were going to be on the ship list, whether you'd be that lucky, and, of course, if you were an aviator and you were on the ship list, your qualifying command was going to be one of these seaplane tenders, because that's all we had. It was kind of funny to recall that when I left the job of flying Admiral King around, one of the jobs I could have had then, just for the asking, was command of an AVP, because at that time they were all commanded by commanders.* They were just involved in the advance base support of the patrol planes and seaplanes that we had in quite some numbers in those days. But I had turned that down out of hand for the command of the air group on the carrier. And here, about ten years later, I was sweating out the matter of whether or not I would be able then to get command of one of these little AVPs. I was lucky, and I did.

Q: Yes, but with a different view of the assignment.

Admiral Hyland: I'd always enjoyed the active flying so very much that I shied away from duty on board ship. But I'll have to say that when I finally got to be captain of a ship, the picture was absolutely, entirely different.

_____
*AVP is the designation for a small seaplane tender.

There isn't any job that is more pleasurable and more rewarding than being the skipper of a ship. And being the skipper of a very small ship is far better than being exec of the biggest ship that ever floated. There's just no comparison at all. Now these little AVPs were designed to support PBYs, and they could just barely support PBMs, but really couldn't hoist a PBM aboard, whereas they could hoist a PBY aboard if that ever was necessary.* So they were used for a variety of tasks. They had a very easy schedule and a very predictable schedule.

Q: Wasn't this in the declining days of the flying boat?

Admiral Hyland: Yes, it was. There were just a few squadrons left, and they were all PBM squadrons by that time. As I say, the little AVPs were really not capable of taking full care of them, but they could bunk the crews and fuel them and help to maintain them. They couldn't get one aboard. So we were used for a variety of tasks, such as station ship at Hong Kong, which I had with my little AVP twice for periods of six or seven weeks at a crack and one of the most lovely times you could ever have. I just love Hong Kong and can recall those periods there at a buoy right close to the city--hardly a more favorable setup anywhere in the world.

---

*The PBM Marlin had an empty weight of 32,378 pounds; the empty weight for the PBY-5A Catalina was 20,910 pounds.

We did a certain amount of seaplane tending here and there, up in the Pescadores Islands and elsewhere. But really the little ships were beginning to outlive their usefulness, and most of them were later turned over to the Coast Guard and became first-line, long-endurance cutters for the Coast Guard. They were diesel-driven ships. For their size they had an enormously long range and endurance, and really were very, very well suited for this Coast Guard duty a little later on.

Q: That prompts me to ask you, then what was available for aviators to command as a ship?

Admiral Hyland: Of course, shortly after I had my so-called qualifying command, which was this little seaplane tender, the whole system in the Navy was changed. They then started to assign aviators to command of tankers, supply ships, ammunition ships--all the service force ships. And now the aviators, I think, have about 50% of those ships on the average. There are no assignments now in the qualifying command level that are strictly aviation oriented. We don't have any seaplane tenders active any longer, and there are no other specialized aviation ships that you get at that point in your career.

I took over the Onslow in Hong Kong, and just about a

year later I very unhappily released her to my successor in Hong Kong. So I'm one of the more experienced Hong Kong sailors who operated in the Navy really. I know a lot of people, and I know a lot about the place because of those long, long periods that we spent there.

One of the ways to appreciate the tremendous size of the Pacific Ocean is to sail across it in an AVP. The thing would only go about 16 knots max. I would normally cruise at about 13 or 14, and I'll tell you it's a long ride from Alameda to Honolulu to Yokosuka, then to the Philippines or to Hong Kong or wherever you're going next. But they were very fine little ships, very easy to maneuver, good training ground for getting a certain amount of respect for ships that's absolutely essential to get one place or another.

There's a type of naval aviator who just figures to himself that, "If I can fly these high-speed fighters and bombers, and if I can just with my eye solve the relative motion problems that are involved in joining up with other airplanes and making landings and takeoffs and approaches and all the rest of it, certainly there'd be nothing to handling a ship that at best will only go 30 knots or 35, and whose maneuvers take minutes and minutes rather than seconds, so there shouldn't be anything to it."

What that aviator ought to learn, and if he doesn't, he has trouble later on, is remember the old formula

MV^2.* The V isn't very high in the case of ships, but that M is really big. And when you get to the large ships such as the carriers, I'll tell you if that thing is going one-half knot and bumps the dock, it'll keep going for about 50 feet before it'll stop. And one of our little problems that we really had, seriously now, is the aviator who never has developed any respect for ships and the problems of handling them. They're just entirely different.

It is true that ships can back down and airplanes can't. It is true that there are a lot of people standing around on the bridge who ought to be able to tell you about potential trouble coming up and, if you don't see it, they ought to see it, and they certainly ought to tell you about it. None of these things is available to that fighter pilot in the cockpit; he has to do it all by himself, and it's very fast moving. But just the same, there's great skill involved, there's great judgment involved, and a big ship that hits anything with any appreciable speed on is really going to have some serious aftereffects. Some aviators who never learn that end up plowing their way halfway through a tanker, or making a great big hole in a pier.

Q: Maybe you can talk about the next assignment, which

---
*The formula for energy is mass multiplied by velocity squared.

looks very fascinating to me, back in Washington on the atomic energy team.

Admiral Hyland: I'll have to say that I was not particularly pleased to go to that assignment. The Navy then, and even today, doesn't have enough absolutely top-notch officers to staff the staff of the CNO the way he would like to have it staffed and also staff the Navy's share of the Joint Staff.* There is almost complete duplication between the two, and something ought to be done about this. Whether it ever will be or not, I wouldn't know; I'm inclined to doubt it. But it was obvious to me from watching the scene for some years, as I got a little more senior, that the really top-notch, first-team people invariably went to assignments on the staff of the CNO. And the somewhat lesser people, with a certain few outstanding exceptions, were given jobs down in the Joint Staff.

It was obvious to me, at that time, that when I went to the Joint Staff, for one reason or another--and I didn't know what the reasons were--I wasn't on the first team. That bothered me just a little bit. Now, however, the particular segment of the Joint Staff to which I was assigned, this nuclear energy team, was the best thing that you could get in the Joint Staff, in my opinion. Then the

---
*CNO--Chief of Naval Operations.

Joint Staff was not organized in the regular J-staff setup the way it is now. It was composed of a number of teams, and they all had the names of various colors--like the blue team, the red team, the gold team, the white team, and so on--and they had the rainbow team.

Rainbow team was the most prestigious one and was involved in the development of managing, and monitoring, and advising about the nuclear weapons. There I was introduced to all the details of what goes on in nuclear weapons. I was able to travel to all the places where they were manufactured. I was able to be privy to the most sensitive information about how much nuclear material we had, and where it was, and in which weapons it was used, and how much we were going to produce, and all the planning for new plutonium reactors, and so on.

There was great competition among the services for nuclear weapons in those days, and it really boiled down to a competition for your share of the nuclear material. Various commanders in the field would put in statements of their requirements for nuclear weapons, and I can remember one of the humorous sides of the thing was that all of them, even the smallest one, had "requirements" for nuclear weapons which exceeded the national stockpile. So there was, of course, the problem of dispensing this material and dispensing these weapons. The Navy was trying to squeeze a reasonably large number of them away from the Strategic Air Command, and so on.

Q: Doling them out. Who was the chief doler?

Admiral Hyland: The way it actually worked out in practice was, this little three-man rainbow team actually dispensed the nuclear weapons among the military, because there would be absolutely wide-open splits among the services. The Navy and the Air Force and the Army would simply completely disagree officially about any partition of this stockpile that was offered up, and which came, we'll say, from the discussions of the various service staffs.

It would get to the late point where it was absolutely necessary to reach some sort of a compromise, and I can remember for a couple of years in a row, the director of the Joint Staff would call us in, and he would say, "You three guys go back into your offices and don't you come out. Don't talk to your service staffs any more [of course, we perhaps would], don't discuss anything further with them. You fellows come up with a compromise. You figure it out for yourselves. Somebody's got to break this deadlock one way or another, so you're all going to have to compromise, but you are going to have to come up, by tomorrow morning, with a solution to this thing. And you're going to recommend for me one way to settle this controversy."

At that time, it was the bloodiest of all the areas of controversy among the services. So we would simply sit down because we had to, and finally we would come up with a solution. It would be fair; it would be equitable. We were quite knowledgeable individuals about these weapons, and we knew a little about the other fellow. So we would offer this up, and at the next JCS meeting the chairman would be able to say, "Look, gentlemen, we're not getting anywhere here.* Now, here we have a proposed solution, and it's been developed for me by this joint team--the rainbow team. They're really just as knowledgeable as your experts up on the staff, and this is a compromise. This is what they've come up with, and here it is. We've got to go on to other business. We do have to make a decision here, so I just recommend we accept this relatively unbiased solution." And, by gosh, that's what they would finally do. It happened twice while I was there.

So, of course, the individuals involved in that bloody battle would become a little better known than perhaps the average fellow down in the Joint Staff, and your own service wouldn't be able to hold too much against you for what you'd done and what you'd given away that the Navy really wanted to get. They would have to understand that what they were trying to get was simply not possible to

---
*JCS--Joint Chiefs of Staff.

get.

Q: You really had to divorce yourself from your service orientation, then?

Admiral Hyland: In fact, your advice when you went to the Joint Staff was that you really were supposed to do your level best to wear a purple suit.* You weren't supposed to think of your parent service entirely. You were supposed to represent them, but you were really supposed to try to be unbiased and to be joint. It can be done. I think any officer in a situation like that has to recognize that he's going to come back to the parent service sometime, and he can't have represented them poorly down in the Joint Staff and expect to have them delighted to see him when he comes back to the service and to give him a good job because of it.

Q: Who was the exec of the Joint Chiefs? Was it Count Austin at that time?**

Admiral Hyland: Yes, part of the time.

---
*"Purple suit" is a slang term for the uniform of an officer on joint-service duty. The idea is that if the colors of the uniforms of the individual services were combined, the resulting color would be purple.
**Vice Admiral Bernard L. Austin, USN, was the director of the Joint Staff Office, Joint Chiefs of Staff from 1956 to 1958. His oral history is in the Naval Institute collection.

Q: Well, that certainly was his philosophy, that when you served on the staff there you served the Joint Chiefs and not the Navy or the Army.

Admiral Hyland: Yes. He was the director of the Joint Staff part of the time I was there, and the other part of the time it was Air Force General Ollie Picher.* Both of them were simply marvelous officers. They had learned to be "joint," if I've ever seen two who had learned it. Picher was a little more of a dramatic type than Count Austin, and he was sort of famous for being so tough on the air force position all the time. He leaned over backwards to make sure that nobody ever accused him of favoring the Air Force. He had an acid tongue and a very, very fine vocabulary--a little like Buckley and a little like Westbrook Pegler--and he would take off on some of the claims and statements that were made by air force action officers, and they were just priceless things to listen to.** He was a very, very gifted fellow with words. But he was very objective and very, very fine.

Q: In one sense, I suppose your task was made more

---
*Lieutenant General Oliver S. Picher, USAF.
**William F. Buckley, Jr., journalist, author, and editor-in-chief of the National Review; Westbrook J. Pegler, Pulitzer Prize-winning newspaper journalist from the 1930s to the 1950s.

difficult because the CNO at that time was Arleigh Burke, and he was Navy all the way down the line, was he not?*

Admiral Hyland: Yes. I don't think that tour of duty in the Joint Staff really did me any harm with my parent service at all, and I got to enjoy it very much. And, as I say, we all felt that we were in a very, very fortunate part of the Joint Staff. Some of the teams just really had very little to do. The team that handled the South American countries--there just wasn't anything going on, and you might sit there and might be a very able person, but there just wasn't anything going on. Fortunately for us, the nuclear business was just "Subject A" in the highest levels all across the board, so we got in on some very, very hot actions and some very bloody, bloody battles.

Q: This was the time of Raborn, too, was it not, or did it predate that and the Polaris?**

Admiral Hyland: No, this was before that.

---
*Admiral Arleigh A. Burke, USN, was Chief of Naval Operations, 1955-61. His oral history is in the Naval Institute collection.
**Rear Admiral William F. Raborn, Jr., was director of the Navy's special projects office, responsible for developing the Polaris missile and the submerged launching system. He has done a Naval Institute oral history concerning the Polaris project.

Hyland #4 - 227

Interview Number 4 with Admiral John J. Hyland, Jr.,
U.S. Navy (Retired)

Place: Admiral Hyland's home in Honolulu, Hawaii

Date: Friday, 10 March 1972

Interviewer: John T. Mason, Jr.

Q: We want to resume your very, very interesting story. Last time, you were with the Joint Chiefs of Staff in a very special capacity. I think perhaps you did deal pretty thoroughly with that assignment. Is there anything else?

Admiral Hyland: I think I mentioned, really, everything about that tour of duty that was of any special interest at all. I was very lucky when I left that assignment down in the Joint Staff, because it was then that I got command of the Saratoga, which was a very fortunate and relatively prestigious command for me to be able to get.*

Q: Weren't you rather young for the command of a carrier at that point?

Admiral Hyland: No, I really wasn't especially young. It was just about my time to get a major command. There was one little problem that stood in the way. At the time that

---
*The USS Saratoga (CVA-60) was then one of the Navy's newest aircraft carriers: length, 1,063 feet; beam, 130 feet; draft, 37 feet; standard displacement, 56,000 tons. She had been commissioned on 14 April 1956.

there was this opening to have that command--and, of course, she was one of the few bigger carriers, one of the few Forrestal-class ships that we had at that time--I had done only 14 months of duty down in the Joint Staff. And there was a temporary crisis in my life when the director of the Joint Staff refused to release me. Then the Navy sort of officially went to work to try and have me released from duty down there, because it was working out that if I didn't go to my major command then, within a very short time I might be too senior for one, or there might not be one available and the navy scheme of things would be upset.

Q: And you'd lose out in the end.

Admiral Hyland: Yes. Now the point of view of the director, who was General Picher, an air force general, was simply that the Navy was, clearly to him, using the Joint Staff as a parking place for officers for whatever period the Navy chose to use it for.* He felt the Navy very seldom let an officer really do a complete tour of duty down there, which General Picher thought should be at least two years, and in the case of officers in the other services was normally three years. So I can recall being told that Admiral Burke went to bat for me and talked to General Twining, who was the chairman at the time, and they

---

*Lieutenant General Oliver S. Picher, USAF.

then had to come to a meeting of the minds between the Joint Staff and the Navy.*

Henceforward, it was firmly agreed that when a naval officer was sent to the Joint Staff, he was going to stay for a full tour of duty--that meant at least 24 months--and there would be no exceptions. The Navy would continue to send good people, and so on, but they would have to stay and do a job once they got there. But since I had apparently done a good job for the rainbow team, the Navy was saying that this was an unusually golden opportunity for me, and they didn't want to be unfair about it. In this one case they would make an exception and let me go. I apparently was the last one who escaped the Joint Staff with an uncompleted tour of duty.

From there I did go to the Saratoga. I took her over down in Jacksonville when she came back from Europe, and, of course, what followed was a year or so of simply great command duty. It was during that tour of duty that I was selected for flag rank, so I could hardly have been luckier than to have had it all work out: to be able to get out of the Joint Staff and to go to this great ship and have good luck with her.

---

*Admiral Arleigh A. Burke, USN, Chief of Naval Operations. General Nathan F. Twining, USAF, was Chief of Staff of the Air Force, 1953-57, and Chairman of the Joint Chiefs of Staff, 1957-60.

Hyland #4 - 230

Q: Where did you take her? What were some of your experiences?

Admiral Hyland: She had just come back from a deployment over to the Mediterranean, and lying alongside of the pier down in Mayport a serious error was made.* Down in one of the engineering spaces they had opened up a condenser to inspect the inside of it as part of a regular engineering check, and they failed to take proper precautions when a young sailor came along checking the operation of electrically operated valves. He went through his regular checkoff list and went ahead and pushed the button which opened the main injection valve to that engine space, so the water rushed in through the condenser and filled up number four, the after engine space in the ship. Temporarily, the ship was completely disabled and out of commission, because filled with that much water she actually went down and rested on the bottom. It was through this particular engineering space that the shafts for the other three engines passed, so she actually was out of commission for the time it took to de-water the space and to try and repair this damage.

Well, I think in the old Navy, an oncoming captain would certainly never accept command of a ship that was

---

*Mayport, Florida, is the site of a naval station near the Jacksonville Naval Air Station. When the carrier is in her home port, her air group operates from the air station.

actually resting on the bottom, that was aground, that was out of commission, immobilized, couldn't move an inch. He would insist on the previous captain at least getting her afloat and getting her in such shape that she could move. The accident had happened. It was a horrible error, and it was shown later that some of the safety precautions simply weren't good enough, and we would have to take steps to make sure that a very, very costly mistake like that couldn't happen again.

Q: You had not actually taken command?

Admiral Hyland: No, but within a few days she was pumped out. Obviously there was major damage in that engineering space, but the ship could operate on three shafts, and she was scheduled to leave within a week or so and go up to Norfolk for a regular overhaul anyway. I was, in the first place, so anxious to take over that ship that I really didn't think too seriously about the fact that she was out of commission, because I wasn't going to be held to account for that. We just did the best we could with the ship to get her in shape. We rushed to Norfolk as many days ahead of time as we could, and emergency measures were taken in every area that you could think of to try and minimize this damage from the salt water immersion that she'd had.

Unfortunately, that engineering space did suffer great

damage and was a relatively serious problem in the ship and in the engineering department for the rest of the time that I had the command. However, we were able to get it all in shape, and there was nothing to do but go ahead and follow the schedule. I was pleased to have the command, and, as I say, the only sea duty I was going to get in the immediate future anyway was this one trip up to the Norfolk Naval Shipyard. Then I'd sit there for four months and watch the ship get repaired and get modernized, and that's just what we did. After the overhaul was finished, we went out.

Q: This did take four months?

Admiral Hyland: Yes. Actually, a regular overhaul, which in those days used to occur perhaps every two years, took between four and six months to do the work anyway. But we went out to sea after the overhaul was over and tried out everything. It was at that time that this particular engine, when it was operated, just wasn't up to snuff. The noise of the turbine was so loud that you just simply couldn't talk to another person when it was just going at normal speed. So then, after the overhaul was over, and even after all these emergency measures were taken to try and make sure that the main engine would be all right, they hadn't been good enough. It was obvious that we had to have an entirely new main engine put into the ship.

The Constellation was being built at that time up in New York.* She was just partly finished and, luckily, on the dock alongside the new Constellation was one complete main engine. So we rushed the Saratoga into the New York Naval Shipyard, and there we got one of the more amazing repair jobs that I've ever seen in the Navy. What was done then was to cut a hole in the flight deck directly above this main engine that had to come out, straight down through the hangar deck, and straight down through all the intervening decks--and there were perhaps three or four of them--right down to where the opening entered into the engineering space. And this entire turbine and the reduction gear and the whole thing was picked vertically up out of the ship, and the brand-new engine that was alongside the dock there, waiting to be put into the Constellation, was put into the Saratoga.

Q: Whose brilliant idea was that?

Admiral Hyland: This was, I guess, the product of the knowledgeable people up there in the New York Naval Shipyard. I can remember Admiral Schuyler Pyne was the shipyard commander, and a fellow named Petrovic, who was

---

*The Constellation (CVA-64) was a slightly more modern ship than the Saratoga. The Constellation was commissioned 27 October 1961.

just a class behind me at the Naval Academy, who's now an engineering admiral in the Navy, was the officer in immediate charge.* The engine change was actually done in about ten days, which was a simply amazing thing to be able to do. Right after it was done and the ship was buttoned up, we went out to sea off New York, and the thing ran absolutely like a clock. By that time, we were a little late for some training operations that we were scheduled to do, so we just rushed on to our regular schedule perhaps these ten days later than we'd expected, and from that time on things ran very smoothly and very nicely in that particular space.

Q: Sounds like a human heart transplant.

Admiral Hyland: It really was almost like that. Admiral Pyne, who was the shipyard commander up there at the time, had had personally quite a bit to do with the construction of the Saratoga, which was built there in the New York Naval Shipyard. And he kind of felt the Sara was his baby, and I certainly felt like she was mine, so we got a lot of help and an awful lot of cooperation. I know that he was personally very interested in getting this job done as

---

*Rear Admiral Schuyler N. Pyne, USN, was the shipyard commander. His oral history, which discusses the Constellation fire in some detail, is in the Naval Institute collection. Captain William F. Petrovic, USN, later a rear admiral.

quickly as it could be done, and they just did miracles.

Q: So you joined your fleet.

Admiral Hyland: We just went back to the Atlantic Fleet, then operated in the normal way in and out of Mayport for a while. We then went down to Guantanamo, and went through the standard training for an aircraft carrier--first with the ship itself and then later with the air group embarked--and then went through a regular deployment over to the Mediterranean.

It seems to me it was July or August that selection boards met at that time. While I was on board as skipper of the Saratoga, I think it was in August of 1959, I was on the list for selection to flag rank. I was able to stay aboard, though, until November, when I finished my year's duty as skipper; that was as long as anybody could hope to hang on to a ship like that. Of course, I was selected a little bit ahead of time, and it was perfectly well known that, since I was way down at the bottom of the list of those who had been selected, it would be at least another year before I'd make my number. I tried to induce the detail people to recognize this fact and just let me stay aboard and continue to be the captain of that great ship. But in those days they took you off almost exactly a year and a day after the time that you took over.

Q: There were too many men pushing up and wanting the berths.

Admiral Hyland: Yes. I was very fortunate, although I didn't recognize it in all respects at the time, but I had on board for most of the time that I was the skipper of that ship Admiral George Anderson as the carrier division commander.* Wherever Admiral Anderson was, he interested himself extremely closely in all the details of the operation. I can tell you that I had a great deal of help and a great deal of advice from him, more than I wanted to get at the time, but he was famous for that. I realized later that, of course, it's professionally really quite an advantage to have a marvelous officer like that. It's an advantage to have the admiral of your division riding in your ship, because he does have a chance to see a lot more of you than he would another captain who had an equivalent command but who didn't have the flag officer aboard and who was just operating by himself.

Now there are many joys concerned with being the captain, and being absolutely the senior officer around, and having no advice from above. I can see that that's very pleasant in some respects, but really it's professionally a big advantage to have the division

---
*Rear Admiral George W. Anderson, Jr., USN, Commander Carrier Division Six, 1958-59.

commander on board. Admiral Anderson was followed by Admiral Moorer.* Both these officers later became Chiefs of Naval Operations. Tom Moorer, of course, was my intimate friend and adviser, and the situation for me on board the ship was different. But in both cases I was lucky to have them right there, so that when they apparently were pleased with the performance of the ship they were able to write it up in fitness reports.

I feel now that the immediate reason why I was fortunate to be selected a little bit ahead of time was the fitness report that George Anderson wrote for me at a very critical time, and which I saw later on, and which seemed to say that I could almost walk on water. It was very nice, and it was very effective. Of course, he was such a prestigious person that it really made a great deal of difference in my young life at the time. No sooner had he left the carrier division command than he was assigned as Commander Sixth Fleet.** Within a month of the time that he left there, we were over in the Mediterranean under him again, so I continued to see a great deal of him.

He had a very appropriate code name, "Fast Charger." I will say that any ship in the Sixth Fleet at that time, when they would have "Fast Charger" aboard, or when they

---

*Rear Admiral Thomas H. Moorer, USN, Commander Carrier Division Six, 1959-60.
**As a vice admiral, Anderson served as Commander Sixth Fleet, 1959-61, and as a four-star admiral he was Chief of Naval Operations, 1961-63.

knew he was coming aboard, would really do everything that they could do to get ready to put on a good show for him. Because he was quite dashing, very knowledgeable, quite demanding, and, as always, not satisfied with anything but the best performance that you could get out of whatever it was. We operated routinely in the Mediterranean. I hadn't been able to get over there ever in my life before that time, and we went to all the larger ports that the carriers normally visited there in the Med, and as far east as Istanbul.

Q: Was that a relatively calm period of time in the Israeli-Moslem feud?

Admiral Hyland: Yes. There were no crises going on at the time, really. It seems to me the Lebanon affair had taken place shortly before that, so the ship on the previous deployment had had a very busy time of it, but there were no problem areas while I had the ship over there.* We just did a routine, standard deployment. It was very, very exciting for me. The air wing on board was absolutely outstanding, and I think I'd had so much duty in carriers and so much experience as a pilot myself that we had a good

---

*U.S. Marines from the Sixth Fleet were landed in Lebanon in July 1958 at the request of the Lebanese Government to help prevent a suspected revolt being engineered by the Soviet Union and the United Arab Republic.

reputation for running the Sara to take care of that air wing. We knew what our main battery was, and that's the way we tried to run the ship, to take care of them.

There have been other carriers where people, even with the best intentions, somehow or other seem to have the whole operation go that the air wing is on board to support the ship, instead of the reverse of that, which, of course, is the way it should be done. It was a very happy ship. It seemed to me all the squadrons were pleased with the support that they got. They were able to fly a great deal, and we had great times at sea, and we had absolutely wonderful and remarkable times and parties ashore here and there. I've never forgotten a minute of that cruise.

Q: Did you touch in at North African ports at all?

Admiral Hyland: No, not a single one. In times just a little earlier than that, it seems to me that the exchange of the incoming carrier with the one going home--and they always had, if they could possibly manage it, a head-to-head meeting of the ships--they actually got together physically for one day and exchanged notes and information and instructions and all that sort of thing, and then the turnover would take place. That used to be done in a North African port, but we didn't do it there. They had changed the site of those things for one reason or another, and I can remember our turnover with the ship we relieved was done in Pollensa Bay.* I can't recall any really noteworthy things that happened to the ship or to the wing.

Just as almost always seems to be the case in those cruises, we did lose a very few pilots, and that's always so sad when that happens, but that's just kind of a by-product of operating these very high performing airplanes from ships at sea and trying to do it day and night. I was astonished to find out how rough it can be in the Mediterranean. To this day, including a good deal of sailing out in the Pacific where the typhoons come every now and then, I've never seen water any rougher than we had on a couple of occasions in the Mediterranean. West of Sardinia and east of Spain, these mistral storms would come down from the north, come down through France, and actually on a few occasions the water was so rough that the Saratoga would actually be taking green water over the bow, and we would decide, just because there was no real absolute necessity to continue to fly, we would stop flying the airplanes just because the motion of the deck was so extreme that you were taking too much of a chance of having landing accidents. But I hadn't realized that what I'd always heard of as an inland lake--a large one, but nevertheless, an inland lake--inland sea, could be as rough as it was.

---
*The Bay of Pollensa is on the north coast of the island of Majorca in the Western Mediterranean.

Q: Did the Sixth Fleet at this time use the facilities at Malta at all?

Admiral Hyland: We didn't go to Malta then. Some of the smaller ships did, but really not very much. We pretty much were a sea-based outfit. We did all the replenishment at sea; they were quite rigidly against replenishing in port if it could possibly be avoided, although once in a while when you were in port you'd certainly pick up a few fresh provisions from the local port. By and large, the policy and the doctrine was that all major replenishment would be done from the accompanying service force and would be done at sea, so, of course, we had a great deal of underway replenishment, day and night. It was just standard to do it. It seems to me almost every day you'd have some ship pull alongside, but those things have become so completely routine in the Navy now that they're not difficult, and normally there's no problem concerned with them at all.

When we went to Istanbul, I was introduced to the Premier of Turkey, who was really an effective dictator; the Premier was Menderes at the time.* I was very impressed with him. He was clearly quite a strong fellow,

---

*Adnan Menderes became Premier of Turkey in 1950. His restrictive policies led to a bloodless coup and his ouster and arrest in 1960.

and he was running a one-man show in Turkey and without any question was the boss of the country. I had a few pictures, which I still have in an album somewhere, showing me standing up on the flight deck alongside Premier Menderes and his little group who came to visit the ship. I'm sort of proud of being able to show that. But within a month or two after we left, he ran into difficulty at home, and he was deposed. Then, shortly after that, he was given a fair trial and was hung. So it's kind of a thrill to look at those pictures and see this very strong man and realize that, however their political system works, he hadn't managed it quite perfectly, because he was just gone.

I was relieved of command of the <u>Saratoga</u> in Barcelona, and from there I went up to Argentia, where I was commander of the Atlantic Barrier Wing, as it was called in those days.*

Q: That's an interesting shift, isn't it? What was the Atlantic Barrier Wing?

Admiral Hyland: The Navy operated an aerial barrier which flew between Argentia and the Azores Islands. The particular job was to keep four of these early-warning Lockheed Constellation airplanes in the air at all

---
*Argentia, Newfoundland, Canada.

times.* They would just fly a sort of a racetrack pattern from Argentia down to the Azores and turn around and come back.

Q: Where were you based in the Azores, Terceira?

Admiral Hyland: The field that we used when we would have to land down there was the field at Lajes, which is on the island of Pico.** The mission was really just that of early warning. It had been decided that there was a possibility that the Russians would attack the United States, and this barrier of radar-equipped airplanes flying across a possible area of approach of bombers coming from Russia would be through this barrier, so they had mathematically figured out that if you had four airplanes in the air at all times and they were spaced properly, there was a very, very high probability that any raid of any size would be detected. It was just the early warning which would give the United States perhaps two or three hours' additional warning that would be provided from the operation.

Personally, I never thought that barrier was

---

*The Lockheed WV-2 Warning Star was a propeller-driven four-engine airplane, one of the military versions of the civilian Constellation airliner. It had a maximum speed of 321 miles per hour at 20,000 feet and a maximum range of 4,600 statute miles.
**Pico is about 40 miles west-southwest of Terceira.

necessary, and, in a sense, the Navy backed into it. When the concept was first suggested--that it was necessary to fly a barrier like that--I think the Navy disagreed in the Joint Staff that it really was necessary. But when it became a little more clear that someone was going to do it and it really was a chore over the sea, the Navy decided that since it was inevitable that it was going to be done, it would be better for the Navy to do it than for some other service to go ahead and do it. So that's how the Navy got the chore. As I say, I never felt it was necessary. I never felt the Russians were really honestly capable of an attack of that nature at that time, or that they would do it in the first place. But, of course, again, one of the things you'd better be careful about is making your decisions on what you're guessing about the enemy intentions; you'd better not do it.

Q: How were you able to maintain an alert attitude and keep morale high when you did this on a routine basis, back and forth, back and forth?

Admiral Hyland: Of course, you've hit on what really was one of the major problems of the whole thing. By virtue of various competitive exercises and various schemes of one sort or another, and running unannounced tests which you could run from time to time, you would be able to establish that the barrier was, in fact, alert and was, in fact, effective. And in all cases when these tests were run, it was very gratifying to see that these youngsters were on the ball.

Each airplane had about 22 or 24 people aboard, and they did trade off. In other words, they had substantially a double crew, and they took turns off and on. The patrol would take perhaps 10 or 12 hours to make the complete circuit and was a boring, a tiring, and a repetitive thing that didn't have very much excitement to it. The flying operation itself was really one of the most impressive things I've ever seen done in the Navy.

The job was to keep these four airplanes airborne, and for each launch that you would make--which was done every few hours--we would arrange to have a backup airplane for the one that was due to go on patrol which could be launched within 15 minutes of the first one if something went wrong with the first one. Then we had still another backup airplane that could perhaps get in the air inside of a half an hour if something happened to the number one backup airplane.

To look back over the long history which went on for six or seven years of doing this flying, the barrier was maintained upwards of 97%, or some such very high figure like that, through a prolonged period. There were something like 36 of these airplanes, so we discovered that in order to keep one airplane in the air all the time and have it relieved on station and have the mission continued, really takes about nine airplanes to keep one going, if you include all the checks and overhauls and all the things that have to be done to keep airplanes running.

Q: Where was the maintenance done, at Argentia?

Admiral Hyland: Yes, it was all done at Argentia, except that major maintenance was done down in New York by the Lockheed Company. You mentioned offhand here just a second ago that it was expensive, and, boy, I'll say it was expensive, if you look at the size of the tubing that carries the fuel to the engines on a Constellation. It used to bother me because other segments of the fleet were very hard up for aviation fuel at that time, and here and there in other areas we were having to curtail the flying of some of the tactical airplanes, and perhaps some of the carrier airplanes. This task of running the barrier was considered a priority one, and we just continued to do it.

Q: Almost a combatant state, wasn't it, where they were concerned?

Admiral Hyland: Yes. Of course, the weather in Argentia is just about the worst for flying that you can find if you go all over the globe looking for the place that's least favorable. I've never seen so many very low, real honest-to-goodness bad-weather approaches and landings, and also real honest-to-goodness extremely low ceiling conditions for takeoff. I've never seen so many of those done for real anywhere else so frequently as at Argentia. There was almost no need to ever go out and, for instance, put up a hood and practice instrument flying. You got so darn much of it just by virtue of doing the operation that every one of these plane commanders and all these copilots and so on became just marvelously proficient at making real low GCA approaches.* I remember their code, with respect to whether or not they'd go on a flight was whether or not they could see to get out to the end of the runway. If they could see enough to taxi out and get to the end of the runway and get pointed in the right direction, they would go. We had a deviation which allowed us to take off under worse conditions than normally you'd be permitted to make a takeoff, just because we had people that had gotten so wonderfully experienced at it.

Q: If the weather did turn so bad that you couldn't even do this, then what happened?

Admiral Hyland: There were other alternate airfields in
___
*GCA--ground-controlled approach, a system of using radar and radio for guiding aircraft to landing.

Newfoundland--the international airfield at Gander, the Air Force had a base over at Stevensville, and there were a few other places. And it's a lucky accident of the weather up in Newfoundland that it almost never is the case that all places are shut down at the same time. As long as people were careful, and as long as they made the decision to go to an alternate in good time, there never was a problem about getting down. All the time I was there, we never had any accidents at all, and in the long history of the barrier there were very, very few really bad accidents. Perhaps we had a few blown tires from hard landings and so on, but never a major accident.

Q: Did you have any similar problems in the Azores, in terms of weather?

Admiral Hyland: The problem down in the Azores as far as flying was that this field at Lajes was a one-way strip. It was very nice and very long, but occasionally very, very strong crosswinds would come in, and the field would have to be closed because the wind was just too strong, and at 90 degrees to the direction of the runway. There's some maximum limit; it seems to me it's about 30 or so knots of direct crosswind, and beyond that a Connie cannot be controlled for a landing or a takeoff, and you simply have to stop flying. It was very nice having this southern terminus, because once in a while we would base airplanes down there, and we would make the flight from Lajes up to Argentia and go back and land at Lajes. This was often in the very unpleasant weather up in Argentia. The weather down in the Azores would be very nice and very sunny, semi-tropical conditions, and it was a very nice alternative to be able to send people down where they could actually sunbathe and go for a swim, and so on. But generally the flights were all flown from Argentia and terminated in Argentia.

Q: What's the distance between the two points, about 800 miles?

Admiral Hyland: It's longer than that, over 1,000.

In addition to the four airplanes that were flying at the time, there were also four ships, which were little DERs, which were positioned at intervals on the sea down the line, and they had good radar equipment on them.*
They were a supplementary assist to the airplanes, because they could look up and see certain targets that the Connies couldn't see with their radar. It was those people in the seaborne part of the barrier that really got some rough weather to go through. In the middle of winter in the

---
*DER--destroyer escort radar picket ship.

North Atlantic there isn't anyplace that's more difficult and more unpleasant--terribly cold, terribly rough, and terribly windy--and these very small ships would go out and stay for several weeks at time, and then come back to port.

Some of them would come back to Argentia, but for the most part they were based in ports on the East Coast and would go back there when their time on the barrier was up. As time went on, it became too expensive to keep these ships going. They were removed, and the flying continued. And then gradually the flying was reduced, and finally the whole barrier concept was stopped.

Q: When did that come to an end?

Admiral Hyland: That was a couple of years after I left. I think that was about in 1962 that we terminated that operation; maybe it was as late as '63. Just why the thing was terminated, I'm not sure. It seems to me there was at least a temporary easing of tensions, and the whole thing had been studied a little bit more. The cost of the thing came under more and more scrutiny, and so on, and it just was decided to accept the risk and not have that protection for the United States.

When the decision was made, it was stoutly opposed by the Air Defense Command, because they felt that if the Russians did attack, it would be of great value to have that couple of hours' additional warning. But then, of course, we got further into jet flying, and it was obvious that if the Russians were going to use it, they would be flying jets and not old prop airplanes, and the warning that you were going to get from it would be much less. And they also had gone on and completed most of that distant early warning line that was built across Canada and across Greenland--the DEW Line.* It was just decided that the coverage was there, and the flying barrier wasn't necessary anymore.

Q: That was a fascinating assignment.

Admiral Hyland: Well, I was so impressed with the flying performance that I couldn't get over it. But all the time I used to have many, many second thoughts about the enormous cost of the thing and whether or not it really was necessary. Now, of course, you'd never communicate this to the people who were doing the flying, and I made quite a number of flights myself. I'd never been in anything as large as a Connie, but I was up there and was able to get checked out in the airplane and make patrols and so on, so it was very enjoyable from that point of view.

The youngsters who did the job were able to feel proud of this amazing record. They were supposed to keep four

---

*DEW--distant early warning.

airplanes in the air all the time, and the percentage of the time that they were able to do that was so high, and it drew so many admiring comments from people that there was lots of area for you to use to pump up morale and to get them to believe that it really was worthwhile. At the same time, we had a policy that safety was first, and if icing conditions or storm conditions were really so forbidding that flying shouldn't go on, the plane commander was completely free to make the decision to come on back, and he'd never be questioned or criticized about it, except to just learn from it whatever we could.

Of course, each airplane that just started a patrol would be able to talk in the air to those three other airplanes, one of which was ahead of him on the outgoing leg and perhaps two of them were on their way home on the other leg. He'd be able to talk to them and find out what sort of weather was ahead of him. Some of them were fatalistic in their attitude; they wouldn't talk to the other airplanes, because their feeling was they were going to go anyway, and there was no sense in finding out ahead of time that it was going to be terribly rough and terribly difficult, because that would just make them worry that much more. They knew they were going to do it, because these fellows had done it, so they just went ahead and plowed along. But most people would want to know what Joe noticed when he was down near the Azores, so the thing was a self-supporting community.

Argentia is a very bleak place, and when I was sent up there, of course, I felt a little like I'd hardly been selected for flag rank and they were taking their pound of flesh from me immediately to make me pay back this lucky thing. But, honestly, we had a great time up there with our family and with the other people there. It was the sort of place where you had to make your own fun, and you had to mostly do it indoors, but we had one of the most enjoyable family times that I've ever had while we were there for almost a year.

Q: Thrown on your own resources for your own entertainment?

Admiral Hyland: Yes. It was an absolutely great place for people who liked the outdoors. It was wonderful for fishing and hunting, two things that I had never been able to do very much, but I remember finally getting enough interested in it to go out and get myself a complete fishing outfit. I was going to go out into the outside and enjoy this thing, and it was about that time that I was detached and sent out to Omaha, Nebraska. So I never got to enjoy this fabulous fishing that I'd heard about all the time I was there.

Q: Omaha was more of the same thing, in a sense, wasn't it? Was this part of the CinCPac command?

Admiral Hyland: No. The reason I was sent to Omaha was to represent the Atlantic Command at a brand-new centralized targeting staff which had been formed out there.* It was decided that the nuclear planning for the United States should be centralized, and predominantly should be done by the Strategic Air Command.** But all other commands which had nuclear weapons should offer whatever weapons and whatever delivery vehicles they had--should offer them to this central planning committee or planning group to form a Single Integrated Operational Plan. The acronym you get from whose words is SIOP, and that still is the name of the most sensitive and most important single plan that the United States has.

My job was to represent the Atlantic Command, which was headed by Admiral Dennison at the time.*** The Navy didn't want to engage in this centralized targeting; the Navy felt that it could be done just as well by each service separately and that a simple coordinating committee could very easily manage to put all the forces together and

---
*The name of the new organization was the Joint Strategic Target Planning Staff (JSTPS), established in August 1960.
**The Strategic Air Command is part of the U.S. Air Force.
***Admiral Robert L. Dennison, USN, was Commander in Chief Atlantic Fleet, Commander in Chief Atlantic Command, and Strategic Allied Commander Atlantic from 1960 to 1963. He is the subject of a Naval Institute oral history.

to have a very workable and a very effective nuclear strike plan. I think the worry, of course, was that the navy nuclear effort, which was then quite small, would be swallowed up by the huge Strategic Air Command and that the Navy's assignment in this very important plan perhaps would be minor.

Q: Am I right in understanding that the Navy did cooperate because it seemed that the Air Force wanted the job entirely to itself?

Admiral Hyland: The decision to go ahead and do it was made by Mr. Gates, and I'm told--and I don't know whether this is so--that Admiral Burke took advantage of the prerogative that he had as head of a service to go directly to the President, and that on that one occasion, in protest against the setting up of this centralized targeting, he did go to see President Eisenhower and say that he didn't think that this was in the best interests of the United States.*

The President, of course, couldn't very well go against his Secretary of Defense, who was Mr. Gates and who had made the decision that we would at least give it a try, so the Navy was turned down and we were more or less forced

---

*Thomas S. Gates, Jr., was Secretary of Defense from 1959 to 1961; earlier he had been Secretary of the Navy from 1957 to 1959. Dwight D. Eisenhower was President of the United States from January 1953 to January 1961.

to go along with it. Then at that time, the Navy went to general quarters, because they felt that since we were going to do it, the Navy's representation out there had better be very knowledgeable people and very experienced people in tactics and so on, and that the Navy's contribution to that staff ought to be as top-notch as it could possibly be or the Navy's interests would be sort of swallowed up.

The Polaris submarines were just then starting to be built, and some of the early missile firings had been made, and we were just really getting into the nuclear deterrent business in a big way.* So a bunch of young officers who were squadron commanders having the types of airplanes that the Navy would use to deliver the weapons, and one or two Polaris skippers and those kinds of people, all highly select, were sent out there to Omaha. I don't believe I've ever seen a finer bunch of young people assembled than the group that was assembled out there in Omaha. Almost every one of those officers that I can think of now has gone right on up, and for the most part they're flag officers or close to it, and they've all done very, very well in the Navy. Most of them were assigned directly to this planning

---

*The <u>George Washington</u> (SSBN-598) was the first U.S. submarine designed to fire Polaris ballistic missiles against targets in the Soviet Union. She was launched 9 June 1959 and commissioned 30 December 1959. On 20 July 1960 she successfully launched the first Polaris missile from a submerged submarine.

staff, which came under the Strategic Air Command, and which ran it in a sort of a two-hatted fashion.

It was one of our concerns in the Navy that every single key job on the staff was held by a SAC officer, who on the SAC side of the house did his job for SAC and with his other hat did his job as part of the planning staff. All of the navy representatives were submerged at least one--and it was usually more than one--level below these various key jobs. So we were concerned about having a proper voice in the whole matter. One of the devices to try to make sure that that was so was that each separate command who contributed forces, such as the Atlantic Command and the Pacific Command, would have representatives who answered to their commanding officer and who did not come under the jurisdiction of the SAC people.

So I was a young flag officer independently working in Omaha for Admiral Dennison and charged with, in effect, getting a proper place in this SIOP for the Atlantic Command's forces. I had wonderful assistants. I had three younger fellows with me, and they were all top-notch. Things for perhaps the first year that we were there were quite unpleasant. The head of the Strategic Air Command was General Power, and his reputation had been that he had been hatchet man for General LeMay when the Strategic Air

Command was formed, and he later succeeded LeMay.*

Unlike LeMay, who was a very inspirational leader and actually very much admired and even beloved--tough as he was--by the people who worked in SAC, General Power was much more the coldly analytical, completely unreasonable and demanding, killer type. They feared him, whereas they sort of revered General LeMay. General Power's scheme of running things was really to conduct a kind of a reign of terror and to ruthlessly punish anyone who failed to live up to the standards.

He ran a number of surprise inspections and, we'll say, a select crew--one which had done very well in bombing and which may have even had a few people promoted and so on--when they were next examined, if they didn't perform up to this same high standard, they would all be immediately removed from their select crew status and put down at the bottom of the barrel, and heads would roll, and so on. So the people in the various elements of that command were very much in awe and very much in fear of General Power. Now, he was an outstanding man and really quite a fellow. I don't believe he even finished high school, and yet he was one of the most articulate, one of the most highly educated men I think I've ever seen.

---

*General Curtis E. LeMay, USAF, commanded the Strategic Air Command (SAC) from 1948 to 1957 and went on to become Chief of Staff of the Air Force. General Thomas S. Power, USAF, commanded SAC from 1957 to 1964.

He didn't really, himself, want anybody in that business except his own Strategic Air Command. He really believed, I think, that naval forces, by the nature of what they do, didn't have a proper place in a plan like that, because you can't, for a year ahead of time, tell where, for instance, a carrier is going to be. He would be able to tell you where every B-52 was going to be for the next year, and he would be able to tell you the number of the weapon they were going to pick up, and where they were going to take it, and when they were going to start--so many minutes after the button was pushed--and so on.* He could make a firm plan that you could put down on paper and then examine, whereas when it came to the naval forces, as he would say, he couldn't get the Navy to say where that carrier was going to be.

So Tommy Power's opinion was that these were not the kind of reliable, constantly available forces that he needed for a plan like that. He had a relatively low opinion of what their potential was. My job was just simply to do my best to convince him that some of those things he was saying were undoubtedly true. You didn't know where that carrier was going to be, but you did know there were going to be two or three of them at least out in the Far East; you did know what their response time could be. They did all carry nuclear-capable aircraft and

―――――――
*The Boeing B-52 has been the Strategic Air Command's principal manned bomber since the early 1950s.

trained pilots and, of course, it would be absolute folly not to take advantage of these things and write them into the plan one way or another.

I tried to show him how that could be done very readily, and although it was difficult for anybody to guarantee that such and such a target would be eliminated at "X-time plus so many hours," it was still relatively inevitable that it was going to be eliminated if the forces were ordered to strike, and that the survival of carriers was somewhat better than forces based on a fixed airfield. Just what percentage better that would be, it's hard to say. I always thought it was high, and he always thought it was low and not significant.

So we had a lot of very bitter exchanges. From our point of view, it seemed at first like the boys on the other side of the fence were trying to give us the worst targets and maintain at all times that our likelihood of success was the least of anyone's and could hardly be counted and was relatively insignificant, whereas you could relieve a lot of the complications if you'd just turn it over to SAC and let them do it. If we would just go home and go back to whatever we were doing out there on the briny deep and just not bother anybody, that would be a lot better.

Q: There was a CinCPac navy man, too. Was he of any great help to you in this whole project?

Admiral Hyland: Oh, yes. He was at that time Rear Admiral Bob Stroh--he later became a vice admiral--and he was the number two navy man in this job in Omaha.* The head man was the commanding general of SAC, and the number two man was a vice admiral in the Navy.

Q: This is at Offutt?

Admiral Hyland: Yes, at Offutt Air Force Base; it's in SAC headquarters. Our first officer there was Vice Admiral Parker, who was one of our admirals who has a wooden leg, and who is a distinguished officer.** Well, that integrated targeting has actually turned out to be a good thing for the United States. I guess we'll have to say that the Navy was wrong in opposing it, but there were some good reasons to oppose going out there and doing it that way at the time that it was started.

Now the capabilities of Polaris submarines and their

---

*Rear Admiral Robert J. Stroh, USN.
**Vice Admiral Edward N. Parker, USN, was the top-ranking navy man in the Joint Strategic Target Planning Staff when it was established. His foot and part of one leg were amputated in the mid-1950s as a result of cancer; fitted with an artificial leg, he remained on active duty but was limited to shore billets. He has been interviewed for the Naval Institute's oral history program.

missiles are fairly well established. The capabilities of all the tactical airplanes, both in the Navy and the Air Force, are fairly well known. The country is concerned about a possible nuclear superiority on the part of the Russians, and so now, anyone and everyone who has nuclear capability at his disposal is most welcome to offer it to the planning people there in Omaha so that this centralized plan for nuclear war can be just as strong as it could possibly be.

Now, I'm told, it's all sweetness and light, and everyone mutually respects the other guy, and everyone is trying his best to make sure that whatever it is that's going into the plan is used to the best advantage of the plan. The longer we stayed there, the better things became. We would spend days fighting with our air force counterparts and calling them every kind of a bad name we could think of, and then we gradually began to get together in the evenings and find out that the other fellow was human, too, and really was a very able and very fine type. Then gradually the thing all worked out.

But in all the time that I've observed officers--very senior officers--I don't believe that I have ever seen one so coldly ruthless and tough and single-minded, and yet really dedicated, as General Power. All the senior SAC officers actually had to keep themselves in readiness 24 hours a day. Their rule was that they had to be within three rings of the telephone, and if they went out to play golf, or if they went out to play tennis, they had to have a two-way walkie-talkie with them so that they were absolutely available all the time. Every feature of the operation of the Strategic Air Command is that of centralized, rigid control; everything comes from the top and is dispensed downward.

The navy scheme of things has always featured decentralized execution. Perhaps we would agree that centralized planning was a good thing, but when it came to the execution of things, it's far better to decentralize, because sometimes communications from the central control point are going to be interrupted, and people are going to have to make decisions. If they don't train in making these decisions, they're not going to be able to make them when they have to make them in real life. So the two philosophies about how you control forces were just simply opposed, and they still are.

The Air Force still, for many good reasons, believes in centralized control, and we in the Navy have always thought it was far better to have it decentralized as much as you can. In some areas the Navy simply can't have its way any longer and knows that it will lose out if it doesn't develop certain capabilities for centralized control, because that might be the fashion, that might be the name of the game today, and if you're not able to take part in it, you just are sort of left on the outside and you don't get to play your share of whatever the big game is. So we're being maneuvered into running the Navy as a highly centralized thing when I think the majority of us really don't feel that's good.

Q: May I ask a question which is a footnote for Offutt? What percentage of the men developed ulcers?

Admiral Hyland: I don't remember any real difficulty with that. There were some terribly hard-working people there, and I guess I must have overemphasized how difficult things were at the time.

Q: How much time were you there at Offutt?

Admiral Hyland: Actually, I had a two-year tour of duty there. I lived right on the base, and as far as living with my family there was concerned, it was very pleasant. The quarters were quite adequate. There are very fine facilities for all sorts of things there on that Offutt Air Force Base. The Navy had a reserve training command on the other side of the city of Omaha, and we used to see a few of our friends over there from time to time.

It was interesting that the people in the Strategic Air Command at Offutt, because of this philosophy that they had to be so completely prepared and so ready all the time, really didn't socialize with the civilian community nearly to the same extent that the Navy had been able to do. There in Omaha, which was the meat capital of the United States, are a lot of very well-to-do people, there are a lot of very vigorous industries there, and it's really quite a town. It's come along way from the days when it was mainly, I guess, a railroad center, a railroad terminus. I don't think I'd ever choose to retire in Omaha, Nebraska, which is about as far from salt water as you can get.

Q: Your next tour of duty was Carrier Division Four?

Admiral Hyland: I went from there and got command of Carrier Division Four. My flagship during that tour of duty was on board the Forrestal most of the time, some of the time aboard the Franklin D. Roosevelt.

Q: Now this was really a prestigious appointment, wasn't it?

Admiral Hyland: Yes, it was the one that I'd been looking forward to for a long, long time. Some of us who had that duty in Omaha, and who weren't above exaggerating perhaps how difficult it was and what a great job we'd done for the

Navy out there, we joke now that at least we used it to get good assignments when we left, because invariably the people leaving Omaha would get a good assignment. And I got the one for me which was best of all at the time, which was command of an attack carrier division. I had a wonderful time with that.

I made another Mediterranean cruise in the <u>Forrestal</u>, and it was during that one that my wife took three children and went over to Europe and followed the ship around the Mediterranean as she went from port to port. One of our three children we put in a school in France, in Cannes, and the other two youngsters just went around with their mother, following the <u>Forrestal</u> and going to every port that we went to.

Q: It was educational for them, I'm sure.

Admiral Hyland: It was a very, very nice tour of duty. In fact, when the deployment to the Med was over and the ship came back, my wife stayed over there to let this one daughter finish her year in the school in Cannes. From that one year in a French school, where they all spoke French, she's remained quite fluent in French and enjoys that very, very much.

Q: You were attached, in the Mediterranean, to the Sixth

Hyland #4 - 267

Fleet?

Admiral Hyland: Yes.

Q: There's a certain amount of social life attached to that assignment, isn't there? I mean, the ports of call and the diplomatic courtesies?

Admiral Hyland: Yes. Everywhere we went we were very, very nicely received. Normally, the port visit, of course, always includes calls on the local mayor, or the local governor if there is one there, or whoever the local native dignitaries are, and they all return the calls. Also, normally it includes liaison with our State Department people who are stationed in those various ports. We went to all of them that are common on such a cruise while I was in that job.

Toward the end of the time in the Mediterranean on that deployment, we went through the Cuban Crisis.* That's one of the most vivid recollections of that tour of duty. We received messages from Washington, from Admiral Anderson, who by that time had become the CNO, and from other places which were just in the most deadly earnest

---
*The Cuban Missile Crisis came to a head on 22 October 1962 when President John F. Kennedy ordered a naval and air quarantine of the island of Cuba because of evidence of Soviet offensive missiles being installed there. The Soviets agreed to remove the missiles, and the crisis ended on 28 October.

language, that we might very well be right on the verge of a nuclear exchange. Precautionary messages were sent to make just absolutely certain that none of these large carriers was lost at the outset, that we just absolutely had to have them, and so on. We were able there in the Mediterranean to sort of follow the Cuban Crisis almost minute by minute.

Q: You didn't come out into the Atlantic?

Admiral Hyland: No, we didn't. At one point in the proceedings, I can recall the Forrestal was scheduled to go into Genoa. We hadn't been there before, and we were due in Genoa the next morning. I thought personally, in view of the situation which was described to us in these messages, that it was absolutely the height of folly to take the Forrestal into Genoa and come to anchor there, and more or less be a sitting duck, assuming the other fellow might have some way of knowing that you were there. I think Admiral McDonald, who was the commander of the Sixth Fleet at the time, agreed.* But contrary orders came from highest levels.

---

*Vice Admiral David L. McDonald, USN, was Commander Sixth Fleet from 1961 to 1963. As a four-star admiral, he served as Chief of Naval Operations from 1963 to 1967. His oral history is in the Naval Institute collection.

Q: Was that the White House?

Admiral Hyland: I believe so. At the same time that this crisis was going on--and it was understood that it was truly a crisis; it was a showdown between the two countries, and a lot of it had sort of come out in the press and was known, and the tensions were very high--it was just decided that if a big ship like that which was expected to come into port didn't, it could be misunderstood one way or another. And we were told that despite the risk we were to go ahead in and anchor, do whatever we could without causing any undue attention, but just do our best to remain ready to get out quickly. We were to go ahead with a routine port visit as best we could, and still try not to be relaxed as much as you might otherwise relax when you go into a port.

Now that worried me very much. I think the military man is supposed to think principally of military risks and military factors. He can't be oblivious to the fact that other things come into the equation, but they're not really for him to decide. But since I'd expressed my concern to Admiral McDonald, and it was well known that any simpleton would be concerned over doing what we were about to do, I didn't worry about it much from then on. It just was decided, and I realize it was decided in very, very high places that we weren't going to act like we were panicked, we weren't going to act like we were upset or that we were about to launch an attack or any such thing. We were just going to try to make it look like business as usual. So that's what we did. Within a few days, the crisis period passed, and we just went on about our business for the rest of the regular deployment over there.

Q: Were you charged in any way with following some of the merchant ships? I think there was one that made its way through the Bosporus about that time and was en route.

Admiral Hyland: No. We had by that time in the Sixth Fleet generally gone to a plan that one of the two carriers would be at sea all the time, and the other one would be in port. It worked out because of money available and so on. The money for operations was enough to keep the ships at sea about half the time and in port the other half the time. In the earlier years, the whole fleet would go to sea. Both carriers and all the destroyers would go to sea, and they'd operate together, and then they would all disperse and go into various ports. But it had been decided, just for whatever protection you might get from this, that half would be at sea and half would be in port. So when we went into Genoa, the FDR was at sea and was in the central Mediterranean.* We were not assigned any

---

*FDR--USS Franklin D. Roosevelt (CVA-42), which was the other aircraft carrier then in the Sixth Fleet.

specific feature of trying to keep track of any Russians or any such thing as that. In fact, in those days the Russians didn't have any presence that amounted to anything in the Mediterranean.

Except for that one time of the Cuban Crisis, the time in the Med with the Sixth Fleet on that cruise was just routine normal training--very interesting, very nice to take part in. And, again, we got to the same general ports that I'd visited earlier when I was on the <u>Saratoga</u>. I've always enjoyed the Mediterranean ports very, very much. As a sailor, if given a choice, assuming you're just going to be doing peacetime readiness training, I far prefer to sail in the Mediterranean than to sail around in the Far East. The ports are many more, and they're closer together, and they're all so developed and such wonderful cities, whereas out in the Far East there are only a few of them, and they are a long ways apart. It's hard to get all of them into your schedule when you're on a regular deployment. Everything about the duty in Europe, I think, is a little more to my liking, although, of course, all of our real wars and all of our real actions--as far as the Navy is concerned--have been in the Pacific.

Q: From that assignment you went to strategic plans in Washington, in the office of the Chief of Naval Operations.

Would you tell me about your duties there?

Admiral Hyland: I went to the Strategic Plans Division, which had the designation OP-60.* I went in there as the assistant director of the division. My immediate superior was Admiral Wally Wendt, who had been in strategic plans on three other tours of duty before that.** Except for my tour on the Joint Staff, which was a somewhat abbreviated tour, I had not had any Pentagon duty until I went to this assignment. I was there in Washington for about three years on that tour of duty, and almost all of the time I remained the assistant director of this division. Finally, Wally Wendt was promoted and went down to be deputy commander down at CinCLantFlt in Norfolk, and at that time I succeeded him as the director of the Strategic Plans Division.

That division handled all of the JCS matters that are of any concern to the CNO. They handle all the JCS papers that the CNO is going to have to discuss with the other chiefs.

Q: You mean they develop the papers?

---

*OP-60—the various divisions and offices of the staff of the Chief of Naval Operations are identified by numerical "OP" codes.
**Rear Admiral Waldemar F. A. Wendt, USN, later a four-star admiral.

Admiral Hyland: We did the Navy's part in developing the papers, yes, and, of course, did all the briefing, all the generation of all the point papers which the CNO would read before he went down to the tank to engage in these discussions with the Joint Chiefs. While I was there that time, Admiral McDonald was the Chief of Naval Operations. We used to call OP-60 a night-oil-burning circus, because the deadlines on many, many of these papers were very short.

It was a kind of a unique division in that it was never possible, for instance, to have a division party, because there were always so many people working through the night to get ready for some emergency meeting of the joint chiefs the next morning, or doing some overtime work for one reason or another that you just couldn't assemble all of the people. It never was possible.

However, because you were involved in all of the JCS papers, you certainly were in the know on what was current, what the current problems among the services were, what the current difficulties between the military and other civilian departments in the government were, what our international problems were, and so on. Of all places to do staff duty, assuming that it must be done and that you must sometimes do your share of it, I always thought that the Strategic Plans Division was by far the best place to be assigned.

Q: Can you give me an illustration of some specific project you did work on?

Admiral Hyland: As assistant director--and that really means "executive officer" in navy lingo--I didn't personally handle any papers but, of course, got to review and see all of them that were being generated by our younger people who were called action officers. We came in touch with everything concerning the nuclear business and the dispensing of the available stockpile of weapons, all that sort of business. More and more, the Joint Chiefs of Staff were getting into the daily operations of the forces, and we would find ourselves involved in advising about that sort of business.

When I was in OP-60, the Tonkin Gulf affair took place, and, of course, we were privy to all the discussion that went into deciding what to do about it--deciding what the response of the United States was going to be, and to have something to do with what was recommended.*

It's really hard to pick out any specific things. Two of the most important plans that are generated every year in the Joint Chiefs of Staff are the Joint Strategic Capabilities Plan and the Joint Strategic Operations Plan.

---
*The Tonkin Gulf Resolution authorizing President Lyndon Johnson to take military action in Vietnam was passed by Congress on 7 August 1964 after North Vietnamese gunboats reportedly attacked U.S. destroyers.

The first simply sets forth what you're going to do with the forces that you have; in other words, that's the plan that you can carry out, because you actually have the forces to do it. The other, longer-range plan, called the JSOP, is a future look, perhaps five or ten years into the future, and there you're not constrained by your actual capabilities. You just do a little crystal ball gazing with forces which may not be in being, but which you would urge be put into being.

Q: What values does that plan have for the budget people?

Admiral Hyland: You do have to put a dollar figure on some of these occasionally grandiose plans. You have to examine whether even though the possible military situation in the future might require X numbers of forces, it may become apparent that that number of forces is just not feasible for the United States to afford. You don't go too far; you don't just go crazy devising impossibly large and expensive forces. But the Navy's part in these major plans is handled in the Strategic Plans Division. If there is any controversy, or any problem, or any changes in the way that the services operate together, such as in the Unified Command Plan, which sets out the roles and missions of the services--if there's going to be any change in that, again, that would be a matter that would be handled by people in this Strategic Plans Division.

It's always been considered a prestige assignment to be in it, and while I was there it was the only division, I believe, that had the prerogative of screening ahead of time the people who were going to come into the division. That policy had been started some years before by Admiral Burke who, I think, at one time was disappointed here and there with the support that he got in getting himself prepared to go down and argue in the tank with the other chiefs.* He realized that it was very, very important to have people who wrote well and people who understood command relationships. It was very important to have high-class people of that persuasion and that experience to help out. He favored officers returning to OP-60 from time to time so that they would immediately be able to pick up the ball and run with it, so to speak. So we had absolutely first-class officers in the division.

Q: And there were repeaters?

Admiral Hyland: Oh, yes. I was relatively a newcomer, and I had to do some struggling to get up to speed there. As I say, when I first went there, my boss, Wally Wendt, had

---
*The "tank" is a slang term for the Pentagon meeting room in which the members of the Joint Chiefs of Staff get together on a regular basis.

been there three other times, and in all occasions he'd been in OP-60. He used to call himself a "four-time loser" in the business. I relieved Dave Richardson there, who's now the deputy out here at CinCPacFlt, who's a younger officer than I but who happened to be there in the number two slot in OP-60 when I came.*

I think I mentioned that the hours were really very long hours, but just the fact that you were so close to the CNO himself, and so close to the vice chief, who sometimes alternated with the CNO down in the tank, you were so intimately involved in all the problem areas that the Navy got itself involved in, no one complained about these long hours. And, generally speaking, when the officers left they got good assignments again. They were clearly, in most cases, right out of the very top perhaps 5% of officers available in the Navy.

It was really a first-class division, so it was very easy to be involved in the administration of a thing like that. You'd never have to talk to an officer about keeping proper hours, or not having initiative or not having willingness to work and all that, because they were all just overflowing with it. It was more of a problem to watch some of them and to stop them from completely exhausting themselves on something because they'd gotten involved in it and they were going to see it through to the

---
*Rear Admiral David C. Richardson, USN, later a vice admiral.

end, regardless of whether they should have been in bed the day before. You'd have that sort of a problem, but, of course, those kinds of problems are much easier than the other kind.

Admiral Sharp was there as the Deputy CNO for Plans, OP-06, when I first got there.* Then he later was succeeded by Andy Jackson.** Of course, in both those cases you have absolutely first-class performers. In fact, I got to OP-60, I'm sure, by virtue of Admiral Sharp's influence. Then he went on to higher things shortly after that, and that's the last I saw of him until I got back from my job out in the Seventh Fleet, and I relieved Admiral Johnson here as the fleet commander and Sharp was CinCPac.***

---
*Vice Admiral Ulysses S. Grant Sharp, USN.
**Vice Admiral Andrew M. Jackson, USN, whose oral history is in the Naval Institute collection.
***Admiral Roy L. Johnson, USN, was relieved in 1967 as Commander in Chief Pacific Fleet by Admiral Hyland. Johnson's oral history is in the Naval Institute collection.

Interview Number 5 with Admiral John J. Hyland, Jr.,
U.S. Navy (Retired)

Place: U.S. Naval Institute, Annapolis, Maryland

Date: Tuesday, 29 May 1984

Interviewer: Paul Stillwell

Q: Admiral, I know it has been quite some hiatus since you had your last session with Dr. Mason in 1972. Rereading your transcript, I was fascinated by your discussion of the test pilot time at Patuxent and your mention of Fred Trapnell.* What can you say about his particular gift in that role?

Admiral Hyland: Well, in those days he was more or less our idol. He was still a very active pilot and a very skilled one. He flew as much as any of us. He was the deputy commander there. Mel Pride was the boss down at Patuxent.** But Trap had a top reputation as a pilot himself.

When we would do tests and write reports about them, we would finally get them worked up and into the smooth, and we would go ahead and publish them. Trap would never do anything about those reports that we had written and

---
*Captain Frederick M. Trapnell, USN.
**Rear Admiral Alfred Melville Pride, USN, was Commander Naval Air Test Center, Patuxent River, Maryland, in 1952-53. Pride was later Commander Seventh Fleet and was promoted to four stars upon retirement. His oral history is in the Naval Institute collection.

thought were almost perfect until later. He would always get a copy of the smooth report after the thing was printed. Then he had a habit of taking that copy of his and, with very tiny writing in red pencil, he would look over the whole report and he would suggest ways of saying the same thing that we had tried to say--better ways to say it, or shorter ways to say it, or more accurate ways to say it. With some of us, it was always an aggravation to have to put up with that kibitzing of our wonderful English. But, when you would simmer down after the sessions, you had to admit that every single time he had a better way of putting it.

Then he would send this copy back to you. If you wanted to argue about anything--for instance, he certainly would occasionally make an error, and we would really leap on that to go back and explain to him that we had said it properly and he had misunderstood. He was always very gracious about that. But Trap was just a distinguished guy. We really almost idolized him. He was never sarcastic or biting about things. However, he was not a patsy either. He was very firm about how things ought to be done. He kept up with everything so well.

I personally think I owe him my life because of an accident I was involved in one time. I told Dr. Mason about the time I ran into a bird when I was flying an F2H at Patuxent in the late Forties, but I didn't mention Trap's role in it.* If you look at that airplane in profile and the tail is missing, there is just as much area of fuselage in front of the wing as there is behind the wing. So it had an equal tendency to fly frontwards or backwards or sideways or anyways.

I tried to simulate a landing up there at altitude a couple of times. Each time I would get relatively slow the plane would yaw. It would yaw around, I'd say, as much as 60 or 70 degrees away from the direction it was going, and then it would do a violent snap roll because of the slow speed. I would end up just about heading straight down. I would be able to pull it up. The minute I would get it up into level flight again, it would repeat this maneuver, this violent yaw away one side or the other.

About that time I can still remember Trap hollering over the radio--he was our senior man in leading this aerial demonstration--yelling, "Johnny get out of that airplane! Get out!" And I finally opened the canopy and got out. I've been amused and listened to other test pilots talk about how they got out of an airplane that they did abandon. They would say, "I went over the left side, then I walked along the wing until I got to where I was sure to clear the tail, and then I jumped off and pulled my chute."

---

*The rest of the account of this accident is to be found on pages 173-176 of this transcript.

I haven't really any idea how I got out of that airplane. I just remember that I opened the canopy, I undid the safety belt. We did not have ejection seats. It was just before that era. And I stood up, and there was, to me, a sort of a violent loud report. The next thing I knew, I was out, and the airplane was about 10 or 15 feet to the right of me, and it was rotating. My first thought when I looked at it was, "Golly, it's going to hit me, and I've got to get away from it." I suppose this must have occurred in seconds. I thought, "God, I've got to pull the chute." So I was able to do that. I found it right away.

One of the marks of a very cool and collected pilot is when he pulls the chute he is supposed to be able to retain the hand grip that you pull the chute with, because it comes loose. Well, I didn't. I don't know where the handle went, but I know the chute was pulled properly, because the next thing I knew I was floating down in the chute and landed in the water. The impact was very, very much harder than I thought it was going to be. I was just coming down like an express train it seemed. Of course, it couldn't have been. I hit the water and went down, seemingly almost to the bottom of Chesapeake Bay. I thought I'd never come back up. But finally I did come up and inflated my life jacket.

Floating around there in the water, I got free of the

chute. In those days right after the war, there were few experienced boat handlers, and it happened that our crash boat was manned by rank amateurs. It was an adaptation of a PT boat and was a very fast and powerful boat. The coxswain, in his best effort to pick me up, almost ran me down. Finally, I managed to wave them away, because simultaneously a little Grumman amphibian airplane had come out and landed on the water and was circling right close at hand. I paddled myself over to this little amphibian, and they hauled me aboard and flew me back to the field at Patuxent River, right in front of operations.

They were waiting there with a couple of doctors and the ambulance and insisted I go up to the dispensary, although I apparently wasn't injured. I hadn't realized then that my right arm was badly bruised. I didn't even know I was hurt. But they insisted that I go up to sick bay and have an exam. Getting into the ambulance from the back, I bumped into the bumper of the ambulance with my right knee and darn near broke the kneecap. So the worst injury I got in that whole episode was I had my knee banged upon the bumper of the ambulance when I was already back on the ground. Later on that same day they let me go.

That afternoon there was a meeting of all the dignitaries who attended the air show, and I got to it as it was ending. Admiral Soucek saw me and asked me to relate the whole experience to them.* When it was all over, I realized that that episode probably helped me very much in my career in the Navy. All of those very senior officers probably remembered my name, because they had seen the accident and just an hour or two later, here I was standing up in front of them telling my story. A whole bunch of senior guys probably ended up with a favorable impression of Johnny Hyland, the test pilot. I really hadn't done anything very wonderful. I just ran into a bird and had a dire emergency. Thank heavens I was able to get out.

I remember Charlie Minter was there in another testing unit at the same time.** My wife was off shopping in Leonardtown, I think it was. Anyway, my son Jay, who is now a captain in the Navy, a nuclear submarine officer, was just a kid down at Patuxent.*** His remark to Commander Minter was, "Wasn't that neat the way that bird knocked my daddy's tail off? Wasn't that neat?" Charlie has never forgotten that. He always teases my son over that remark that he made. I guess he was about 10 or 12 years old at the time.

I enjoyed that Patuxent River duty. At that time, I was in flight test. Later on, I came back for two more years as head of the tactical test division. Trap was

---
*Rear Admiral Apollo Soucek, USN.
**Commander Charles S. Minter, USN, later vice admiral, whose oral history is in the Naval Institute collection.
***Captain John J. Hyland III, USN.

there both the times that I was there. He had a lot of duty there, too. Tactical test didn't have a very well defined role. Admiral Pride was anxious to just put it out of commission. He didn't think it was fulfilling any requirement. Flight test, armament test, service test, and electronics test were actually measuring every airplane against the specifications for it.

Tactical test's role, as I saw it, was to test the entire airplane qualitatively. For instance, you might have a new airplane that passes all the tests, but it's a dog. And there might be another airplane that doesn't pass some of the requirements, but it's a beautiful airplane from the pilot point of view. So this unit was supposed to be able to make a contribution in that area.

Well, Admiral Pride just didn't think it was worth the expense. I can remember almost the whole time I was there trying to fend off his move to disestablish this outfit. About a month after I was relieved and went to the National War College, Admiral Pride did away with tactical test. When Admiral Pride was asked about this decision, he said, "You know, I wanted to do that for quite a while. I didn't think we really could afford a special unit like that when other units in the fleet were doing overlapping work." But none of us wanted to admit anything like that.

He also said, "You know, I wanted to get rid of

tactical test for quite a while, but I just couldn't do it with that damned Johnny Hyland still here." I thought, well, okay. In a sense, I guess he meant it as a compliment. So tactical test was done away with right after I left in 1953. Those of us who are still around believe that we did make a significant contribution, even though Admiral Pride thought that what we were doing was really not properly done at Patuxent River.

We pioneered in the air-to-air refueling techniques, which later became standard procedure in the fleet. We looked into the problems of making dead-stick landings in the early jets and made recommendations which were very well received by the fleet squadrons which later got those airplanes. We published many reports on the best ways to maximize range and endurance in those early jets, carrying various loads, which were also well received. We published reports on all the early jets which examined the airplane from a qualitative pilot's point of view, rather than from the standpoint of whether it met the quantitative specifications called for in the contract. Those reports were written in plain English, rather than in the more technical aeronautical language, and in all cases were praised by fleet squadrons.

Q: Do you have any other recollections of Admiral Pride? I interviewed him a few months ago.

Admiral Hyland: A very, very staunch and proper New Englander. He had a rather gruff and austere exterior. I think actually he was a softy, but he certainly never showed it. He had a very lovely wife. I understand they are still going.*

I can remember one time when I had TacTest a Canadian pilot on exchange duty had to bail out of one of the early F9Fs, a Grumman fighter, at night.** He bailed out of the airplane and landed in the water right off Mattaponi, which is the admiral's house down there at Patuxent River. As quickly as he could, he shed all his clothes except his underwear. He didn't know where he was, but he saw lights and swam ashore and walked up the beautiful lawn. And here he was, right at the admiral's house. He rang the doorbell. He felt he had to report in right away, because no one knew whether he'd survived or not. Mrs. Pride answered the door, and here was this young Canadian in his underwear saying, "May I use the phone, Madam?" She thought that was just hilariously funny. I guess the admiral did, too.

Admiral Pride was a strict guy and for me was a hard

---
*Admiral Pride died at the age of 91 in December 1988; his wife died two years before.
**The Grumman F9F-2 was the first U.S. Navy jet fighter ever used in combat when it went into action in the Korean War. It was succeeded by the F9F-5, which had a wing span of 38 feet and maximum speed of 579 miles per hour at 5,000 feet.

man to get close to. Of course, we had the difficulty that he sincerely thought my outfit was not in its proper place. He felt you shouldn't do work like that at Patuxent. There were plenty of other things to do. I and all my pilots were supposedly top-notch aviators, and we had a very unique situation in that we didn't have to just go up and see if the airplane would climb at a certain rate and so on. We could evaluate the airplane as a whole article. We had some top-notch guys. We had Paul Pugh, who later got to be a flag officer.* We had Alan Shepard, the first astronaut, and several other guys who got to be flag officers, too.** They all enjoyed the work and didn't want to be put out of commission.

Admiral Pride, you know, had a distinguished record himself as a test pilot in much, much earlier days. I remember taking him up a few times in various airplanes. One was the old AJ, the first airplane the Navy had that could carry a nuclear weapon, and he was curious about flying it.*** I took him up in that.

One of the nice things he did say on a fitness report

---

*Commander Paul E. Pugh, USN, later a rear admiral.
**Lieutenant Alan B. Shepard, Jr., USN, served at the test pilot school from 1951 to 1953 and as a lieutenant commander from 1955 to 1957. He was the first American in space, a sub-orbital flight of 15 minutes on 15 May 1961. Shepard retired as a rear admiral.
***The AJ Savage, built by North American, entered the fleet in 1949. It had a wing span of 75 feet, gross weight of 55,000 pounds, and maximum speed of 400 miles per hour.

was, "This officer is an excellent pilot and can fly anything the Navy has and does it most enthusiastically." Nice words like that, which I thought was very, very nice. He was the sort of officer that if he thought you were a fine officer, he would write, "This is a very fine officer." And it was in an era where if you didn't write up everyone as if he could walk on water, you were going to hurt him. And he wrote this fitness report on me: "This is a very good officer who does his duty and is industrious." I remember going home and talking to Floss and saying, "My God, I'm finished in the Navy.* I'll never be able to survive this kind of report, and I'd better see if Grumman is serious about some of those nice things they have been saying."

One of the things the companies would do was to flatter you and say, "Oh, you could get out of the Navy and make a lot of money test flying."

Every now and then, I would say, "Oh, is that so? Well, when and for how much?" Well, they had their own test pilots who were perfectly able, most of them, and had a navy background anyway. They weren't serious, but they would say these flattering things. Anyway, I didn't have nerve enough to get out of the Navy, and I didn't want to, and I just hung on. Later on, darned if I didn't get selected a little bit ahead of time for my group. I met an

---

*Floss is the nickname of Hyland's wife Florence.

officer later on at Omaha who'd been on my selection board, Butch Parker, and I can remember asking him about that relatively reserved report.* I said, "I've often been curious about that selection, because I got a report from old Mel Pride that I thought I'd never be able to survive."

And Butch Parker told me, "Oh, yes, old Mel Pride, we found out about him. We just had to factor him." They caught on right away, because he hadn't written up anybody as if he could walk on water, not a single one. He was just a terse, factual old New Englander: a lot of "yups" and "nopes" and not very much discussion. He was just writing people honestly. Well, if you did that in all the years I was in the Navy, you stood a darned good chance of hurting them quite badly, because everybody else was getting, you know, virtually a perfect reports in words that would describe him like he was the second coming.

He just wasn't one of those. So I'll have to say I admired the old bird, and I liked him, and mostly I respected him, because he did have integrity. But I was worried about him all the time, because he didn't let you know whether you were doing well or not. Most seniors you can get a pretty good clue on how you're doing after a while. With him I never could. But I understand he's still going. Gosh, he must be in his 80s.** Well, he was

---
*Vice Admiral Edward N. Parker, USN, whose oral history is in the Naval Institute collection.
**Pride was born 10 September 1897 and died 24 December 1988.

a wonderful old officer.

Later on, I saw him when he returned from assignment as ComSeventhFlt and came through Honolulu.* At that time I was on Admiral Felix Stump's staff. I can remember having a chance to talk to him then and ask him some questions. The Navy was very anxious to get a field on Okinawa. He was all for it. Well, that's about all I can remember about Admiral Pride.

Q: You mentioned Alan Shepard. What do you remember of him from that period?

Admiral Hyland: Well, the very first thing when I reported for duty, Admiral Pride was there, and I went to call on him and present myself. He said, "Look, there's only one thing about that little outfit down there that I want to talk to you about. You've got a youngster down there. His name is Shepard." And Shep had been caught just a week or so before for flathatting for the second time.** His wife's family had a place over at Ocean City, right on the surf. And Shep had gone over and beaten up the beach. He flew so low that all kinds of people could copy down the number of the airplane, and they knew it was Navy. They

---

*As a vice admiral, Pride was Commander Seventh Fleet from 1953 to 1955.
**Flathatting is a term for flying low and stunting, particularly in a dangerous manner.

were calling in and reporting him.

So Admiral Pride said, "I want you to straighten that kid out, because we just can't have that sort of thing." This was when there was a Navy-wide campaign against flathatting. Flathatting has been going on over the years. I presume it still does go on. I hope so in many ways. I remember just getting Shepard in and saying, "Now look, Shep, Admiral Pride has made a point of talking about you, and this is the second time you've been caught. We cannot have this happen again. It may happen again, but you can't get caught again, no matter what the excuse is. Now do you understand that?" Sure he did, and he never did it again. I said, "If you want to fly low and do slow rolls at low altitude, for God's sake, go out to sea and do it where no one can catch you, but don't get caught again, because you're going to have to be detached overnight."

Of course, Shep was one of the finest young pilots that we had there. But I was surprised meeting Shep. He's not a very big guy, yet he was the stroke of the crew at the Naval Academy. He was that talented an oarsman. He had a genius IQ. I found that out later on. I don't know what IQs really mean, but it is something that they can test, and very few people have this extremely high number. He had it. I don't know what a genius IQ is, but he was way up there in a very rarefied group. And Shep had a marvelous flying ability. Very smart, and he turned in some of the very best reports we had.

I can remember he's one of the first guys that thought of the idea that it was the total momentum of an airplane, of a fighter airplane in particular, that mattered. For instance, if you were a lot higher than your opponent, you could use the altitude to gain speed and help you get behind this guy and shoot him down. If you were flying faster than he was at the same altitude, you had an equivalent sort of momentum or potential. And if you were down lower than he was and flying a lot faster than he was, you still might not be at a real disadvantage. With your momentum you could pull up and join him. So they developed this very clever way of showing fleet pilots that mainly the thing in fighters is to have altitude advantage if you can get it, have speed advantage if you can get it. But, in any case, try to have momentum, total momentum, which is a product of your speed and your altitude, or a combination of the two. That's one project that I can remember.

We were involved in some of the very earliest air-to-air refueling tests. He was involved in that.

We went out one time to Muroc Dry Lake to test a jet airplane with its engines shut down. We would fly to altitude at Muroc and deliberately shut the engines down and have another similar airplane that wouldn't do that, and we would develop a situation that a pilot could set his airplane with the engines running, which would be equivalent to what it would be if he had flamed out and had to make a dead-stick landing. We practiced the technique of landing a jet dead-stick. It was amazing how in a short time you could get pretty darned good at doing that. Finally, we graduated, and instead of landing out in the seven miles of beautifully flat desert land, we would come in and land on the runway. The final test would be to actually shut the airplane down and then come in and land on the runway and stop.

Then we published a report for all the pilots in the fleet about how to simulate a flameout and practice their technique for getting down. It was very, very well received all around the fleet. They thought it was very, very good that that report came out and they could just go ahead and just look at it and go up in the air and set the airplane with the wheels and the flaps down, put them partly down so that you could simulate the way the plane would actually operate with the engines off. Shep was involved in that.

I can remember the old F7U, which was a real dog.* But it was coming along as an airplane. Whenever they flew a jet for the first time after it was built, it was always taken out to Muroc to fly out there. The test pilots

---

*The F7U Cutlass, a fighter built by Vought, was unconventional-looking in that it had no horizontal tail separate from the wings. The first F7U-3, which proved to be the definitive version of the plane, flew in December 1951. Top speed was 680 miles per hour at 10,000 feet.

wouldn't do it from a regular field, because they never knew what the airplane might be like. Admiral Pride decided that that was silly. It was so expensive to take them way out there. Why the hell not test them right at Patuxent? We had a 10,000-foot runway there.

However, the pilots rebelled at this. I can remember the Vought Company at one time was going to test the F7U at Patuxent, and a fellow by the name of Eddie Owen, who was an ex-navy guy, who was their chief test pilot, refused to make the flight.* And they got another guy to do it, and they actually flew the airplane from Patuxent River. But to do these tests of engine-off performance, later on Admiral Pride thought it ought to be done at Patuxent River. He said, "What the hell do we have Patuxent River for? We don't want to get out there and beg the Air Force for the use of their field." I don't think he understood what a tough airplane that was to do that kind of testing in. I know they did not do it at Patuxent, but by that time I had been transferred. I just had one or two flights in that airplane. When everything was working properly, it was a fine airplane, but it was not suitable for the carrier at all. It was terrible.

Q: It was a strange-looking plane.

---

*Edward M. Owen was Vought's chief experimental test pilot. During World War II, he was commanding officer of VF-5, a Hellcat squadron that operated from the USS <u>Yorktown</u> (CV-10).

Admiral Hyland: Yes. A big, long nose strut on to get the angle of attack that you needed. It was a good try, but it was one of the real dogs that was ever put out. After a certain amount of experience, I think it was on the old Hancock, they finally decided that it simply wasn't carrier suitable, and they put them all ashore.* She was out there on a deployment to Japan, and they put them ashore at Atsugi, and they did whatever they could do for the rest of that deployment.**

Q: Why do you say that you hope navy pilots are still flathatting?

Admiral Hyland: Well, I really don't mean that, but there is a kind of a top pilot who will do the best for you in wartime and who will be your best test pilot, too. There's a need for a certain amount of flair. There's a certain amount of adventuresome feelings that seem to be built into the right kind of guy. And someone who might be absolutely straightforward and methodical and never did anything except by the book, he probably isn't going to be your best investigator when you're looking to evaluate an airplane.

---
*The USS Hancock (CVA-19) was an Essex-class attack aircraft carrier.
**Atsugi is the site of a U.S. naval air station on the island of Honshu, Japan. It is near the port of Yokosuka.

It's a feeling that sometimes comes over the young pilots, and they just go ahead and do it. However, they should know that they're going to face the penalty if they get caught, because that just simply isn't permitted now. And I'm not so sure it's really going on so much.

These airplanes are so darned expensive. You can't tolerate the kind of an error that might lose an airplane, just to give someone a good feeling. It's not sensible. In those Patuxent days of mine, we didn't think anything of flying four or five different airplanes in the same day. In fact, I found out in TacTest there was one fellow who was a fine pilot, but he had flown an airplane when he hadn't even bothered to read the handbook. He just had a friend check him out in the cockpit and said, "Okay, fine." You know, they used to joke about it in early jet flying-- kick the tire, light the fire off, and you go. You can't have that in a testing establishment.

I had to raise hell with this guy over that, that he would have that much irresponsibility to get in an airplane without ever looking at the book. You don't need to read the book to know how to fly the airplane; anybody can fly any airplane usually, but what do you do if something goes wrong? You have to have studied the various systems. In those days particularly, the hydraulic system and systems for emergency lowering of the gear and that kind of thing, you'd have to know what to do.

Now everything is so carefully managed, I imagine, not only do you study the book and get yourself checked out very thoroughly, but now if you have any real trouble and you can communicate with the ground, they run to the tower and open up the emergency procedures, and they give you a hand if you can't recall exactly what the right thing to do is. They will help you. That procedure, of course, saves a lot of airplanes. They do that regularly in the fleet now. Something goes wrong, and if the guy doesn't have to jump out, or if he isn't in a complete emergency where he must land immediately, I think they almost always check with the ground and see if they're doing the right thing.

Now, I shouldn't say I encourage flathatting--hell no, that's going just a little bit too far. I do think, though, and I used to say this occasionally when I was still on active duty, that when you're practicing in peacetime, you should fly the airplane to whatever limits it's allowed to go to. You should check out the envelope and so on. We had made a great thing about safety, and awards were given annually. I think the guy who got the safety award got the best fitness report. Well, of course, in theory if you want a perfect safety record you just put everything in the hangar and talk about it. I used to say that we had to be careful that we're not emphasizing safety so greatly that we're not flying airplanes.

We should get out there, and guys should dogfight with

one another. This isn't done with the intention of flathatting or anything, but I mean we should really fly the airplane and pull the G's as much as they're allowed, see what happens, and get to know the airplane.* That's what you're going to need in wartime. This sometimes can conflict with the goal of a perfect safety record.

You're in a fighter squadron, and the skipper is absolutely intent on winning the safety award, he'll probably fix it so you won't have any dogfighting, you won't do any low-altitude strafing, you won't do things that are part of the military abilities of the airplane. So I used to make a speech about that. I'd get a few "hear hears" from the audience for that sort of thing. But I do think that you damned well better accent safety also and try to make a good compromise, because airplanes just cost so damned much. We don't have any spares.

The thing I used to worry about the most when I was on active duty was that if we had a first-class enemy and we went to war, I think we'd run out of airplanes in about two weeks. You can't build these babies like we could in World War II. What are you going to do when you run out of airplanes? That would be my question when we were talking about how many to buy. But, of course, sometimes the

---

*One G is, according to Webster's New Collegiate Dictionary, "a unit of force equal to the force exerted by gravity on a body at rest and used to indicate the force to which a body is subjected when accelerated." In flying, it is a measure of the strain on both plane and pilot from maneuvering.

civilian masters will say, "How many can you put on a carrier? Show us a diagram of how many airplanes and you fill up the carrier. Okay, that's the maximum that you're ever going to buy."

We would say, "Well, you certainly ought to have at least double that, keep them somewhere, out on the beach and have replacements." That's been very carefully handled. They never have bought enough for many, many years. I think the other guy would run out of some airplanes also in that first week or two or three of the war, assuming it was nonnuclear. But the Russians have built for numbers and not for super technical excellence like we do. I think we'd run out before they would. But no one will ever know until we have a go.

Q: Well, speaking of people in aircraft, did you encounter Admiral Thach during your years at the Pentagon?*

Admiral Hyland: No. No, when I was in OP-60, he was OP-05. I knew his name, of course, because when I had Air Group Ten during the last part of the war, we were using

---

*Vice Admiral John S. Thach, USN, was Deputy Chief of Naval Operations (Air), 1963-65. He was a top fighter tactician during World War II, inventor of the Thach Weave. His two-volume oral history is in the Naval Institute collection.

the Thach Weave. Gayler had been in his squadron.* He had a fine name. He was a very quiet guy. I knew who he was, and we had been introduced. But I don't think he knew who I was. He was a four-star guy. He was over there in England.** But, unfortunately for me, I was never with him. The best known pilot that I was with was Jimmy Flatley.***

Q: He and Thach were very close.

Admiral Hyland: Yes, they were close friends. Thach was a little bit senior to Jimmy.**** Jimmy Flatley was one of the better pilots. He was in the first squadron I went to. He was so much better than the rest of us that it was comical. I can remember having a position of advantage. It didn't matter to him as far as fooling with me was concerned. I could have the advantage in altitude or not, but in about two or three minutes he'd be right behind me. Then later on, he'd explain what I'd done wrong.

---
*Lieutenant Noel A. M. Gayler, USN, was in Fighting Squadron Three, commanded by Lieutenant Commander Thach, at the beginning of World War II. Gayler, who eventually retired as a four-star admiral, has been interviewed as part of the Naval Institute's oral history program.
**Thach served as Commander in Chief U.S. Naval Forces Europe, with headquarters in London, 1965-67.
***Lieutenant Commander James H. Flatley, Jr., USN, was also a fighter tactician and squadron commanding officer during World War II. He eventually reached the rank of vice admiral.
****Thach was in the class of 1927 at the Naval Academy, Flatley in the class of 1929.

Jimmy Flatley had some envious contemporaries, and they all said that one of the reasons he was so good is he is such a small guy. He didn't weigh anything--130 or something like that. They claimed that in those old fighters that made a big difference. Well, that was a lot of baloney. He was just an extremely skilled pilot. You know, he has a son who is now a flag officer in the Navy.* His son is also a hell of a pilot and has done all the things. He's a Patuxent graduate and all that. He's the one who took a C-130 aboard ship one time. He took that thing and put it on the Forrestal; this was years and years ago, just to show it could be done.**

One time young Jimmy was recommended to me for my aide when I was CinCPacFlt. I wrote him and said, "I'd be delighted to have you, but do you want to come?"

He wrote back a very nice letter and said no, he didn't. He'd been doing a hell of a lot of flying. Then he was graduating from a wing command, as I recall it. He'd been on one deployment after another for various reasons, and he said, "No, I don't want to do that right now," and he hoped I'd understand. Of course, I did.

---
*James H. Flatley III, a 1956 graduate of the Naval Academy, retired from active duty in August 1987 as a rear admiral.
**In October-November 1963, Flatley was one of the pilots from the Naval Air Test Center, Patuxent River who conducted carrier suitabiliity tests of the KC-130F Hercules tanker on board the USS Forrestal (CVA-59). The full-stop landings were done without a tailhook, relying instead on special brakes and maximum reversing of the propellers.

I can remember then another one down at Patuxent when I was there. Wes Byng was the exec, and he later got to be a flag officer.* He has a first-class son who became a naval aviator.** So Wes Byng's boy was recommended to me. He was not a volunteer at all to be anybody's aide. He seemed to think he'd been selected and he was about to be ordered. I didn't want to have anybody do that if they didn't want to. Anyway, before I could do anything about it, I found out that young Byng had said he didn't want to be aide for CinCPacFlt. He didn't want to be aide for anybody. He wouldn't be aide for anybody. He would get out of the Navy if they ordered him to be an aide. He wouldn't do it if it was the last damned job in the world. That was about the tone of his letter. I said, "Fine, that's about the way I felt when I was his age." So I didn't get him. One of my aides is now down at Patuxent River. Ned Hogan is the skipper, the admiral down there now.***

Q: When you had stopped with Dr. Mason, you were in the midst of that tour in OP-60, and the head of that was Admiral Wally Wendt.**** What do you recall about him?

---
*Captain John W. Byng, USN.
**Lieutenant Weston H. Byng, USN.
***At the time of the interview, Rear Admiral Edward J. Hogan, Jr., USN, was Commander Naval Air Test Center.
****Rear Admiral Waldemar F. A. Wendt, USN.

Admiral Hyland: Well, he was an old hand in OP-60. That was a very specialized area of the CNO's staff. He was an old pro in that business of handling joint papers. There was a system that you had to learn. I had to learn in a great hurry and from scratch. He and I thought that OP-60 was the most important of the divisions.

OP-60 had various sections that took care of all the Navy's input into all the joint plans, into all the joint nuclear business, and all sorts of things that were covered with blood down in the JCS tank in those years. Wally Wendt was just an old pro at that. He was wonderfully nice to me. I hadn't known him before I got there. He was a regular surface officer. Of course, I was an aviator. He was the least prejudiced one of those surface guys about aviators that I've ever run into. A lot of them had a grudging feeling about how the aviators had sort of taken over the Navy.

We had a succession of CNOs that were all aviators. After Admiral Burke, we had George Anderson, we had Dave McDonald, Tom Moorer, and so on.* I think the fact that here there was a succession of them, one after another, didn't go down so well with the other parts of the Navy. He was a very level-headed, unbiased guy, one of the nicest men to work with that I ever ran into in the Navy. I know

---
*Admiral Arleigh A. Burke, USN, 1955-61; Admiral George W. Anderson, Jr., USN, 1961-63; Admiral David L. McDonald, USN, 1963-67; Admiral Thomas H. Moorer, USN, 1967-70.

the reason I got to be OP-60 finally was he got promoted. Tom Moorer was CinCLant at the time, and he got Wally down. They were classmates.* He got Wally as deputy, and that's when Wally got his third star. Then, about six or eight months later was when I got my third star. I got to go out and take command of the Seventh Fleet. That was a lot of good luck for me. The incumbent, Vice Admiral Paul Blackburn, was very ill with a terrible case of pneumonia which lingered on, so I was sent out to replace him.**

Now, back to the business with Wally Wendt. We worked very hard. We got in first thing in the morning, and it was very unusual to leave before about 7:00 o'clock in the evening. I practically never saw my children. They were practically in bed by the time I would get home. My wife didn't especially like that. We always worked on Saturday mornings, and quite often that would extend into the rest of the day. It wouldn't be too unusual to have to come in on a Sunday, because the Vietnamese War was just getting started then. We had the Tonkin Gulf incident and the Tonkin Gulf Resolution.

And that was the beginning of my experience with

---

*Both Moorer and Wendt were graduated in the class of 1933 from the Naval Academy.
**Vice Admiral Paul P. Blackburn, Jr., USN, was Commander Seventh Fleet from 1 March 1965 until 13 December 1965.

McNamara and the "Whiz Kids."* They were right in the midst of running the show and kibitzing everything that the military services did. That really was troublesome for the standard old navy types in those days. They hadn't been used to that. The older generation before us, they pretty much managed what the Navy was going to buy in the way of weapons and where the flag officers were going to be posted and all that. Gradually, these new people began to get into all that stuff.

I remember being told by one fellow who was leaving and telling his civilian replacement, he said, "If you want to have any hold over these bastards at all, you'd better get control over the personnel assignment business." He said, "Don't let them delegate themselves. Don't let them decide where they're going. You decide. You get control." Of course, for years they had always had the power to do that sort of thing, but most of them had the discretion not to use that power because they're simply not qualified to do it.

We had some gross mistakes made by civilian masters who were anxious to help some favorite of theirs. I'm not going to name any names along that line, but they would be very taken with a guy, and all his peers and his seniors and his juniors knew that he really was not that good a

---
*Robert S. McNamara was Secretary of Defense from 1961 to 1968. The "Whiz Kids" were the group of young scholars from academia and industry that McNamara brought to the Defense Department to introduce systems analysis.

man, nowhere near that good a man. The CNO and the vice chief and other very senior people had a way of getting together and talking about these people. They all knew who the good guys were, who the white hats were, so to speak. I think they did a pretty good job of moving up the people who should have been moved up and stopping others.

Well, you start having a civilian who's only there temporarily, and who doesn't think of his job with the Navy as the ultimate in his career, not by any means. They've all got other things in mind much bigger and better than that. When they decide to tinker with assigning people to duty here and there, it more often than not will be an error and cause a lot of disaffection, I think, in the Navy. Jim Watkins told me it is much worse now: "If you thought it was bad when you were CinCPacFlt, you ought to see it now."* I don't know anything about that. I guess maybe it is. Of course, from the secretariat's point of view, it's probably better. But from the uniformed guy's point of view, it's definitely not.

Well, anyway, Wally and I actually slaved together for a couple of years there in OP-60, or a year and a half. Finally he got promoted, and I fleeted up. I remember a classmate of mine, J. V. Smith, relieved me.** He was the

---
*Admiral James D. Watkins, USN, was Chief of Naval Operations at the time of this interview. He held the office from 1982 to 1986.
**Rear Admiral John Victor Smith, USN, later vice admiral and subject of a Naval Institute oral history.

bridesmaid for only a relatively short time, and then he relieved me, and I went on out to the Seventh Fleet. That was very fortuitous for me.

It was a very awful time to become a relatively senior guy, because very shortly we began getting into that business of fighting a war and risking these marvelous young people, but not having any real intentions of winning it. They absolutely controlled everything we did and fixed things so that we couldn't do what we all knew should have been done if we were going to win it. And mainly it was the idea that if you are going to use something like air power, you'd better use it overwhelmingly, to the full extent that you can do, and do it right away, and do it so hard and so vigorously that maybe the other guy will just fold.

But when you're doing it piecemeal, you're going to drop one bomb today, we'll try two bombs tomorrow, we'll try three bombs the next day, and so on. Pretty soon he's going to get the message, and he'll realize that we don't really mean business. All it really does is give them plenty of time to get ready for the third day and the fourth day and the subsequent days, and so on. And that's exactly what happened. We never were allowed to hit all the targets at once that should have been hit.

They were very selective. They would give you a target list of six or eight targets, and you'd be told to hit them. The next day the weather would be impossible.

You couldn't hit them at all, and we would start getting messages, "Why the hell haven't you hit them? We've given you permission to hit them." Well, there were eight other targets in another area that we knew about that we could have been hitting that day, but the way it was controlled we were never allowed to have the whole target system of the enemy at our disposal. We couldn't always be doing something to them. We could only be lucky if the weather was good and we could have the targets that were important, or we thought they were.

It was kind of an amazing performance. But that particular group, that still now are called the "Whiz Kids," had absolutely no reluctance at all to manage that campaign. They would even be willing to decide at what altitude a photographic airplane should be flying in order to take the best pictures, and they didn't really know anything much about photographing from a high-speed airplane and so on. I think I'm tending here to tell a sour grapes story that, you know, if we'd have been turned loose, we'd have won the war. And I honestly do think we would have ended it a hell of a lot sooner if we'd been allowed to really go after them from the very outset, but we weren't.

Q: Were you clamoring for that opportunity when you were in OP-60?

Admiral Hyland: Well, we began to. I, of course, was an underling in those days. I did write some of the beseeching messages and all that. We had a constant exchange. We would be getting messages back from the people who were actually doing the flying, doing the fighting, wanting to know what was the trouble? Why couldn't they get better targets, more targets? And everybody was working hard on it. You know, to think that that whole mess could have gone on as long as it did without any major protest from, let's say, a very senior officer, I really don't know.

All along we thought they were getting the news. We thought that it was beginning to penetrate to them finally that the only way to do this--if we were ever going to win it--would be to go after them. But by that time it had gone on so long that they began to have doubts about whether it could ever be done. I've asked myself, now that I'm out of it and long gone from it, "What was the matter with you?" I haven't been one of these guys who write an indignant book, but I could. But then the way that's received normally when it's by an officer who's retired and he writes this sort of sour-grapes book, they say, "Well, what the hell's the matter with him? When he was on active duty, why didn't he sound off then?"

Well, the answer is he did sound off then and at great length, but always within the system. We never thought it was proper to go public. And if you had, I'm sure you wouldn't have lasted ten minutes. Those top jobs in the Navy are highly desirable. People have had a whole career to get there, and obviously they like what they're doing. I don't mean to say they will do anything to keep their jobs, but they do like them, and they're not going to throw away their whole careers and lose their jobs because the civilian masters--who must have reasons of their own--just because they won't let you hit a given target.

Now, it might be different if sometime in our history we had--Louis Johnson was SecDef, and he made a firm decision that we would stop building the United States, which was going to be the first big flattop.* He said they would build no more of them. Well, the CNO joined in the protest against it, and he lost his job as a result.** He didn't speak up immediately. People began to talk about it: "What's the matter with him? He's not making any noise about this. Is he going to accept this thing which, of course, would be the end of the Navy practically?"

---

*The keel for the carrier United States (CVA-58) was laid 18 April 1949 at Newport News, Virginia, but construction was halted five days later at the direction of Secretary of Defense Louis Johnson.
**Admiral Louis E. Denfeld, USN, was the Chief of Naval Operations, 1947-1949. He had been expected to be reappointed to a second two-year term, but he was fired instead.

In my years, nothing was ever put up on the front line that was worth making a major squawk. I personally think that if you had attempted it, it never would have been possible. Whatever you said would be on page nine, and the next day you would be completely forgotten. Of course, there would be another officer available right away to relieve you, because a lot of people want to be a fleet commander. They're not going to undermine you to get there, but if you have to leave, they're certainly all set to come in.

Q: One case that's brought up about McNamara during those years is the F-111B.* Did you get involved in that at all?

Admiral Hyland: Well, no, except I followed it closely. It was elsewhere then. The best guy to talk to about that is Tom Connolly.**

Q: We have his oral history.

---

*In search of commonality in regard to weapon systems, Secretary McNamara attempted to get the Navy to develop a carrier version, the F-111B, of an air force fighter plane. His efforts were ultimately unsuccessful.
**Vice Admiral Thomas F. Connolly, USN, was Deputy Chief of Naval Operations (Air), OP-05. He has been interviewed as part of the Naval Institute's oral history program.

Admiral Hyland: Well, he was involved in that. He was OP-05. Of course, to most of us that was the typical example of what McNamara just rammed down the throats of both the Navy and the Air Force. Both of them are developing airplanes, and this is a very expensive procedure. Why the hell can't they build one that will do for both of them? And they built that thing. It wasn't such a bad airplane for the Air Force, I understand. But they don't care whether it takes 12,000 or 20,000 feet of runway to get off. They can always take care of that. And they don't care about the size the airplane. Quite often, if you want to get more and more performance out of an airplane, you have to accommodate a bigger engine. Before you know it, the airplane gets pretty big, and you can't go beyond a certain point on a navy airplane.

Well, I can remember it got to the point where they gave the airplane some carrier tests, and one of the guys down at Patuxent--I had graduated from that long since, but this youngster wrote down in a report about the F-111, "This is absolutely the worst dog I've ever flown!" Which is not a very technical evaluation of an airplane, but it kind of tells the story.

I remember Tom Connolly telling me later that it got to the point in one of those meetings where some of these canny old senators got him up there, and they wanted to know, "Now, what do you really think of the F-111?" And Tom Connolly told them that as far as a carrier airplane, it was a dog, and it was not going to work, and it was not acceptable, and they should do something else. I remember Paul Nitze was Secretary of the Navy then, and he, of course, was in a sense a kind of a captive of McNamara and company.* It seemed to us in uniform that all those guys were fearful of McNamara, just like we were in uniform.

Anyway, after Tom had made this testimony and really told the senators what he thought, Nitze apparently looked at him later and said, "Tom, God, I wish I'd known you felt like that about the F-111." Of course, he had asked Tom about it beforehand, and Tom had told him about it. But he apparently had put it in somewhat more colorful language when he talked to the Senate. Nitze didn't like it. I remember that was the point of what Tom told me. He sure didn't like it, because they had spent so much time and so much dough on it and everything.

I guess they really wanted it to succeed, and in theory there isn't any special reason why you can't have an airplane that is flown by both services. And, golly, for years we used to crow and tease the Air Force about how many Navy-developed airplanes they had to fly. We developed the F-4.** We developed the A-7, the F-8--a

---
*Paul H. Nitze was Secretary of the Navy from 1963 to 1967.
**The McDonnell Douglas F-4 Phantom was a mainstay as a fighter and bomber/attack aircraft for the Navy and Air Force during the Vietnam War.

whole bunch of them.* We developed all sorts of ordnance: Sidewinders and so on, anti-radiation missiles, and all the rest of that stuff that we'd done out in China Lake.

I think, for our size, naval aviation has contributed more than its share, more than its proportionate size, to the advancement of flying and military flying. We were very, very proud of that. But, again, I suppose, there is no theoretical reason why you can't have a common airplane. But if you do have one that's suitable to go aboard ship, the Air Force can certainly legitimately claim that the damned thing is too strong, it's too heavy: "We don't want that weight. We want just about the same airplane, but we don't have to have that kind of structure, so why do we burden ourselves with it?" They've certainly got a point.

I think that as long as the two services are not bankrupting the country, I've never thought of the problem between the two of them as being just pure and simple unacceptable rivalry. I think it's a kind of competition. They each go at the problems, and each one of them has developed many things that were better than what the other guy developed. Then they settle down, and each one can perhaps use it. But I think as long as we can afford it,

---
*The Vought A-7 Corsair II and the Vought F-8 Crusader (previously the F8U) were navy carrier planes that were adapted for air force use from runways on land during the Vietnam War.

and, of course, as long as we think flying off the ships is the way to go, we'd better keep at it, because the Air Forces does not think that way.

They've got all kinds of people who were just as sincere as anybody else, and they just think it's much simpler and cheaper, and better to do it the way they do it. And they can even get by the problems of what do you do about the base that the foreigner won't let you use and that stuff. They say, "Well, hell, if we're in any kind of a real go, we'll use it whether he likes it or not." And that kind of thinking, that's all right, too. But certainly if they were left to foster naval aviation, it wouldn't last very long, because they just don't feel that way about it.

Q: How much relationship did you have with Admiral McDonald when you were OP-60?

Admiral Hyland: Oh, just a fair amount. You see, we were the division that prepared most of the papers that he would use down in the tank, down at the meeting of the Joint Chiefs of Staff. Every time before he went down, we had a meeting in his office, in a little conference room there. My people would brief him on the paper that was going to be considered that day. A young lieutenant commander would get up and brief the thing, and then if Admiral McDonald had questions, he could ask them. Sometimes it was up to somebody more senior than this briefing officer to sort of straighten something out. He noticed me. We had been in contact before, though. He was ComSixthFlt when I had the carrier division over there, and we crossed paths a number of times. I guess he was fairly favorably impressed.

He was the one who was CNO when I got to be ComSeventhFlt. I can remember all sorts of rumors about that. You know, people are gossipy in the Navy. Just like a small town, everybody knows everybody's business. People would ask me, "When are you going out?"

And I would have to ask, "What are you talking about? When am I going out where?"

I can remember one time Tom Moorer, who was CinCLant at the time, came walking down the corridor just as I walked out of my office. We were old buddies. We were roommates a couple of times on ships and all that. I said, "Tom, the damndest thing is going on. There's a lot of talk or gossip about I might get a third star and go to have the Seventh Fleet. What the hell can I do about something like that?"

He said, "Look, I think you're going to get it. But, for God's sake, don't act like you're going to get it. And don't say anything; just put up with this foolishness. Act like you don't know what people are talking about."

I found out later that he'd gone in to see Dave McDonald, and they were at that time worried about Brick Blackburn being ill.* He'd gotten terribly sick up in Korea and was hospitalized to the point where they'd gotten a temporary guy named Joe Williams, a submarine officer, to be ComSeventhFlt.** They decided on the replacement, and it narrowed down, I was told, between me and another fellow. Roy Johnson was CinCPacFlt at the time, and Dave McDonald apparently said, "Well, which one should we send, Johnny or the other fellow?"

And Tom said, "Well, why don't you call up Roy Johnson? I would guess that he will tell you to send Johnny Hyland out there. I don't know, but why don't you just call up and ask?"

Apparently that's what he did; right then and there, he called up CinCPacFlt and said these two guys are available. Nitze was the Secretary of the Navy at that time, and I remember being appalled when I found out that he didn't give a damn who went out there. He didn't care. He said, "Any of those guys are okay. You just select them." He was a nut on studies and all that stuff, and he was very careful about who was going to be there in the Pentagon helping him, but he really didn't much care about

---
*Blackburn was hospitalized with pneumonia and complications on 6 October 1965. Following his relief by Admiral Hyland and his recovery, Admiral Blackburn was assigned as chief of staff, U.S. Strike Command. He retired as a vice admiral in March 1968.
**Rear Admiral Joseph W. Williams, Jr., USN.

who went out to the field. I thought it was the most important thing in the whole world at the time. Anyway, to make a long story short, Roy Johnson said he would like to have me come. (I didn't see Tom after that; I found out about the meeting later.)

The next day, Dave McDonald called me up and asked, "Is there any reason why you can't go out to the Seventh Fleet? Brick is still sick out there, and we want to get somebody out there right away."

In a way, you have to be grateful for the fellow who actually proposed your name to the Secretary of the Navy, and he said, "Sure, he's okay." But it was surprising to realize that Nitze didn't think of that as a very important assignment. He thought his evaluation group in the Pentagon, who were working in the tank, were important. And, of course, they are. Operations? Hell, anybody can do that apparently.

Q: Who was the other contender for the job?

Admiral Hyland: Well, a classmate of mine, Bill Martin. Bill very shortly after that got ComSixthFlt.* I can still tease Bill, because I was in a couple of flight classes ahead of him. I was lucky; I was in the very first

---

*Rear Admiral William I. Martin, Jr., USN. On 10 April 1967, Martin became Commander Sixth Fleet and was in that billet during the six-day Arab-Israeli war of June 1967.

one that '34 was allowed to go to. Also, I had good luck with instructors and so on. I was the first guy in our class to get wings, so I treat these other guys like they're kids--you know, newcomers to the fleet.

Q: We have Admiral Martin's oral history also.

Admiral Hyland: Yes. You'll find him a nifty guy to talk to. He was a great performer in World War II.* He's had all the good jobs. He was OP-05 at one time and ComSixthFlt.** That's where he met that good-looking German gal that he's married to now. I really intended not to mention his name until you asked me who it was. I didn't know at the time that he was the competitor, but I can remember these people coming up and knew all about it, that I was going out there. And I think they were doing the same thing to him. I guess it had been narrowed down to one or the other. It's funny how those things happen.

Q: Do you remember much exchange with Nitze's executive assistant, Captain Zumwalt?***

---
*Martin was an aviation squadron commanding officer and carrier air group commander; he was one of the pioneers in night fighting techniques.
**OP-05--Deputy Chief of Naval Operations (Air).
***Captain Elmo R. Zumwalt, Jr., USN, was a special assistant to Paul H. Nitze when Nitze was Assistant Secretary of Defense (International Security Affairs), 1962-63, and executive assistant when Nitze was Secretary of the Navy, 1963-67. Zumwalt was Chief of Naval Operations, 1970-74.

Admiral Hyland: Well, I can remember knowing Bud Zumwalt then, and knowing who he was. He was very solicitous of me in those days. But that changed a little bit later on. The thing I remember about him was he was one of a case where, when you get a new Secretary of the Navy, one of the first things that the Navy will do is to line up a selection of maybe four or five absolutely top-notch officers, and you offer them to the new secretary. In many cases, you don't know much about this guy. So nowadays I suppose they probably would offer him a black; a Jewish guy; one who had the map of Ireland on his face; a WASP; a tall, dark, and handsome guy; and a short, stocky guy.

This is making light of a pretty serious thing, but the Navy would offer these men. He would interview them if he wanted, and he would take the one that he thought would be best for him. But in this case, you see, the Navy is assigning this guy as the aide to the secretary. Well, Nitze came up from ISA to be Secretary of the Navy; working with him down in ISA was Bud Zumwalt, one of his top officers.* So when this procedure was started with Nitze, he said, "Aide? I've already got one. His name is Zumwalt. I'm bringing him up from ISA with me."

---

*International Security Affairs is a division of the Office of the Secretary of Defense, headed by an Assistant Secretary of Defense. It sometimes is referred to as the "Pentagon's State Department."

Well, you see, this young officer now has been selected and elevated to that very, very important job totally outside the Navy in a sense. You follow that, I think. So when things begin to go wrong and the secretary becomes difficult, if he does, you can't call the guy in and say, "Look, you dummy, can't you convince him of this and this and this? He doesn't seem to understand this and this and this, and that's your job, among other things, for God's sake, to keep us out of trouble." You couldn't do that with him, or they couldn't do that with him to the same extent.

Well, I can remember shortly after that, while I was still in OP-60, I was on a selection board. I was one of the junior members of the board, and we selected Bud Zumwalt among some others. Jerry Miller was on that selection list.* Oh, a bunch of guys. But one of the most astounding things I ever read was the fitness report that Nitze had written about Bud Zumwalt. Talk about being able to walk on water. It was obvious that Nitze was very anxious for this officer to be selected, and it was time for him. He could be selected. It was way ahead of time for his year group and all that, but he could be selected, and Nitze was determined that he was going to be selected.

---
*Captain Gerald E. Miller, USN, who later was promoted to vice admiral and served as Commander Sixth Fleet in the early 1970s. Vice Admiral Miller's oral history is in the Naval Institute collection.

I guess he asked some experts from BuPers and everything else.* He said, "How do you do this now? I don't know how these reports are made." He got some dope, and he got some help from Bud himself. I would have given it to him if he'd asked me for it. So this fitness report went on for two or three pages. It was the most extreme language of extreme capabilities. This officer could do just absolutely anything, and so on. He actually was a hell of a good officer. I think he would have been selected. But, boy, Secretary Nitze was determined to make it so. And it was.

Then, later on, I saw him, heard about him. I remember he got a promotion that Nitze generated. He went out to Vietnam there and got promoted to a third star.** What happened to him is all in that book that he wrote, where he rewrote a little naval history, among other things.*** But I followed him. It's when he was down there in Vietnam that he was elevated above a whole flock of people to be the CNO. I wasn't surprised. But that is what happened.

John Chafee had become Secretary of the Navy by that

---
*BuPers--Bureau of Naval Personnel.
**Zumwalt became a vice admiral in late 1968 when he took over as Commander U.S. Naval Forces Vietnam.
***Zumwalt's book is <u>On Watch: A Memoir</u> (New York: Quadrangle Books, 1976).

time.* Chafee's very fond of Zumwalt, too. Chafee told Tom Moorer one time when Tom was the CNO, "You know, I'm so much younger than you and other people at the top of the circuit. I find it very uncomfortable having to work with men who are so much older than I am."**

You know the answer to that; I'm sure he got it from Tom: "What the hell of it? This is the age that people are when they get to this point in their naval careers." But he was a little bit of a nut on the youth movement. He pushed that pretty hard. I think sometimes that kind of a civilian and a politician--you see all kinds of examples in civilian life where a young man, 35 years old or 40 years old, gets to be the head of a giant corporation or does something extraordinary to get to the top. And they wonder why the hell can't we have that in the Navy.

Well, they never do fully understand the Navy's not a corporation. The Navy doesn't make a product that somebody sells a million copies of. It's an entirely different thing. You shouldn't promote people ahead of time in the Navy, or any other military service, unless they are really and truly extraordinarily capable. If they have the admiration of their peers--and not only people above them, but all of their contemporaries, and even people below

---
*John Hubbard Chafee, former governor of Rhode Island, was Secretary of the Navy from 31 January 1969 to 4 April 1972.
**Chafee was born 22 October 1922; he was 46 years old when he became Secretary of the Navy. Moorer was born 9 February 1912.

them—they will admit in a few cases this guy is really something. He is absolutely fully able to have an advanced rank. They're not going to resent it. But to promote somebody a year or two ahead of a guy who later gets selected, and then he wonders, "What the heck was the matter with me in the first place?" Or to assume out of every year group, and that's what they began to do about my time; they were assuming that there were three officers in each class that were extraordinarily terrific guys. That's a lot of poppycock.

I got it on the second go-around, and all kinds of people looked at me later and wondered, "How does that ever happen? He's not any better than I am, and I know it, and he knows it." And that was true. But if you're offered these opportunities, you can't turn them down. You go ahead and accept it and do the best you can. But, at the same time, you can see in some cases that it's really just as well to have people wait.

One of the hazards if you are selected way ahead of time in the Navy, and then it doesn't seem to work out too well, you have to retire well ahead of time. Even that happened to Bud Zumwalt. He had the top job and, gosh, I think he was still in his middle 50s when he left.* Of course, he was so different from the rest that there just

---

*Admiral Zumwalt was born 29 November 1920. He was 53 when he retired from active duty at the end of June 1974.

wasn't a prayer that he would get to be the chairman or get any other assignment.* So he just had to leave. I think it's too bad. If he'd been assigned to a fleet command and had a little more preparation for being the Chief of Naval Operations, I think he would perhaps have modified some of his views. I don't know. But, again, why in the world would he ever think of refusing it once he was told he was going to get it?

Q: When you were in OP-60, how much relationship did you have with ISA? I would think there would be a lot of interchange.

Admiral Hyland: Well, in those days, surprisingly, there was not much, no. I always thought of ISA as the State Department element in the Department of Defense, just as I believe there must be some type of military element of the State Department. They corresponded with one another. ISA, on the papers that we talked about, that I had anything to do with, or when I was with Wally Wendt, they almost never came into the picture. I think they were another avenue that came into the Joint Chiefs of Staff. What we were involved in was the navy point of view on joint matters.

I can remember everybody was wild about nuclear

---

*This is a reference to the post of Chairman of the Joint Chiefs of Staff.

weapons, because they had been used once or twice, and then they were being developed very rapidly.* The Navy was doing everything it could to get a full place in the use of nuclear weapons. We were the principal service that was trying to push for smaller weapons that could be carried on a tactical airplane. The Air Force didn't want to have any tactical weapons. If they could confine them to large planes like the Strategic Air Command, it didn't matter to them if the weapon itself was quite a big weapon. You might know, the early weapons weighed 10,000 pounds. It was a hell of a big thing. It got down to where they were just hundreds of pounds eventually. That was the Navy pushing for that with quite a bit of help from the Army, because they wanted to be able to fire them out of cannons and have them on ground-based, short-range missiles and that sort of business.

So there was great competition for the nuclear material that was available. The AEC, the Atomic Energy Commission, was making nuclear material as rapidly as it could be made. The military applications division of the AEC was handling the manufacture of weapons that the services wanted. Looking back, you know, everybody wanted the entire stockpile. Everybody had a requirement. Put in your requirements, and they would be ridiculously high. We

---

*The section that begins here supplements Admiral Hyland's discussion in interview number four of his role on the Joint Strategic Target Planning Staff in the early 1960s.

wanted nuclear antiaircraft weapons on every ship. We wanted at least one or two for every airplane. We wanted all this stuff. It was silly. It would finally be beaten down, and each service would get its share of the pie.

In those days, the majority of it was going to the Air Force, to the Strategic Air Command. It would be a paper like that. If I remember anything about that whole period, the nuclear business was the most bloody and the most hotly contested item that the Joint Chiefs would be arguing over, trying to come to an agreement on. Usually, they'd come to some reasonable solution to the thing because they just simply had to. You had to assign some of the material to somebody, and they had to decide to put it into certain kinds of weapons. So there would be a very distinct compromise of all these forces, and they would go ahead and decide on what to do.

The role of the services in the nuclear plan had the nickname SIOP, Single Integrated Operational Plan. It was generated out there in Omaha. The whole process was dominated by the Strategic Air Command. I can remember some of the bloody stuff that went on out there. When I was stationed in Omaha, we'd be fighting with these good air force guys all day long, and then we'd meet them after work and get along fine with them, or play games with them and so on. I found out after a year or so out there that they were human, like I thought I was.

But I remember General LeMay was Chief of Staff of the Air Force. He'd just left SAC, and a guy named Power had relieved him, and Power would make these speeches.* He would say, "I can't figure out what the Navy is trying to do here. You give me a nuclear weapon. I'll tell you what I'm going to do with it. I'll tell you which target it's going to hit and what time of day it's going to hit that target, and I'll tell you the number of the airplane, and the base where it's parked, where we're going to put that weapon. And we're going to take off, and we're going to go there, and we're going to hit that target. You give the same weapon to the Navy and you ask them, 'What are you going to do with it?' and they don't know. They can't tell you what the hell they're going to do with it. So I think in an era where these things are in terribly short supply, I would think it would make sense to give it to the guy that knows what he's going to do with it, not to someone else."

Of course, we would have our arguments, but to him they were ridiculous, or apparently so: "We know what carrier it's going to be on. We can't tell you this spot on the map where that carrier is going to be, but when the war begins we'll have the carrier in position, and it'll operate, and the plane will deliver the weapon. We'll tell

---
*LeMay was the SAC commander, 1948-57, and Power, 1957-64.

you the target. But as far as telling you the time of day or night it's going to be delivered, who needs to know that?" This sort of fighting would go on all the time.

For every one of our types of airplanes that might deliver a nuclear weapon, we had a man who had been skipper of a squadron of that kind of airplane. And for the use of the weapons in the Polaris submarines, we'd have a Polaris submarine skipper who knew how that kind of a ship operated. We had experts in our field helping to put together the navy part of the plan. It was amazing to see that SAC had a bunch of guys planning for their attacks who had never been in a B-52 for a flight. They were all pilots, but they might have come from anywhere. They had just, however, become expert planners. For this B-52 they would even describe the flight profile to take the weapon in to the target.

We used to hear a little grousing from some of the operations people that they weren't even consulted. And sometimes a brilliant staff officer can assign a flight to a B-52 that the B-52 guy knows is not the best way to do that. If they had talked to him, they would have done it a little differently, or maybe very much differently. They had a different system. They could plan things right down to a last little tiny element and were confident that whatever the B-52 driver was told to do, he would do. Maybe that's all right. It's strange to us, though. We thought, "Gosh, if we're going to put a weapon on a little jet airplane, we'd better decide how would be the best way to do it, and would he be willing to do it, or could he do it?"

Somebody who didn't know anything might say, "Well, tell him to go as high as he can and go in there, or go in on the deck," not knowing that if you went in on the deck you would run out of fuel before you even got there. That kind of thing. You know, you ought to have an operational input. We were very careful about that. The big argument was to get for the Navy a proper place in this very, very important plan. Because once the plan was adopted each year, then all things were then planned at lower and lower and lower levels, right down to the operational level to carry it out whenever the balloon went up.

So in my years out there, the Air Force was doing their very best to give us a secondary role in the plan. When McNamara and company and other people like him would come out, they would put on briefings, and then they would always show off all the weapons to be delivered--77% of them are going to be delivered by Air Force; of those, 90% will be SAC-delivered. The Navy would have a role, but of the important targets, most of them were going to be covered by SAC, and only a few were going to be covered by the Navy.

We would always try to present our contribution as

favorably as possible for the Navy. It was in the very, very early days of the development of the Polaris missile system. I, an aviator, became the papa of the Polaris navy--as far as its place in the strategic plan was concerned--there for a while. I was later replaced by a submarine officer.

The Air Force people at SAC were just doing everything they could to discredit the Polaris system. They would have war games. I don't know if you've ever been involved in some of them. They are approximations of what might happen and so on. But then you finally get down to this war game, and you're playing a game, and these two things encounter one another, and you roll the dice. The dice tell you if it's number so-and-so that that time it was a hit. It would perhaps be in the war game that an airplane was flying and dropping a depth bomb on a Polaris submarine that was known to be in the vicinity. The war game would come up with a miss. General Power would be told that, and he would say, "Play that part of the game over." So if you played it about ten times, about twice it may come up a hit. He'd then say, "Okay, publish that part." That would be about the way it went.

I was walking along in front of his office one time, and we knew that there was a Polaris missile that was going to be fired that day down off Cape Canaveral. A whole bunch of them were gathered inside the office there. I don't know who they were. I know he was in there. I just happened to walk by, and they found out the missile had been launched, and the damned thing had malfunctioned, and the safety officer had blown it up in midair. So this one guy came tearing in to tell General Power that the Polaris missile had malfunctioned and had been destroyed. There was a tumultuous cheer which went up from inside the office: "Hurray, the damned thing didn't work. We never thought it would anyway."

I thought that was a shameful point of view. Doggone it, they should want our Polaris. We're spending that dough on them, and we want them to work. We don't want them to fail. But they felt differently at that time. The thing that bothered them was they had never been able to test their system. No one would let them fly stuff out of those holes in Nebraska because of safety considerations. Chances are they would work beautifully, but they wouldn't let them do it. The only time they can test one of theirs is when they fire it out of that place on the West Coast, or out of Canaveral and do it there.

We actually, one time, fired a weapon out of a submerged submarine that went where it was supposed to and exploded a nuclear weapon at the end of the trip. We're the only system that's actually been tested successfully from start to finish. Now, of course, most of the testing when you get to the end of the line, you don't have a nuclear warhead. You have just an explosive or a device that indicates it went off. But we're the only one that did it. It's come a long way.

I understand now that everybody's friendly out there in Omaha. We are really worried about the Russian problem. And everybody wants every weapon now to be utilized the very best way it can. That was not the way it was when I was struggling out there. We felt very sorry for ourselves. We were out there in the enemy camp and all that stuff. Paul Masterton and I were out there together for quite a while.* We used to commiserate with one another. I was the representative from Admiral Dennison of the Atlantic Command, and he was from Admiral Felt, the Pacific Command.** We both got good jobs when we left. We each got a cardiv, which is what we wanted.*** So it was all good stuff on the way up and really quite an experience when I look back on it.

I would think that if certain parts of the media were to find out that that sort of penny ante fighting actually went on, they could really make a big field day out of it. You know, this is typical of the way these guys look at things. This is what the country is putting up with, but they don't know it. I don't know of any rivalry or any

---
*Rear Admiral Paul Masterton, USN, later a vice admiral.
**Admiral Harry D. Felt, USN, was Commander in Chief Pacific from 1958 to 1964. His oral history is in the Naval Institute collection.
***Cardiv--carrier division.

difficulties that are anything like that. But this was the dawn of the nuclear era. We took it seriously. We had kids training in the Navy all over the place that knew exactly where they were going to go. They had a folder to tell them how to get to the target. They studied pictures of their target. They made practice runs where they could be set up for an equivalent ride. All these kids were absolutely ready to go and deliver nuclear weapons all over the place--in Europe, in China, in Siberia, and so on.

But now the emphasis has declined. We're still able to handle those things and are capable of delivering them if it ever has to be done. As long as they still exist, you simply must have a capability to do it. You must be able to do it if the other guy is going to be able to, and if he won't agree not to, and make an agreement that you can check, and all that sort of business. So much more is known about the frightful consequences of a nuclear exchange that it's perhaps the most unlikely thing that any of us have to face. But, at the same time, you have to be fully able to do it if you're going to be in that league.

I certainly hope they're never used, because, among other things, out there and subsequently I've been involved in a lot of war games and a lot of "guess-timates," where you look at how it would be if you respond to a surprise attack, how it would be if you conducted a surprise attack on him, and how would that be done and all that. You know, it just doesn't make a heck of a lot of difference who starts it, or how it starts, or anything. The likelihood is that once it gets started, it will escalate to a full exchange. And it just doesn't make any difference, because both sides suffer such losses that would take centuries to recover from, if they ever did recover.

Now, this business that we've got enough stuff to blow up the world. We don't, but we have enough to blow up anything, and people here, there, and everywhere to such an extent that there wouldn't be any point in going on. That's why it's so worrisome that some nut might get hold of these things--a guy like Qaddafi.* What in the world would you do if he got some of them? Because he might actually go ahead and use them. I think there might be a young group in Russia who never had any wars and don't know the consequences of just a conventional war, and they might be pretty adventurous. They might figure, "What the heck? We can give it to them, and they won't even be able to do very much to us." That could happen, but unless some of these little nutty people get control, I don't think we'll see it.

Q: Admiral, how much of a concern, when you were in OP-60, was the emerging Soviet Navy, which was building up?

---

*Colonel Muammar el-Qaddafi has been the strongman in Libya since overthrowing that country's King Idris in 1969. He has been linked to terrorism in various parts of the world.

Admiral Hyland: Well, it was not particularly of concern. We knew they were certainly advancing, and we were seeing more of them in the Mediterranean than we had before. We saw them occasionally out in the Pacific, but that development, that trend in the Russian Navy, hadn't become as clear as it is now--not at all. While we were in the midst of the Vietnamese problem and I was still around, we had experienced for many years the Russian trawler following you, and observing what you did, mainly from the carriers, and kibitzing on your electronic stuff. All that kind of business. We saw a lot of that.

We had encounters with them. Occasionally, we would have a collision or a near-collision with them. Whenever it happened, when I was in charge out there in the Western Pacific, it would always be the fault of the Russians. It really would. They didn't give a darn about the rules of the road. A couple of times, our ships would be on converging courses; we would hold on, and they would also, and we would bump. I would always send the skipper of our ship a congratulatory message saying, "Good work. Don't let them bluff you. Don't let them push you around." Well, I don't think that encouraged any of them to look for a chance to bump. You don't want to bump anybody when you're skipper of a destroyer or a cruiser or anything else. It's the worst thing that can happen, but if it is one of those chicken games, you really feel--if you're following the rules of the road--why, you should hold on. Go ahead and bump him if necessary. You don't want to.

We weren't as worried about that, because we were fully occupied with that Vietnamese thing. This would span a period from about '63 to '71; all those last years of my active service we were at war, never declared and never prosecuted properly--a very, very sad disappointment. Among my regrets as I got to be CinCPacFlt--I guess I was the third senior officer in the Navy, and I really didn't have anything to say about what we were doing. I could recommend hitting targets and so on. I could agree or comment. I could do that, but everything was decided in Washington, and then told to us.

One of the things I can remember that was disappointing was the way things would be leaked. I don't know who would do it, but you would be about to hit a bunch of targets perhaps that hadn't been hit earlier, and if somebody back in Washington didn't like that, it would be leaked. It could be somebody in the State Department, or it could be a mole in the Pentagon. If could be anybody--I don't know who--but they would leak it. And before you knew it, columnists would be sounding off about this, about expanding the war. So just the most amazing and ridiculous efforts would have to be made to keep things quiet.

Just as I was nearing the end of my career, I remember

a couple of times a flag officer, in this case it was a brigadier in the Air Force, would come out in person. He'd make a trip to Hawaii, and he would stop in CinCPac, and he'd tell them what they were going to do. Then he would continue on out in an airplane, and he would go see Abrams and his people and tell them what was going to be hit.* They were supposed to pass it on down to those who really needed to know. Well, this was done in place of a system that normally would send that kind of directive in a super top secret message, a "burn before you read it," and all that business. But that wasn't good enough, because directives sent on those systems would somehow or other get out. Then people would set to work to foil it, to stop it.

So I felt, again, here I was very senior and really not having any ability to change the way things went. I suppose there are officers in similar jobs now who must sometimes feel the same way. You just simply were not consulted. If you were a loyal officer and you did it the way they wanted it, you might squawk, and you might comment, and you might bemoan what was happening--but all within the system.

Well, as I say, I tend to go from one thing to another. I guess you can detect I still have got these very regretful feelings about what went on and what I might

---

*General Creighton W. Abrams, USA, was Commander U.S. Military Assistance Command Vietnam (MACV) from 1968 to 1971. He later became Chief of Staff of the Army.

have been able to do about it. It's sort of Monday morning quarterbacking. However, I never had any job, and particularly the more senior ones, when later reflecting on what had happened, I didn't feel that if I could do it over again, I could do it better. I didn't see some things, and I made some decisions and so on, and they just weren't right. I could have sounded off, I suppose, but I didn't. I could have decided that, but I didn't. So I thought if I could just do that one more time, if I could have command of the Seventh Fleet another two years, I'd really be a whiz-bang at it, instead of having a certain amount of feeling that I'd fouled up here and there.

Q: You've talked about the desirability of hitting harder with the air offensive earlier. Was there any thought given to, say, amphibious operations or ground operations against North Vietnam?

Admiral Hyland: Yes, there was. And a couple of times, to my recollection, there was a plan--actually, sort of a skeleton and an outline plan--made for an assault on North Vietnam. We had plenty of people that thought that would be a good thing to do. We also had some suggestions that one thing we might do that would be very effective would be to do everything that would indicate that you were going to do it. You can't make a really big amphibious assault anywhere without it becoming known that you were going to do it. There's no way to disguise that. So this idea was you would assemble the ships, and you would practice, and you would deliberately leak some information here and there and act in every way that an assault was pending. And that will really convince them that they better look out and better be worried. However, it never was done.

All the time I was ComSeventhFlt, and subsequently, we did a lot of amphibious landings for practice. Every time the Marines, the amphibious ready group in the Seventh Fleet, would go ashore somewhere in South Vietnam, we would operate by the book. It was amazing to me, but you'd never know whether there was any enemy there or not. They were so good at concealment, or there was something the matter with our information, but you never would know.

We would always say we're not going to have a lot of young Marine kids go ashore and then suddenly get slaughtered because there's a real force waiting there for them, and they know they're coming. So we always prepared the beach with gunfire support. We'd just blast the hell out of a whole area, and then we would go ashore. Everything would be done by the book. All the precautions would be taken. Then we would go in and land these troops, and they would make their way inland. And maybe, after searching and destroying, or whatever it would be for a certain area, they would withdraw.

We always did it exactly like we thought it would have to be done if you had real opposition. We never had any, but we certainly practiced it. Of course, that sort of thing is the lifeblood of the Marines. They're all just really happy to do that. I guess if you're floating around in those amphibious ships with nothing to do but be ready, why, you're delighted to go ashore and do anything to stretch your muscles. We did a great deal of that.

But back to that other point, I think that the administrations--and, of course, we went through quite a number of them, both Democrats and Republicans--always were secretly afraid that China would come into that thing, and here we would really be stuck forever and ever. So they didn't dare to do anything very adventurous. You know, you might go ahead and land in North Vietnam. And there are ways, I'm sure, to send the word privately to the Chinese and say, "Look, we are not going to do anything to China. We are not going to do it." But would they believe it? Chances are, no. When they saw you landing 100 miles south of Hanoi, they'd probably come down across the border north of Hanoi. And there you would have one of these possible faceoffs that would lead to something really big.

I guess our political leaders must have been worried about that, because I don't think it was ever really seriously thought of. It was certainly talked about a lot, and a lot of people thought it could be done and should be done, because practically the only way to defeat somebody is to take over his territory and run it. I'm inclined to believe if you really want to conquer someone, you can't do it solely from the air. You can give him such a beating from the air so quickly, and you can in some cases that he and his people just can't tolerate it, and they'll quit. They'll sue for peace, or they will be willing to negotiate.

Late in the war, when Nixon went back to that fairly large bombing of Hanoi and Haiphong, that was followed by them coming to the table and talking turkey.* I always felt that if that had been done within the first year, and if we'd mined the harbors and really given some heavy blows, that they probably wouldn't have been able to do successfully what they later did. They couldn't have. But I'm inclined to agree with the Army and the Marines that if you're going to win a war, you're going to have to get the enemy-held land. You have to go in there and take it. Now, the air power and certainly nuclear weapons can fix it so they can't do anything to prevent that. But you do eventually have to go in and take charge of the territory if you want to bring someone to his knees and make him do your bidding.

---

*Richard M. Nixon was president from 1969 until his resignation in 1974. He renewed bombing of North Vietnam on a massive scale in late 1972, ending the bombing halt ordered by President Lyndon Johnson in 1968. The peace accords were concluded in early 1973.

It might be possible--it used to be a part of the air force theory, I believe--that you could actually do it from the air. Just make the bombardment so intolerable that nobody could put up with it, and he'd negotiate. The evidence in both cases, from Japan and from Germany, is you can give them a frightful pasting, and they still won't quit. And they can still produce; amazingly, they can still produce things. So perhaps that's just not so, that you can do it entirely from the air. I think that would be my view--you have to get them on the ground also. But in order to get them on the ground, you support that with air.

Q: How much consideration was actively given to mining during the Sixties?

Admiral Hyland: Well, quite a lot of talk went on about it. And it was urged as the thing to do, but it wasn't until much later that it was actually done.* It was after my time when it was actually done. Now, there was an adaptation of, I guess, the standard 500-pound bomb. It had a hydrostatic fuze that you could put on it. In my day, we dropped thousands of them in various rivers and bays to try and stop the coastal traffic and try to stop the river traffic. By and large, I don't think it really had very much of an effect. But it was just one of those

---
*On 9 May 1972, U.S. Navy carrier-based planes mined Haiphong and other harbors in North Vietnam.

things--a little like the effect of the New Jersey bombarding the beach.*

There's no way to check on how effective it was. We didn't have any spies. We didn't have any observers. We didn't have anybody who could infiltrate into those areas and actually check. So you just never knew. It didn't appear to be very effective, however. But you couldn't help but think to yourself that, "If I had a river, a small river, which I was using to transport goods up and down, and to get people across, I certainly wouldn't want to have many mines in that river." And if you know there are some mines, you're going to be a little more cautious about crossing it, or sailing on it. It's just the idea that if somebody knows that you've dropped a mine, he can't tell whether it's a mine that will really work or not. He has to assume that it will.

It might just be a dummy. It would almost have the same effect as if you did it in broad day and a lot of mines; you'd probably get all the foreigners to stay out. They don't want to go in there and take that chance. And the ones that are in may decide to stay in for a while, because they don't want to come out. However, if you're going to put on the effort to do it, it would be silly not

---

*The battleship New Jersey (BB-62) was reactivated from the mothball fleet and recommissioned in 1968. She made one combat deployment that was largely confined to South Vietnam because North Vietnam was put off-limits to bombardment in 1968. She was decommissioned in 1969.

to use real ones so that if they do decide to take the risk, why, you're going to get them anyway.

We've never been as avid about mining in the Navy as we perhaps ought to be. That's one element of the Navy that gets shortchanged from time to time. We didn't have very much of a mine-laying capability. Most of what we did was with the 500-pound bomb business. That was all done by air, and usually done by low-altitude attacks. Again, I say, we had no way of checking whether it was being effective or not. I had one civilian engineer who was attached to CinCPac's staff, and he had the idea that after you'd laid all of these hundreds of 500-pound mines, that one way to check might be to use your ASW capability and follow that up by spreading a bunch of sonobuoys around, and then listen with airborne listeners to see whether you heard any explosions.*

Well, if you know as much as I know about that sort of business, that is absolutely the silliest notion in the whole world. I can remember this fellow was really upset. He was really angry that I wasn't willing to lay on that kind of an effort from our ASW carriers. We always had one of them in the Gulf, too.** They were mainly using their windmills to deliver the mail and move the chaplains around and that sort of business, and help to replenish--not for

---

*ASW--antisubmarine warfare.
**The Gulf of Tonkin adjoins Vietnam.

ASW. But the idea that this kind of an effort ought to check on whether these mines were working or not was ridiculous. All my guys felt the same way. But this one scientist really wanted to give it a go. We were really pressed doing what we were doing, never mind something like that.

You know, when I was in those last two jobs, we put on a large-scale coastal patrol effort called Market Time, and we had a lot of destroyers and smaller boats, Swift boats, patrol boats, and all that going up and down the coast and being out there all the time.* My private view of that was it simply wasn't worth the effort. I don't think there was very much infiltration by the sea from north to south. There may have been some. Occasionally, they would run into a North Vietnamese boat; they would see it and chase it. It would run aground somewhere in South Vietnam, and we would capture it. Usually the people would get off it and disappear. Occasionally, the boat would be found with some ordnance on it. Those incidents were so few and we put on such an effort. I just never thought they were doing it that way. I think they were just plain infiltrating over the ground, down the Ho Chi Minh Trail and Cambodia and Laos, doing it that way. There wasn't much question about it.

---

*The Market Time coastal surveillance patrol was designed to interdict the supply of weapons and supplies by boat to Viet Cong and North Vietnamese forces in South Vietnam.

Q: Well, you can ask the counter question, though. Was it that they sought other means because Market Time was effective?

Admiral Hyland: Well, the Market Time man certainly has an argument when he says that, because you'll never know. You'll never know whether the enemy even knew that it was there. But I think he probably did, though. But we flew a lot of airplanes. We sailed a lot of ships, and a lot of people did a hell of a lot of sea duty.

Now, we always were told by the Marines that these same ships--the destroyers and cruisers and anything that had a good-sized gun--were needed for gunfire support. We always were told by the troops ashore that it was effective, that it really did help them. It was very expensive, and it just wore out all of our guns. It used a hell of a lot of ammunition, and it kept a lot of people up all night. But they claimed it was worthwhile. And, you know, I'm not a Marine or a soldier, and I couldn't see how I had the knowledge to say, "Look, this is ridiculous. It's not doing enough good, and it's costing a billion dollars a week. We're going to stop it."

They would have howled. I decided that if they want it, and they claim that it's helping them, they are going to get it. I'm not going to kibitz that. I had my own private doubts about how valuable it was. Of course, that's Marine dogma. You have to have gunfire support from the ships. They want you to keep alive every caliber gun. They feel you should keep the New Jersey alive solely to have a capability with these really big guns to help them if necessary, and also have a couple of cruisers with their eight-inch guns, some with their six-inch guns. We ought to keep the whole thing alive. I certainly didn't have any knowledge that can disprove that at all.

Q: Well, there was General Greene who, as Commandant of the Marine Corps, coined this term "gun gap" at that time to increase requests for reactivation of the battleships and cruisers.* Were you, as the Seventh Fleet Commander, consulted on that?

Admiral Hyland: No. Actually, the New Jersey didn't come out until after I'd left the Seventh Fleet. By that time, I was CinCPacFlt. One of the most amazing things to me was when that ship on her first trip came into Pearl Harbor.** You know, it's a beautiful ship to look at if you're a mariner or a navy guy. It's a very good-looking ship, so powerful and all that. It drew the biggest crowd that ever assembled at the entrance to Pearl Harbor. Both banks were

---
*General Wallace M. Greene, Jr., USMC, Commandant of the Marine Corps, 1964-67.
**The New Jersey stopped at Pearl Harbor in September 1968 on her way to the gun line in Vietnam.

just jammed with people. We were told that old sailors, all these old turret captains, had volunteered to come back on active duty if they could get the job as turret captain that they had when the battleship navy was in its heyday. That's how they manned the ship. She went out to Vietnam. She'd just arrived, as far as I was concerned. Nobody asked me beforehand if I thought we needed her. I understood that certain politicians thought she was needed.

Q: Senator Russell was instrumental.*

Admiral Hyland: Yes. He was very fond of battleships, and, by God, he wanted a battleship, and he got one. When a war like that is going on, you're not going to fight it if they are going to give you a battleship and you know they are not going to use the same money for anything else. It gets to that point, you know, that it's going to cost a lot, and you think you could use the money better another way. One guy might say you can buy a lot of airplanes for that. The question finally will be asked, "Look, we've talked this from A to Z. Do you want the battleship, or do you want nothing?" So, of course, there is only one answer to that. You take the battleship.

---

*Senator Richard B. Russell (Democrat--Georgia) served in the U.S. Senate from 1933 to 1971.

My father was a battleship skipper way back.* Ever since World War II, I always thought they were definitely over the hill. I didn't have, personally, much use for them. There was a whole group of people in the Navy who did a great deal to hold back the whole development of naval aviation. They just wanted it to be a little support/observing force for them. They didn't see anything further than that. So that bothered some of us. When she came out, she was fairly useful, particularly firing the big guns.

I've been on board a couple of times. I think you ought to support everything you've got. I saw them and made a speech to the crew and all that stuff. I even went down and pulled the trigger firing them. I'll tell you, it's an impressive thing when nine 16-inch guns go off all at the same time. But nobody knew where the hell those shells landed. Only God knows where they landed, because we didn't have any ability to see them hit. You couldn't fly an airplane over the potential target and have him adjust the range or deflection and all that sort of thing like you would if it were a contest at sea. They fire sometimes up to about 20 miles. A lot of people don't understand that a 16-inch gun is like a rifle. It's a naval rifle. It's a hell of a big rifle. The farther away something is, the more it's going to miss.

---
*Captain John J. Hyland, USN, was commanding officer of the USS Nevada (BB-36) from 12 July 1930 to 30 April 1932.

The shells weigh 2,000 pounds. So the dispersion at 15 or more miles is rather large. If you're going to hit anything, you'd be much better advised to put that shell on an airplane and fly over there and drop it on whatever you wanted to hit. If you had no way of observing the fall of the shot, you might just as well not do it, except as a sort of a terror weapon. Just the sight of that magnificent ship offshore--maybe that put the fear of God in a few North Vietnamese. I don't know. But I noticed after a while, just, oh, a year or so, she was recalled and put back out of commission again.* That also cost a lot of money. I remember columnists all the way from Art Buchwald on up jiving at the Navy for having spent all this dough on the rejuvenating of this monster that was out of date.**

Now, I don't know much about their missile battery. There's where the thing is worthwhile, if it's worthwhile at all. Of course, we don't use them in a situation like we had in Lebanon. I notice the big guns were used very briefly in Lebanon, and they weren't effective.*** They stopped using them. But now, because there is enthusiasm

---

*The New Jersey was recommissioned on 6 April 1968 and decommissioned on 17 December 1969. Her combat deployment lasted from September 1968 to May 1969.
**Art Buchwald is a syndicated newspaper columnist who writes in a satirical, often biting style.
***In February 1984, the New Jersey fired about 300 rounds of 16-inch shells at Syrian gunnery positions overlooking the Beirut airport, where the U.S. Marines were based.

for them, they are going to reactivate several of them.* It doesn't do any good even to try to tease somebody about what are they doing all that for, because the present secretary is very full of himself and very sure that that is a good way to get a lot of firepower without too much money.** It is a lot of money, but it's nothing like another way to get it. So I don't know whether they're really worthwhile or not. It's one of those things.

They're very good, strong, and can take a lot of punishment. Some of them have taken some punishment in World War II, and it didn't bother them at all. Their engines have not been run very much. It's sort of like finding an old 1925 Rolls-Royce that's been parked on blocks in some old lady's garage. It's a beautiful thing, and it still runs beautifully. I think they're a little like that. I hope the Tomahawk missiles will work. I think they're still working out the tactics. You know, you have a missile that will fly several hundred miles. How does the ship know where there's a target? So how do you do it?

But the New Jersey was not worth the expense of bringing it out during the Vietnamese War. There was no

---
*At the time of the interview, the New Jersey and the Iowa had been recommissioned. Since then, the Missouri was recommissioned in 1968 and the Wisconsin in 1988.
**John F. Lehman, Jr., was Secretary of the Navy from 1981 to 1987 and a very enthusiastic proponent of the battleship program. He has written about them in his memoir Command of the Seas (New York: Charles Scribner's Sons, 1988).

way to use the ship effectively. If you were going to assault, if you're really going to go in and hammer away at Haiphong and you were willing to risk just driving that baby right up close and just let them have it, you could have knocked the airfield for a loop. You could have knocked down almost everything in the port structure, and so on. But we just never were allowed to do anything like that. So there she was with a fairly large crew. I guess those guns are unique. You don't want to wear them out for nothing. I suppose even the ammunition, I remember, was in relatively short supply. That's a very special kind of bullet.

Q: Admiral, we just had seven bells. Reluctantly, I guess, we call it off for today.

Admiral Hyland: Well, let's see, do you think this session has really been worthwhile?

Q: To me it's fascinating. And I can compare this with other individuals, and you have that unique perspective that people are going to be interested in.

Admiral Hyland: Well, let's hope so.

Index

to

Reminiscences

of

Admiral John J. Hyland, Jr., U.S. Navy (Retired)

AJ Savage (North American)
   Hyland took his boss, Rear Admiral A.M. Pride, for a test flight in this plane in the early 1950s, 288

Aircraft Carriers
   Billet of operations officer instituted in carriers with some trial and error in the late 1940s, 178; U.S. carriers not challenged during the Korean War, 187; see also Barnes (CVE-20); Constellation (CVA-64); Enterprise (CV-6); Forrestal (CVA-59); Franklin D. Roosevelt (CVA-42); Intrepid (CV-11); Kearsarge (CV-33); Lake Champlain (CV-39); Lexington (CV-2); Saratoga (CVA-60)

Aircraft Development
   Relationship between aircraft manufacturers' representatives and the Navy, 57-60

Air Force, U.S.
   Cooperation between the Navy and Air Force in aircraft development after World War II, 162; studied navy dirigibles when developing big bombers in the mid-1940s, 163; established a useful base on Okinawa shortly after World War II, 199-200; teased by the Navy about all the navy-developed aircraft and ordnance they use, 314-315; Hyland sees relationship with Navy as competition, not rivalry, 315-316; interest in nuclear weapons, 327-332; see also Strategic Air Command

Air Forces, U.S. Army
   Operations in the Philippines in 1941, 73, 77-78, 85, 94

Air Group 14
   Carried back home from Saipan at end of World War II by carrier Intrepid (CV-11), 151

Air Group Ten
   Trained at Atlantic City in 1944, 137, 141; contrary to normal practice, kept on board the Intrepid (CV-11) after arriving at Pearl Harbor in January 1945, 142; returned to San Francisco with the Intrepid after she was damaged by a kamikaze attack in April 1945, 142-143; launching attacks on the Japanese home islands when the war ended, 144-145, 148-; mediocre pilot lucked into a group of unskilled kamikazes and became an ace, 146-147; joint hit of Japanese plane near Kyushu, 147-148; postwar air displays over China and the Soviet Union, 149-151; air group disestablished in Alameda after brief time in Saipan, 151-152; casual contacts with air group members after the war, 153-154

Air Warfare
   Hyland sees fallacy in air force theory that a war can be ended solely by intense air attacks, 343-344

Amphibious Operations
   Practice landings conducted by U.S. Seventh Fleet units in the mid-1960s, 340-342

Anacostia Naval Air Station
   Used to iron out bugs in new aircraft in the late 1930s, 60-61; test center moved to Patuxent River early in World War II, 156; Hyland turned down further patrol squadron duty in 1942 to become operations officer at this air station, 123-124; Hyland's experiences piloting for CNO Ernest King and other high officials, 125-140; Hyland's duties when he wasn't flying dignitaries around, 134-135

Anderson, Rear Admiral George W., Jr., USN (USNA, 1927)
   As Commander Carrier Division Six in the late 1950s, concerned himself with the operations of his flagship, the Saratoga (CVA-60)--sometimes to skipper Hyland's distress, 236; Hyland attributes his early selection to flag rank to a glowing fitness report by Anderson, 237; assessed by Hyland, 237-238

Antisubmarine Warfare (ASW)
   Hyland flew an ASW patrol over the Queen Mary when she brought a load of American troops to Australia in 1942, 119; American PBY mistakenly attacked a U.S. submarine off Australia in 1942, 120; possibility offered, but not considered, to use ASW capabilities to determine effectiveness of aerial mining during the Vietnam War, 346-347; see also VX-1

Argentia, Newfoundland
   Home base of aerial barrier patrol between Argentia and the Azores in the late 1950s and early 1960s, 242-243, 246-249, 252-53

Arkansas, USS (BB-33)
   Used for midshipmen summer training cruises in the early 1930s, 17-21

Arresting Gear
   Carriers Enterprise (CV-6) and Yorktown (CV-5) had both fore and after arresting gear in the late 1930s, 54-55

Atlantic Barrier Wing
   Navy-run patrol between Argentia and the Azores in the late 1950s and early 1960s, designed to detect incoming Soviet bombers, 242-53

Atomic Energy Commission (AEC)
   Prolific production of nuclear weapons in the early
   1960s, 327

Austin, Vice Admiral Bernard L., USN (USNA, 1924)
   As director of the Joint Chiefs of Staff in the mid-
   1950s, insisted on a joint approach, rather than service
   bias, 224-225

Australia
   Hyland rescued a downed Australian pilot in early 1942,
   98-102; Patrol Squadron 102 personnel evacuated from Java
   to Australia in the spring of 1942, 111-114; Hyland put
   in charge of a small contingent of planes at Geraldton,
   patrolling the west coast in mid-1942, 116-118;
   infiltration of U.S. military into Australia, 119;
   American submarine attacked by U.S. plane off Geraldton
   in 1942, 120; American desertions during the war, 120-
   122; several American military personnel married
   Australians, 118, 122

Azores
   Navy-operated patrol between Argentia, Newfoundland, and
   the Azores in the late 1950s and early 1960s, 242-243,
   248-249

Barnes, USS (CVE-20)
   Transported Air Group Ten and captured Japanese aircraft
   to Alameda at the end of World War II, 152

Battleships
   Hyland didn't approve of the reactivation of battleships
   for the Vietnam War, or in the 1980s, 345, 349-354; see
   also Arkansas (BB-33); New Jersey (BB-62)

Blackburn, Vice Admiral Paul P., Jr., USN (USNA, 1930)
   Relieved as Commander Seventh Fleet in 1965 due to poor
   health, 305, 318

"Black Cats"
   Success of these nighttime versions of the PBY in the
   Pacific late in World War II showed the benefit of
   experience, 104-105

Black Market
   Semi-official recognition of black market exchange in
   Saigon in the mid-1950s, 209-210

Blue Angels
   performance in Japan in the early 1970s had to be
   canceled due to size of the crowd, 49-50

Brazil
   Brazilian government duplicated the salary of the American naval officer in charge of the U.S. naval mission in the late 1930s, 52-53; discussion of Brazilian naval aviation in the late 1930s, 53; daughter of president allowed to go out on the Enterprise (CV-6) in 1938 to watch flight demonstration, 53-54; see also Rio de Janeiro

Brooks, Ensign Eldon E., USNR
   Pilot in Air Group Ten in 1945 finished off a Japanese plane--that Hyland had riddled with bullets--and got the credit for the kill, 147-148, 153

Burke, Admiral Arleigh A., USN (USNA, 1923)
   As CNO from 1955-61, overwhelmingly interested in Navy concerns, to the exclusion of joint service matters, 226; went to bat for Hyland to get him released from JCS duty so he could command a carrier in 1958, 228-229; went to President Dwight Eisenhower with his opposition to centralized nuclear targeting, 255; started policy of allowing preselection of officers for the Strategic Plans Division (OP-60), 276

Byng, Lieutenant Weston H., USN (USNA, 1956)
   Turned down offer to become Hyland's aide as Pacific Fleet commander in 1967, 303

Carl, Lieutenant Colonel Marion E., USMC
   Characterized as one of the best military pilots ever, Carl was one of a number of quality aviators at the Navy's test flight center in the mid-1940s, 172; flew photo reconnaissance flights over Communist China in the mid-1950s, 201-202

Carrier Division Four
   Hyland was thrilled to receive this plum command in 1962, 265-266; social life while attached to Sixth Fleet, 267; conducted normal operations during the Cuban Missile Crisis of 1962, 268-270

Chafee, John H.
   As Secretary of the Navy from 1969-72, uncomfortable working with older naval officers, 324

Chichi Jima
   Though difficult to approach, Pacific Fleet staff officers visited this island in the mid-1950s to apprise nuclear storage possibilities, 211-212; natives are descendants of English whalers, 212

China
    Hyland and other Patrol Squadron 102 pilots took several
    Chinese Army officers, who'd been in the United States,
    from Olongapo to Hong Kong in the early 1940s, 81-82;
    American pilots put on air displays over China
    immediately after World War II, but were not permitted to
    land there, 149; U.S. pilots conducted photo
    reconnaissance of Communist China in the mid-1950s, 201-
    202; fear that China would get involved in Vietnam War
    colored U.S. policy, 342-343

China Lake, California
    See Naval Weapons Center, China Lake

China Station
    Allure of duty in the Asiatic Fleet in the mid-1930s, 33-
    34

CinCPac
    See Commander in Chief Pacific

CinCPacFlt
    See Commander in Chief Pacific Fleet

Cloukey, Lieutenant Malcolm M., USNR
    Hyland got his only "down" during flight training from
    this instructor in the mid-1930s, 40-41

Coast Guard, U.S.
    Recognized merits of helicopters in the early 1940s
    before the Navy caught on, 169-171

Commander in Chief Pacific
    This billet was combined with Pacific Fleet command when
    Hyland worked on Admiral Felix Stump's staff in the mid-
    1950s, 197-198

Commander in Chief Pacific Fleet
    This billet combined with Pacific Command when Hyland
    worked on Admiral Felix Stump's staff in the mid-1950s,
    197-198; Hyland's duties as air operations officer, 198-
    213; staff officers in the mid-1950s, 213-214

Connolly, Vice Admiral Thomas F., USN (USNA, 1933)
    Fellow naval aviator informally taught Hyland to fly
    helicopters in the mid-1940s, 170; as Deputy Chief of
    Naval Operations (Air) in the mid-1960s, testified before
    Congress that the F-111--strongly supported by the
    Secretary of Defense--was a dog, 312-314

Constellation, USS (CVA-64)
   Engine meant for this carrier, which was under construction in New York in the late 1950s, was put into the damaged Saratoga (CVA-60) instead, 233-235

Cook, Captain Arthur B., USN (USNA, 1905)
   Impressive as commanding officer of the Lexington (CV-2) in the mid-1930s, 27-28

Cooke, Rear Admiral Charles M., USN (USNA, 1910)
   As a top-level planner for CNO Ernest King during World War II, frequently accompanied him on trips, 126-127

Crommelin, Lieutenant Charles L., USN (USNA, 1931)
   Member of flight demonstration team while stationed at Pensacola in the mid-1930s, 48

Cuban Missile Crisis
   Hyland's recollection of this 1962 incident from his vantage point as Commander Carrier Division Four, 267-270

Dahlgren, Virginia
   See Naval Proving Ground, Dahlgren

Davis, Captain William V., Jr., USN (USNA, 1924)
   Favorable assessment of aviator attached to the Patuxent River test center in the mid-1940s, 162-163, 176-177

Defense Department
   Struggle over civilian versus military control of personnel assignments in the mid-1960s, 306-307; question of military officers publicly criticizing civilian officials, 310-312

DeFoney, Lieutenant Commander Clinton G., MC, USN
   Navy doctor at Pensacola in the mid-1930s remembered as a character because of the psychological tests he conducted on pilots, 41-42

Demobilization
   Release of Navymen from active service at the end of World War II, 154

Denfeld, Admiral Louis E., USN (USNA, 1912)
   Hyland sees CNO Denfeld's dismissal after he protested the cancellation of the carrier United States in the late 1940s as an example of the peril of military officers criticizing the civilian hierarchy, 311

The Depression
    Effect on number of applicants to the Naval Academy in the late 1920s-early 1930s, and on the Navy's retention of graduates, 3, 7, 21

Desertions
    Some American submariners deserted in Australia during World War II, 120-122

Distinguished Flying Cross
    Hyland received this award for his difficult rescue of a downed Australian aviator in the early days of World War II, 98-102

Donaho, Lieutenant Commander Doyle G., USN (USNA, 1927)
    Patrol pilot Donaho's plane was destroyed by Japanese fire during the last few minutes of a trip from Pearl Harbor to the Philippines shortly after the outbreak of World War II, 103-104

Douglass, John J. (Democrat-Massachusetts)
    Representative Douglass had to be convinced to give his Naval Academy appointment to Hyland in the late 1920s, 5-6

Doyle, Lieutenant Austin K., USN (USNA, 1920)
    Popular aviator, stationed at the Naval Academy in the early 1930s, influenced Hyland's choice of service selection, 23

Dutch East Indies
    Served as base for U.S. Navy patrol plane operations in late 1941-early 1942, 87-112

Education
    Quality of Brookline High School in Massachusetts in the mid-1920s, 3-4; Hyland's father tried to help his sons get appointments to the Naval Academy, 5, 7; quality of course at the Naval Academy in the early 1930s, 12-13

Edwards Air Force Base, California
    Navy planes tested at Muroc Dry Lake since 1947, 160-161, 187-188, 293-295

Eisenhower, General of the Army Dwight D., USA (Ret.) (USMA, 1915)
    CNO Admiral Arleigh Burke voiced his opposition to centralized nuclear targeting to President Eisenhower in the late 1950s, 255

Elliot, USS (DD-146)
    Towed targets during exercises in the mid-1930s, 31; value of destroyer duty to officer training, 32-33; commanding officer Charles L. Hutton tried to dissuade Hyland from going into aviation training, 34-35

Enterprise, USS (CV-6)
    Shakedown cruise to South America in mid-1938, 51-54; social schedule during shakedown, 52; daughter of Brazilian president allowed to go out on carrier to watch flight demonstration during shakedown, 53-54; forward and after arresting gear, 54; transferred out to the Pacific in 1940, 61; air operations prior to World War II, 62-66

Entwistle, Rear Admiral Frederick I., USN (USNA, 1921B)
    Assessed as head of the Operational Development Force in the early 1950s, 181

Ewen, Lieutenant Commander Edward C., USN (USNA, 1921B)
    As senior officer at the U.S. naval mission in Brazil in the late 1930s, lived in luxury, since the Brazilian government was doubling his salary, 52-53

FF-1 (Grumman)
    First navy plane with retractable landing gear, entered the fleet in 1933, 56

F4B (Boeing)
    These small biplanes compared to the newer Grumman F3F-2, which entered the fleet in the late 1930s, 55

F4U Corsair (Vought)
    Fighter used by Air Group Ten of the Intrepid (CV-11) during operations against the Japanese in the summer of 1945, 145-149

F9F Panther (Grumman)
    Canadian test pilot forced to eject from an F9F during a night flight at Patuxent River in the early 1950s, 287

F-111 (Boeing/General Dynamics)
    Hyland blames aircraft procurement methods for this plane that was intended to be used by both the Air Force and the Navy in the 1960s, 158-159

FR-1 Fireball (Ryan)
    Description of Fireball plane from the mid-1940s, incorporating both reciprocating and jet engines, 167

F7U Cutlass (Grumman)
    Judged to be unsuitable for carrier duty by navy test pilots in the early 1950s, 294-296

F3F-2 (Grumman)
    Takeoff performance of this plane in late 1930s
    operations, 55; Hyland received model of this plane from
    Grumman in the late 1960s, 56-57

F2H Banshee (McDonnell)
    Hyland is forced to eject from his XF2H-1 when he
    collided with a bird during a flight demonstration in May
    1948, 173-176, 280-284

Fighting Squadron Five (VF-5)
    Rivalry with VF-6 in the late 1930s-early 1940s, 66-68

Fighting Squadron Six (VF-6)
    Accompanied the Enterprise (CV-6) on her shakedown cruise
    to South America in mid-1938, 51; planes flown in the
    late 1930s-early 1940s, 55-58; operating routine in
    Hawaii in 1940, 62-66; rivalry with VF-5, 66-68

Fitness Reports
    Potential for good reviews for the skipper of a flag
    ship, 237; Hyland thought his career was sunk when he got
    a favorable but bland fitness report from Rear Admiral
    A.M. Pride in the early 1950s, 289-290; Hyland doesn't
    agree with usual correlation between best flying safety
    record in a squadron and best fitness report, 298;
    Captain Elmo Zumwalt's glowing report from Navy Secretary
    Nitze in the mid-1960s, 322-323

"Flathatting"
    Future astronaut Alan Shepard reprimanded for stunt
    flying at a Maryland beach in the early 1950s, 291-292;
    while not condoning stunt flying, Hyland acknowledges
    that that type of flair is apparent in most excellent
    pilots, 296-299

Flatley, Lieutenant James H., Jr., USN (USNA, 1929)
    Described as the best pilot in Hyland's first squadron in
    the late 1930s, 67, 301-302

Flatley, Lieutenant James H. III, USN (USNA, 1956)
    Compared, as a pilot, to his illustrious father, 301

Focke-Wulf 190
    German jet studied by U.S. Navy test pilots immediately
    after World War II, 156-158

Forrestal, USS (CVA-59)
    Commander Carrier Division Four Hyland objected to his
    flagship, the Forrestal, going into Genoa, Italy, for a
    port visit during the 1962 Cuban Missile Crisis, but he
    was overruled, 268-270

Franklin D. Roosevelt, USS (CVA-42)
    Rotated in and out of Mediterranean ports with the
    Forrestal (CVA-59) in the early 1960s, 270

Gallery, Rear Admiral Daniel V., Jr., USN (USNA, 1921B)
    Colorful officer served with Hyland on the staff of the
    Operational Development Force in early 1950s, 184-85

Gates, Thomas S., Jr.
    As Secretary of Defense in the late 1950s, supported
    joint nuclear targeting, 255

Gehres, Lieutenant Commander Leslie E., USN
    Member of flight demonstration team while stationed at
    Pensacola in the mid-1930s, 48

Genoa, Italy
    The carrier Forrestal (CVA-59) visited this port in the
    fall of 1962, even though Hyland was concerned about her
    safety during the Cuban Missile Crisis, 268-270

Germany
    German jets, studied at the Navy's test flight center
    immediately after World War II, were superior to anything
    the United States had, 156-158

Gershowitz, Lieutenant (junior grade) David, USCG
    Premier Coast Guard pilot taught navy pilots to fly
    helicopters in the mid-1940s, 170

Gliders
    In the early days of naval aviation, gliders were
    considered invaluable in training pilots, 38, 42-43

Great Britain
    Quality of early British jet aircraft compared to
    Germany's in the post-World War II period, 158

Grumman Aircraft Company
    Design of the F3F-2 fighter in the 1930s, 56; presented
    Hyland with a model of the F3F-2 in the late 1960s, 56-
    57; tried to recruit Hyland for employment in the early
    1950s, 289; see also FF-1; F9F; F7J; F3F-2

Gunfire Support
    Marines insisted the bombardment of the coastline was
    effective during the Vietnam War, but Hyland doesn't feel
    that can be proven, 345, 348-349

Hague, Rear Admiral Wesley M., USN (USNA, 1920)
   As commandant of the Industrial College of the Armed
   Forces from 1952-55, favored rigid scheduling of
   students, 191

Hart, Admiral Thomas C., USN (USNA, 1897)
   Hyland's recollections of Naval Academy Superintendent
   Hart from the early 1930s, 13-15; Hyland had pleasant
   associations with Hart when both were stationed in the
   Philippines in the early 1940s, 14; foresaw threat from
   the Japanese as Commander in Chief Asiatic Fleet in the
   early 1940s, 75-76; conferred with Hyland shortly before
   sending him to Spratly Islands to look for rumored
   Japanese buildup there, 79-80; message about Pearl Harbor
   attack, 81

Hawaii
   See Pearl Harbor

Helicopters
   Casualness of training when helicopters were first tested
   in the mid-1940s, 168-169

Hong Kong
   Hyland flew Chinese officers and civilians from the
   Philippines to Hong Kong in 1941, 81-82; visited by the
   seaplane tender Onslow (AVP-48) in the mid-1950s, 216-218

Hutton, Lieutenant Charles L., USN (USNA, 1920)
   As commanding officer of the Elliot (DD-146) in the mid-
   1930s, tried to discourage Hyland from choosing aviation,
   34-35

Hyland, Captain John J., USN (USNA, 1900)
   Duty in turbine experimental laboratory at the
   Philadelphia Navy Yard in 1912, 2; assisted sons in
   procuring appointments to the Naval Academy, 5-7; advice
   to son who was faced with being expelled from the
   academy, 25; recalled to active duty during World War II,
   35; supported son's decision to go into aviation, 35-36;
   changed his opinion of Ernest King after the CNO wrote
   him to praise John, Jr.'s flying skills, 128

Hyland, Admiral John J., Jr., USN (USNA, 1934)
   Birth and early years, 1-3; siblings, 3-4; wife and
   children, 73, 115, 266, 284; high school in
   Massachusetts, 3-4, 7; Naval Academy midshipman from
   1930-34, 8-25; duty in the Lexington (CV-2) from 1934-35,
   26-31; duty in the Elliot (DD-146) in 1935-36, 31-35;
   suffered seasickness, 32; flight training at Pensacola in
   the mid-1930s, 38-50; duty with Fighter Squadron Six in
   1937-40, 50-68; duty with Patrol Squadron 26, July to

December 1940, 70-72, 78-80, 105; pilot with Patrol Squadron 102 from 1940-42, 72-114; attached to Patrol Squadron 101 from March to June 1942, 116-122; operations officer at Naval Air Station, Anacostia, from 1942-44, 116, 123-141; Commander Air Group Ten from 1944-45, 137, 141-154; air officer in the Lake Champlain (CV-39) from January to August 1946, 154-155; assistant director of flight test at the Naval Air Test Center, Patuxent River, from 1946-49, 155-177, 279-284; operations officer, USS Kearsarge (CV-33), 1949-59, 178-180; staff, Operational Development Force, 1950-51, 180-185; director of the Tactical Test Division, Naval Air Test Center, Patuxent River, 1951-53, 185-188, 284-299; student at the National War College, 1953-54, 188-194; air operations officer on the staff of Commander in Chief Pacific Fleet, 1954-55, 194-214; commanding officer, USS Onslow (AVP-48), 1956-57, 214-19; member of the Atomic Energy Team, Joint Strategic Plans Group, Joint Chiefs of Staff, 1957-58, 220-226; commanding officer, USS Saratoga (CVA-60), 1958-59, 227-242; Commander Atlantic Barrier Wing, 1959-60, 242-253; Commander in Chief Atlantic Representative, Joint Strategic Target Planning, 1960-62, 253-265, 326-336; Commander Carrier Division Four, 1962-63, 265-271; assistant director and director, Strategic Plans Division, OpNav, 1963-65, 271-278, 304-317, 326-328, 336-337; Commander Seventh Fleet, 1965-67, 317-326, 338-349; Commander in Chief Pacific Fleet, 1967-70, 338-339, 349-350; consultant to Vought Corporation after retirement from the Navy in 1971, 59

Hyland, Midshipman John J., III, USN (USNA, 1962)
Hyland compares his son's experiences at the Naval Academy to his own, 8-9, 11; as a boy he was impressed by his father's collision with a bird, 284

Hyland, Captain William W., SC, USN (Ret.) (USNA, 1935)
Followed his father and his brother to the Naval Academy in the early 1930s, 3-4, 7; swim team captain at the Naval Academy in the mid-1930s, 16

International Security Affairs (ISA)
Former Defense Assistant Secretary Nitze kept his ISA executive assistant, Captain Elmo Zumwalt, when he became Navy Secretary in 1963, 321-322; characterized as State Department element of the Defense Department, 326

Intrepid, USS (CV-11)
Kept air group aboard after arriving in Pearl Harbor in January 1945, 142; returned to San Francisco for repairs after kamikaze attack in April 1945, 142-143; operations against Japan in the summer of 1945, 144-145; postwar operations out of Okinawa, 149; carried Air Group 14 back to the States from Saipan in late 1945, 151; see also Air Group Ten

Japan
The U.S. Navy's Blue Angels flight demonstration team drew large crowds at the Nagoya air show in 1971, 49-50; Japanese ships shadowed U.S. naval vessels and aircraft prior to World War II, 63, 75-76; Hyland didn't foresee imminent war with Japan prior to the Pearl Harbor attack, 64, 74-75, 80-81; night flying by Japanese pilots before the outbreak of World War II, 65; Japanese planes attacked U.S. Navy planes at Manila shortly after the Pearl Harbor attack, 85-86; Japanese planes outperformed U.S. Army Air Forces P-40s, 94; Japanese pilots defended Jolo in December 1941, 96-98; Japanese planes attacked American pilots off Darwin, 106-108; U.S. Navy pilots attacked Japanese ships at Menado, 109-111

Java
Patrol Squadron 102 relocated to Surabaja when it became too dangerous to operate from the Philippines in 1942, 103, 108; planes were able to be hidden in swampy inland areas of Java, 108-109; hospitality of the Dutch to American pilots, 109; patrol operations from Surabaja, 109-111

Jet Aircraft
Various countries' early jet engines compared from the post-World War II period, 155-158; dead-stick landings, 187-188, 293-294

Johnson, Louis
Hyland sees Defense Secretary Johnson's firing of CNO Louis Denfeld after he protested the scrapping of plans for the carrier United States (CVA-58) as an example of what happens when military officers publicly criticize civilian officials, 311

Johnson, Admiral Roy L., USN (USNA, 1929)
As Commander Pacific Fleet in 1965, approved choice of Hyland as Commander Seventh Fleet, 318-319

Joint Chiefs of Staff (JCS)
Hyland thought it was a dubious honor to be assigned to the Joint Staff in 1957, because he felt the quality of naval officers sent there was slightly less than the best, 220; discussion of the "rainbow team," which allocated nuclear weapons in the mid-1950s, 221-224, 226; Navy accused of using Joint Staff duty as transient assignment, 228-229; inter-service disagreements in the mid-1950s over the value of an Atlantic barrier patrol, 244; Joint Strategic Capabilities Plan, 274-275; Joint Strategic Operations Plan, 274-275; see also Strategic Plans Division

Joint Strategic Target Planning Staff (JSTPS)
Navy opposed centralized targeting in the early 1960s, 254-255, 261-264; Navy sent top-notch representatives to make sure they weren't shortchanged on nuclear responsibility, 256, 261, 326-336; Hyland charged with assuring prominent role for Atlantic Command in nuclear planning in the early 1960s, 257; see also Strategic Air Command

Jolo, Philippines
Target of unsuccessful attack by U.S. PBYs in late December 1941, 95-98

Kamikazes
USS Intrepid (CV-11) attacked by kamikazes on 16 April 1945, 142-143; characterized as a manageable menace in closing days of the war, 145-148

Kearsarge, USS (CV-33)
Position of operations officer instituted in the late 1940s, 178; mothballed as an austerity method right before the outbreak of the Korean War, 179

King, Admiral Ernest J., USN (USNA, 1901)
Hyland apprehensive when selected to be CNO King's private pilot in 1942, 124-125, 132; typical flying schedule. 125, 127; frequently met with Admiral Nimitz in San Francisco, 125-126, 137-138; assessed by Hyland, 127-136, 138-140; wrote to Hyland's father to praise pilot Hyland's skills, 128; anecdote showing King's character by Hyland's predeccesor as pilot, 132-133; faith in his close subordinates, 134; possessive about use of his plane, 135-136; mildly pressed for landing at Quebec in August 1943 despite poor weather, 138-139; offered Hyland choice of assignments when his tour as pilot was up in 1944, 137, 140

Kirkpatrick, Commander Charles C., USN (USNA, 1931)
   As aide to CNO Ernest King during World War II, advised pilot, Hyland, about their boss's schedule, 131-132; sent to discuss Hyland's choice for next in 1944, 137

Korean War
   U.S. aircraft carriers not challenged during war, 187

Krulak, Midshipman Victor H., USN (USNA, 1934)
   Like Hyland, almost required to resign from the Naval Academy due to his height, 24-25; background of nickname, "Brute," 25-26; assessed by Hyland, 26

Lake Champlain, USS (CV-39)
   Decommissioned in 1946 shortly after completing Magic Carpet runs, 154-155

Land, Rear Admiral Emory S., USN (USNA, 1902)
   As chairman of the U.S. Maritime Commission during World War II, often flown around the country by Hyland, 136

Lanman, Lieutenant Commander Charles B., USN (USNA, 1932)
   As CNO Ernest King's aide during World War II, advised pilot, Hyland, of his boss's schedule, 131-132

Leahy, Rear Admiral William D., USN (USNA, 1897)
   As Chief of the Bureau of Navigation in the mid-1930s, approached by Hyland's father about his son's potential expulsion from the Naval Academy, 25

Lebanon
   Use of the New Jersey (BB-62)'s 16-inch guns in February 1984, 352

Lee, Lieutenant Fitzhugh, USN (USNA, 1926)
   Remembered favorably as a flight instructor at Pensacola in the mid-1930s, 44-45, 48

LeMay, General Curtis E., USAF
   Leadership style as commander of the Strategic Air Command in 1948-57 compared to his successor, General Power, 257-258

Lexington, USS (CV-2)
   Hyland was further influenced to become a pilot during his first officer assignment, to this carrier in the mid-1930s, 26-30; Pacific operations in the mid-1930s, 31

Libby, Captain Ruthven E., USN (USNA, 1922)
   Accompanied CNO Ernest King on many of his frequent trips during World War II, 126-127

Lighter-than-air
    Air Force studied and utilized apparatus from dirigibles
    during development of big bombers in the mid-1940s, 163;
    debate over value of this program continued well into the
    1970s, 163-164

Lomasney, Martin M.
    Political boss of Boston in the early 1930s helped the
    Hyland boys get appointments to the Naval Academy, 5-7

Los Angeles, USS (ZR-3)
    The Air Force studied the trapeze apparatus of this navy
    dirigible in the mid-1940s when developing big bombers,
    163

MacArthur, General Douglas, USA (USMA, 1903)
    Kept his dependents in the Philippines much later than
    the Navy did prior to World War II, 73-74, 84; reportedly
    wanted to use nuclear weapons during the Korean War, 205

McDonald, Admiral David L., USN (USNA, 1928)
    Hyland believes that Commander Sixth Fleet McDonald
    agreed with him that it was foolhardy for the Forrestal
    (CVA-59) to proceed with an Italian port visit during the
    1962 Cuban Missile Crisis, but both were overruled, 268-
    269; dealings with Strategic Plans Division in the mid-
    1960s, 273, 316-317; approached Hyland about becoming
    Commander Seventh Fleet in 1965, 318-319

McNamara, Robert S.
    Imposed much more control on senior naval officers as
    Secretary of Defense in the early 1960s than his
    predecessor had, 305-306; criticized for pushing the F-
    111 down the throats of both the Navy and the Air Force
    in the 1960s, 313-314; supported strong Air Force role in
    nuclear delivery, 331

Marine Corps, U.S.
    Conducted photo reconnaissance of mainland China in the
    mid-1950s, 201-202; practiced amphibious landings in the
    Seventh Fleet in the mid-1960s, 340-342; appreciated the
    value of naval gunfire support in the Vietnam War, 348-
    349

Market Time Operation
    Hyland felt this large-scale coastal patrol during the
    Vietnam War wasn't worth the effort, 347-348

Martin, Rear Admiral William I., USN (USNA, 1934)
    After being considered for Commander Seventh Fleet, which
    Hyland got in 1965, was chosen as Commander Sixth Fleet
    instead, 319-320

Masterton, Rear Admiral Paul, USN (USNA, 1933)
    After serving in difficult position as Pacific Fleet
    representative on the Joint Strategic Planning Team in
    the early 1960s, rewarded with command of a carrier
    division, 334

Mediterranean Sea
    Rough sea conditions encountered by the carrier Saratoga
    (CVA-60) in 1959, 240; see also Sixth Fleet, U.S.

Menderes, Adnan
    Hyland met the Premier of Turkey in the late 1950s
    shortly before he was deposed, 241-242

Me 262 (Messerschmitt)
    German jet was studied by U.S. Navy test pilots
    immediately after World War II, 156-158

Mines
    Use during the Vietnam War, 344-346; civilian scientist
    suggested impractical method of checking effectiveness of
    aerial mining, 346-347

Minter, Commander Charles S., Jr., USN (USNA, 1937)
    Hyland's son's comment to test pilot Minter after Hyland
    collided with a bird in 1948, 284

Mississippi, USS (AG-128)
    Aviation equipment tested on this ship by the Operational
    Development Force in the early 1950s, 182

Moorer, Admiral Thomas H., USN (USNA, 1933)
    Hyland relieved Moorer as a fighter squadron section
    leader in the late 1930s, 56-57; Moorer was helpless when
    a Japanese fighter attacked his patrol plane during World
    War II, 106-108; sent home with Hyland in mid-1942 in the
    West Point (AP-23), 114-115; Hyland enjoyed having his
    friend, Moorer, riding in his carrier as Commander
    Carrier Division Six in the late 1950s, 237; advised
    Hyland when rumors of his consideration as Commander
    Seventh Fleet were being circulated in 1965, 317-318;
    young Navy Secretary Chafee told CNO Moorer he was
    uncomfortable working with older officers, 324

Mothballing
    Kearsarge (CV-33) mothballed just prior to the outbreak
    of the Korean War, 178; time necessary to de-mothball a
    ship, 179-180

Munsch, Warrant Officer Albert S., USMC
    Reputation as an good, but tough, flight instructor in
    the mid-1930s, 46-47

Muroc Dry Lake
   See Edwards Air Force Base

National War College
   Background of naval students compared to other service students, 189; Hyland's experiences there in 1953-54, 189-94; value of joint service exposure, 192-193

Naval Academy, U.S.
   Hyland boys had some difficulties in getting political appointments in the early 1930s, 5-7; hazing in the early 1930s, 9-10; discipline, 10-11; regimen in the early 1930s, 12-13; Hyland's involvement with athletics, 15-17; summer cruises in the early 1930s compared to the 1970s, 17-21; applicants and graduates affected by the Depression, 3, 7, 21; flights during summer break to recruit naval aviators, 22-24

Naval Air Test Center, Patuxent River
   Tested early jets in the mid-1940s, 155; foreign aircraft studied, 156-158; equipment studied in the mid-1940s, 159; cooperation with the Air Force, 162; test pilot school established in the mid-1940s, 166-167; helicopter training, 168-170; mission of the flight test division, 171; when Hyland's plane collided with a bird during a May 1948 flight demonstration he was forced to eject, 173-176, 280-284; tactical test division, 185-188, 286, 288; practiced dead-stick landings, 187-188, 293-294; Hyland punished pilot who flew a test plane without reading its handbook, 297

Naval Aviation
   Dubious reputation of aviation community in the mid-1930s, 34-36; safety of flying in the mid-1930s, 37; flight demonstration team in the mid-1930s, 48-49; camaraderie of aviation community prior to World War II, 68-69; Hyland is critical of current aircraft procurement methods, 158-159; some pilots mistakenly assume that if they can fly, then maneuvering a ship will be easy, 218-219; Hyland feels there should be a balance between safety and fully utilizing aircraft, 298-299; Hyland worried that in a real war situation, the Navy would run out of airplanes, 299-300; contribution to aviation at large, 314-315; Hyland sees relationship with Air Force as competition, not rivalry, 315-316; see also Training--Aviation; Night Flying; Jet Aircraft; Lighter-than-air; Helicopters; "Flathatting"

Naval Proving Ground, Dahlgren, Virginia
   Aircraft bomb performance studied here in the mid-1940s, 160

Naval Weapons Center, China Lake
   Worked on armament developments in the mid-1940s, 161

New Jersey, USS (BB-62)
   Hyland doesn't believe the reactivation of this battleship for the Vietnam War was worth the cost, 345, 349-354; attracted huge crowd when she visited Pearl Harbor in September 1968, 349-350; see also Lebanon

Night Flying
   Bare minimum of night flying done prior to World War II due to risk, 62-63, 66; during World War II, 65

Nimitz, Admiral Chester W., USN (USNA, 1905)
   As Commander in Chief Pacific Ocean Areas, had frequent meetings with CNO Ernest King during World War II, 125-126, 137-138

Nitze, Paul H.
   Navy Secretary Nitze put in an awkward position on the issue of a joint Navy-Air Force plane--the F-111--in the 1960s, 314-315; Hyland appalled that Nitze didn't care who became Commander Seventh Fleet in 1965, 318-319; held aide Elmo Zumwalt in high esteem, 321-323

North Carolina, USS (ACR-12)
   Hyland's father served in this armored cruiser in 1915 when she launched aircraft by catapult off Pensacola, 35-36

Nuclear Warfare
   Hyland involved in nuclear strike planning while on Pacific Fleet staff in the mid-1950s, 202-203; attitude towards nuclear warfare in the mid-1950s, 203-204; Hyland's thoughts on the use of nuclear force, 204-206, 335-336

Nuclear Weapons
   Navy worked to get smaller, lighter weapons that could be carried on tactical planes in the mid-1950s-early 1960s, 202, 327, 334-335; allocation of weapons studied by the "rainbow team" of the Joint Chiefs of Staff in the mid-1950s, 221-224; see also Joint Strategic Target Planning Staff (JSTPS)

Okinawa
   Pacific Fleet staff concerned with lack of proper airfield here in the mid-1950s, 199-200

Onslow, USS (AVP-48)
   Hyland considered himself lucky to get command of a small seaplane tender in 1956, though during World War II he turned down an AVP in favor of an air group, 215; duties were modified since seaplanes were on their way out by the mid-1950s, 216-217; at Hong Kong in the mid-1950s, 216-218

Operational Development Force (OpDevFor)
   Discussion of OpDevFor mission in the early 1950s, 180-184; benefit gained by navy testing versus company technicians, 183-184

Ortland, Henry
   As Naval Academy swimming coach in the early 1930s, 16

Owen, Edward M.
   As Vought's chief experimental pilot in the early 1950s, refused to fly an F7U from Patuxent River, 295

PBY Catalina (Consolidated)
   Flown by Patrol Squadron 102 around the Philippines in the early 1940s, 70; Hyland made secret reconnaissance flight to the Spratly Islands in late 1941 in a PBY, 79; the Dutch had a version purchased from the United States, 90; engine replacement, 91; ineffective against fighter attack, 95-98, 105-106, 110-111; Hyland landed a PBY on open ocean to rescue a downed Australian pilot, 98-102; engine fire on flight from Java to Australia, 112-114; Australian PBYs flew surveillance patrols in 1942, 116-117, 119-120; Soviet pilot, flying American-made PBY, fired on U.S. Navy plane in the immediate postwar period, 149-150; see also "Black Cats"

Pacific Fleet, U.S.
   Work of the staff of the commander in chief, Admiral Felix Stump, in the mid-1950s, 194-214

Patrol Squadron 22 (VP-22)
   Flew from Pearl Harbor to Ambon via Australia in the early days of World War II, 103-104

Patrol Squadron 26 (VP-26)
   Transferred from Pearl Harbor to the Philippines in late 1940, 70-71; routine patrols off Hawaii in 1940 used more for training purposes, 71-72; Hyland chosen for secret reconnaissance mission to the Spratly Islands, 78-80; camera gun fighter practice in 1940, 105

Patrol Squadron 101 (VP-101)
    Hyland was in charge of a small PBY contingent flying patrols out of Geraldton, Australia, in the spring of 1942, 116-122

Patrol Squadron 102 (VP-102)
    Squadron moved from Hawaii to the Philippines in late 1940, 71-72; conducted more serious patrols as relations with Japan deteriorated, 72, 75-77, 82-83; morale flagged during constant state of readiness prior to outbreak of war, 74-75, 77; squadron planes ferried Chinese Army officers from Olongapo to Hong Kong, 81-82; disastrous bombing raid on Jolo in December 1941, 95-98; Hyland rescued downed Australian pilot, 98-102; squadron forced to relocate from Ambon to Surabaja due to Japanese successes in the Philippines, 103-104; camera gun fighter practice in the early 1940s, 105-106; operations from Surabaja, 109-111; Hyland's plane caught fire during final evacuation from Tjilatjap to Australia in the spring of 1942, 111-114

Patuxent River, Maryland
    See Naval Air Test Center, Patuxent River

Pearl Harbor
    Few of Hyland's friends foresaw Japanese attack in December 1941, 64, 74-75, 80-81; Patrol Squadron 26 was based on Ford Island in 1940, 70-72

Pensacola Naval Air Station
    Officers stationed at Pensacola in the mid-1930s, 44-47; atmosphere of Pensacola in the mid-1930s, 47; see also Training--Aviation

P-59 Aircomet (Bell)
    First U.S.-built jet attracted many curious pilots at the Navy's test flight center at Patuxent River in the mid-1940s, 167-168

Philippine Islands
    Evacuation of navy dependents from the Philippines long before the Army prior to World War II was indicative of underlying conservatism of Navy, 72-74; few dealings between Army and Navy personnel in the early 1940s, 77-78; Hyland led unsuccessful bombing attack on Jolo in December 1941, 95-98; Patrol Squadron 102 forced to relocate from Ambon to Surabaja in early 1942 due to Japanese successes, 103-104

Picher, Lieutenant General Oliver S., USAF
  As director of the Joint Chiefs of Staff in the mid-1950s, bent over backwards to make sure that he didn't favor the Air Force, 225; conviction that the Navy used the JCS as a temporary assignment almost cost Hyland command of the Saratoga (CVA-60) in 1958, 228-229

Planning
  See Joint Strategic Target Planning Staff; Strategic Plans Division (OP-60), OpNav

Polaris Program
  Successful testing of submarine-launched Polaris missiles coincided with assignment of nuclear responsibilities among the services in the late 1950s, 256, 261-262, 330, 332; Air Force officer cheered failure of Polaris test firing in the late 1950s, 332-333

Power, General Thomas S., USAF
  Assessed as commander of the Strategic Air Command from 1957-64, 257-260, 262; didn't think the Navy was reliable enough to be included in nuclear planning, 259-260, 329-330; cheered failure of navy Polaris test firing in the late 1950s, 332-333

Pride, Admiral Alfred M., USN
  Disestablished the tactical test section at the Patuxent River test center in 1953, 285-286, 288, 295; assessed by Hyland, 287-291; notorious for giving reserved fitness reports, 289-290; concerned about future astronaut Alan Shepard's stunt flying at a Maryland beach in the early 1950s, 291-292

P2V Neptune (Lockheed)
  P2Vs studied at Patuxent River in the late 1940s, 171

Pyne, Rear Admiral Schuyler N., USN (USNA, 1925)
  Commander of the New York Naval Shipyard in the late 1950s when an innovative engine shift was done between the Constellation (CVA-64) and the Saratoga (CVA-60), 233-235

el-Qaddafi, Colonel Muammar
  Hyland concerned that an unstable leader, like this Libyan strongman, could wreak havoc if he had access to nuclear weapons, 336

Quebec Conference
  CNO Ernest King pressed for landing in Quebec for this August 1943 Allied conference despite poor weather conditions, 138-139

Queen Mary
    Hyland flew an antisubmarine patrol over this former
    passenger liner while she was bringing American troops to
    Australia in 1942, 119

R50 Lodestar (Lockheed)
    Executive transport used by Admiral Ernest J. King for
    long flights during World War II, 126-140

Radar Picket Ships
    Modified destroyer escorts used in the late 1950s and
    early 1960s to be ready to detect incoming Soviet
    bombers, 249-250

Radford, Rear Admiral Arthur W., USN (USNA, 1916)
    As Chairman of the Joint Chiefs of Staff in the mid-
    1950s, interested in nuclear storage possibilities at
    Chichi Jima, 211

Rio de Janeiro, Brazil
    Hosted Enterprise (CV-6) crew and air personnel during
    shakedown cruise in mid-1938, 52

Rosendahl, Vice Admiral Charles E., USN (Ret.) (USNA, 1914)
    Outspoken advocate of Navy's airship program until his
    death in 1977, 164

Sabin, Rear Admiral Lorenzo S., USN (USNA, 1921B)
    As Commander Amphibious Force Western Pacific in the mid-
    1950s, visited by Pacific Fleet staff officers after
    evacuating civilians from southern Vietnam, 209-210

San Francisco, California
    Elegant accommodations for CNO Ernest King and his
    entourage when meeting with other ranking naval officers
    during World War II, 138

Saratoga, USS (CVA-60)
    Accidental flooding of engineering space at Mayport in
    1958, 230-232; overhauled at Norfolk in the late 1950s,
    232; received an engine meant for the Constellation (CVA-
    64), under construction in New York, 233-235; operations
    in 1959, 235; value of being a flagship, 236-237;
    Mediterranean cruise in the late 1950s, 238-242

Seventh Fleet, U.S.
    Fleet commander Paul Blackburn temporarily incapacitated
    in 1965 and replaced by Hyland, 305, 318-319; practiced
    amphibious landings in the mid-1960s, 340-342

Sharp, Captain Ulysses S. Grant, Jr., USN (USNA, 1927)
   Came to Pacific Fleet staff in the mid-1950s as deputy
   chief of staff (operations and plans), 207-208; Sharp's
   boss, Admiral Felix Stump, thought highly of his deputy,
   208; trip to Saigon in the mid-1950s, 207-209; Hyland's
   assessment of, 213; Hyland feels that Sharp used his
   influence to bring him to the Strategic Plans Division in
   the mid-1960s, 278

Shepard, Lieutenant Alan B., Jr., USN (USNA, 1945)
   Got into trouble as a test pilot in the early 1950s for
   stunt flying at Ocean City, Maryland, 291-292; assessed
   by Hyland, 288, 292-293; developed fighter tactics as a
   test pilot, 293

Sherby, Commander Sydney S., USN (USNA, 1936)
   Engineer at flight test division of the Patuxent River
   test center became the first head of the test pilot
   school in the mid-1940s, 166-167

Shiphandling
   Hyland's experiences while in command of the small
   seaplane tender USS Onslow (AVP-48) in the mid-1960s,
   218-219; encounters between U.S. and Soviet warships in
   the mid-1960s, 337-338

Sikorsky, Igor I.
   Brought one of his earliest helicopters to the Navy's
   test flight center at Patuxent River in the mid-1940s,
   168

Single Integrated Operational Plan (SIOP)
   Joint-service nuclear weapons targeting plan developed in
   the early 1960s, 254-260, 328-332

Sixth Fleet, U.S.
   Operations of the aircraft carrier Saratoga (CVA-60)
   during a 1959 deployment to the Mediterranean, 237-242;
   operating routine for aircraft carriers in the early
   1960s, 267-271

Soucek, Rear Admiral Apollo, USN (USNA, 1921B)
   Asked Hyland to relate his experiences when he was forced
   to eject his plane after colliding with a bird at
   Patuxent River in 1948, 283-284

Soviet Union
    Soviets hostile to American pilots in immediate post-
    World War II period, 149-150; U.S. Navy maintained a
    constant aerial patrol between Argentia and the Azores in
    the late 1950s for early detection of a possible Soviet
    attack, 242-253; built planes for quantity, not quality,
    300; concern caused by buildup of the Soviet Navy in the
    mid-1960s, 336-337

Spratly Islands
    Hyland chosen to fly secret reconnaissance mission to
    Spratly shortly before the Japanese attack on Pearl
    Harbor, 78-80

Staff Duty
    Value to an officer's understanding of the Navy, 196

Storrs, Vice Admiral Aaron P. III, USN (USNA, 1923)
    Hyland recalls Storr's attractive oriental wife when both
    served on the Pacific Fleet staff in the mid-1950s, 214

Strategic Air Command (SAC)
    Prominence of SAC in Joint Strategic Target Planning
    Staff in the early 1960s caused the Navy concern, 254-
    260, 327-331; rigid standard of readiness demanded of
    officers, 262-265

Strategic Plans Division (OP-60), OpNav
    Mission of navy liaison with the Joint Chiefs of Staff in
    the mid-1960s, 272-278, 304; interest in the Vietnam War,
    310

Stump, Admiral Felix B., USN (USNA, 1917)
    Assessed as Commander in Chief Pacific Fleet/Pacific
    Command in the mid-1950s, 195-196; duties and interests
    as Pacific commander, 198-201, 208-209

Submarine Duty
    Poor conditions on board older U.S. submarines during
    World War II, 120-121

Surabaja, Dutch East Indies
    Base for U.S. Navy PBY operations in late 1941-early
    1942, 89-93, 103, 108-109, 111-112

Taiwan
    Navy photo reconnaissance flights from Taiwan to the
    Chinese Communist mainland in the mid-1950s, 201-202;
    assessment of Nationalist Chinese Air Force in the mid-
    1950s, 206-207

Tate, Lieutenant Commander Jackson R., USN
    Hyland's recollections of Tate as a squadron commander at Pensacola in the mid-1930s, 45, 48

Test Pilots
    Tested new navy aircraft at Patuxent River in the late 1940s, 156-177; tactical testing of planes in the early 1950s, 185-188; 279-299

Thach, Vice Admiral John S., USN (USNA, 1927)
    Skilled aviator's reputation among younger pilots in the mid-1960s, 300-301

Thanos, Ensign James, USNR
    American pilot who married an Australian girl in mid-1942 was killed shortly after bringing her home to the United States, 118

Tibbets, Rear Admiral Joseph B., USN (USNA, 1934)
    Hyland's roommate in the Lexington (CV-2) in the mid-1930s was similarly influenced to go into naval aviation, 30

Training--Aviation
    Summer program for midshipmen in the early 1930s, 22-24; flight training in the mid-1930s, 38-43, 46-48; quality of instructors in the mid-1930s, 43; poor quality of preparation for World War II, 105; test pilot school established at Patuxent River in the mid-1940s, 166-167; haphazard method of teaching naval aviators how to fly helicopters in the mid-1940s prior to establishment of a training school, 168-169

Trapnell, Captain Frederick M., USN (USNA, 1923)
    When Trapnell, head of the Navy's flight test program at Anacostia, went overseas during World War II, the test center was moved from Anacostia to Patuxent River, 156; assessed as aviator and mentor, 162-163, 177, 279-280; Hyland credits Trapnell with life-saving advice, 280-281

Turkey
    Hyland developed a favorable impression of Premier Adnan Menderes during a visit to Istanbul in the carrier Saratoga (CVA-60) in 1959, 241-242

Twining, General Nathan F., USAF (USMA, 1919)
    As Chairman of the Joint Chiefs of Staff in 1958, agreed to release Hyland early from JCS duty so he could command a carrier, but then changed policy to enforce length of duty, 228-229

Typhoons
   Difficulties for airfield on Okinawa in the mid-1950s, 199-200

Ulithi
   The carrier Intrepid (CV-11) used this atoll as an anchorage between operations late in World War II, 143-144

VX-1
   Special squadron organized by the Operational Development Force to test the latest antisubmarine warfare equipment, 181

Vietnam
   Patrols over Camranh Bay in the early 1940s to look for Japanese buildup there, 83; U.S. amphibious ships moved large number of Catholics to southern Vietnam after partitioning took place in the mid-1950s, 207, 209; Pacific Fleet staff officers visited Saigon after evacuation, 207-210; see also Black Market; Vietnam War

Vietnam War
   Hyland feels the late 1960s were not a favorable time to be a flag officer, because they were forced to fight a war with their hands tied, 308-311, 338-339; difficulties controlling leaks to the media, 338-339; choice of targets, 308-310, 338; plan for an amphibious assault on North Vietnam, 340-341; fear that China would enter war colored U.S. policy, 342-343; Hyland's thoughts on how the war could have been won, 343-344; aerial mining operations, 344-347; see also New Jersey, USS (BB-62); Market Time Operation; Gunfire Support

Vought Corporation
   Testing of F7U in the early 1950s was not completely satisfactory, as the plane was judged to be unsuitable for carrier duty, 294-296

WV-2 Warning Star (Lockheed)
   Used for aerial patrol between the Azores and Argentia in the late 1950s and early 1960s, 242-243, 245-252

Wagner, Captain Frank D., USN (USNA, 1915)
   As Commander Patrol Wing Ten in the early days of World War II, 77, 98; in last plane evacuated from Java to Australia in the spring of 1942, 112

Watkins, Admiral James D., USN (USNA, 1949)
   Negatively compared the relations between high-ranking military and civilian defense officials in the 1980s to the 1960s, 307

Weather
　　Difficult flying conditions encountered by planes of the Atlantic Barrier Wing, operating from Newfoundland in the late 1950s and early 1960s, 246-249, 252; effect on bombing operations in North Vietnam in the mid-1960s, 308-309

Wendt, Rear Admiral Waldemar F. A., USN (USNA, 1933)
　　Assessed by Hyland as director of the Strategic Plans Division of OpNav in the mid-1960s, 272, 304-305

West Point, USS (AP-23)
　　Former passenger liner carried American pilots home from duty in the Pacific in mid-1942, 114-115

Whiting, Rear Admiral Francis E. M., USN (USNA, 1912)
　　Duties as ranking officer at Saipan in 1945, 151-152

Whiting, Captain Kenneth, USN (USNA, 1905)
　　Pilot who exemplified the flair associated with the Navy's early aviators, 36-37

"Whiz Kids"
　　Hyland's recollections of dealing with Defense Secretary McNamara's civilian advisors in the mid-1960s, 306; handling of Vietnam War, 309-311

Wyoming, USS (AG-17)
　　Used for summer training cruise in the early 1930s, 17-21

Zero
　　World War II Japanese plane gave temporary advantage over U.S. planes, 63-64

Zumwalt, Admiral Elmo R., Jr., USN (USNA, 1943)
　　Retained as aide by Secretary Nitze after their association in International Security Affairs, 321-322; glowing fitness report from Nitze, 322-323; assessed by Hyland, 323; early promotions resulted in early retirement, 325-325

www.ingramcontent.com/pod-product-compliance
Lightning Source LLC
Chambersburg PA
CBHW080621170426
43209CB00007B/1488